THE HOUSE
OF
COMMONS
AT WORK

John A. Fraser

Les Éditions de la Chenelière inc.
MONTRÉAL • FREDERICTON

The House of Commons at work
John A. Fraser

© 1993 The House of Commons

Coordination: Hélène Day
Copy editing: Sharon Helfer
Proofreading: Antoinette Sevensma
Typesetting: Info-Type inc.
Design: Norman Lavoie
Front cover: National Capital Commission
Back cover: John Evans Photography Ltd.

Canadian Cataloguing in Publication Data

Fraser, John A. (John Allen), 1931-

    The House of Commons at work
    Issued also in French under title: La Chambre
    des communes en action.
    Includes bibliographical references and index.
    ISBN 2-89310-164-X
1. Canada. Parliament. House of Commons.
2. Parliamentary practice — Canada. I. Title.
JL161.F72 1993   328.71'072   C93-096424-1

Les Éditions de la Chenelière inc.
215, rue Jean-Talon Est
Montréal (Québec)
H2R 1S9
Telephone: (514) 273-1066
Fax: (514) 276-0324

ISBN 2-89310-164-X

Legal deposit: 2nd quarter, 1993
Bibliothèque nationale du Québec
National Library of Canada

The Publisher has made every effort to contact the
copyright holders. Further information pertaining to
rights would be welcome.

Printed in Canada
by Métropole Litho inc.

1   2   3   4   5   97 96 95 94 93

The use of the masculine in this book is not
intended to imply discrimination of any sort, but
is used only to make the text less cumbersome.

TABLE OF CONTENTS

I disapprove of what you say, but I will defend to the death your right to say it.

(Attributed to Voltaire, in S.G. Tallentyre, *The Friends of Voltaire*, 1907.)

PREFACE

On a craggy bluff high above the majestic Ottawa River stands the remarkable embodiment of our system of governance: Parliament. Yet, while the vast majority of Canadians recognize the Gothic architecture and many in their millions have made the pilgrimage to the nation's capital and passed through the brass doors beneath the Peace Tower into the historic rotunda, it has long been evident to me that Canadians are eager to know more about their history, more about their country, and more about their parliamentary institutions and how they function.

How much more exhilarating is a personal or armchair visit to Parliament, when the historical drama of the place and the people and events that have shaped us as a people, come alive. How much more meaningful is information, when it is conveyed in context. An article from the *Ottawa Citizen* of February 13, 1937 illustrates this concept perfectly. It is a description of a tour of Parliament given for Torontonian Ned Hanlan, world rowing champion in the 1880s and the first Canadian athlete to gain international recognition. In it, the tour guide recounts that just inside the main tower entrance was "a rosewood stand where we saw Mrs. Barrett with her stock-in-trade: fruits, homemade pies, taffy, rock candy, sarsparilla and ginger beer. She and her pretty daughter Lillie, carried on a good trade..." And later, how they passed through "the smoking room, a popular room with its chest of cut tobacco, a large box of clay pipes packed in oats, and a buffalo's horn full of snuff." Of course smoking is no longer permitted in the Parliament Buildings, but can't you just picture Sir John A. Macdonald buying rock candy from Mrs. Barrett on his way to the House! The fact is that all of us have wanted and needed better information about Parliament, information which for too long has been generally unavailable and inaccessible to the public.

To help meet this essential need, as soon as I became Speaker in 1986, I made a point of setting up a public information office to respond to requests and provide information about Parliament and how it functions. The office has been a great success ever since it opened. The content of building tours has been expanded and improved. Leaflets, fact sheets, and information bulletins have been produced and distributed far and wide. Information officers respond to letters and answer telephone enquiries. The office has been inundated with an intriguing variety of questions, and the number of queries has increased from year to year. The nature and complexity of the questions put to the office prove that Canadians in fact have a very lively interest in their parliamentary institutions. But still more must be done.

Most books on the subject of Parliament are the work of experts in political science. They contain in-depth technical studies, philosophical and political theories, critiques, proposals for reforms: everything, in other words, that one would expect to find in a treatise on political science. Books like these are intended for readers who are already familiar with the subject and want to extend their knowledge, or as professional reference works.

Almost nothing has been published that meets the needs of high school students, their teachers who are always on the lookout for good material, ordinary Canadians who want to look up a practical detail about Parliament, and the many armchair Speakers who assiduously watch the proceedings of the House on television. I thought that a simple, straightforward book describing how the House of Commons works, its organization and structure, and the services that ensure it functions smoothly, would fill a gap and meet a need.

It has been suggested that my experiences as Speaker and, above all, as a Member of Parliament are eminent qualifications for writing such a book. Perhaps I should explain.

The Speaker has a wide range of responsibilities: to represent the House, not the Government, as its spokesperson; as presiding officer, to manage the conduct of debates according to the rules established by the House; as Chairman of the Board of Internal Economy, to administer a budget of $240 million and two thousand employees; to fulfill a quasi-diplomatic role with respect to inter-parliamentary associations and representatives of foreign governments; and, of course, in my case, to meet the obligations that continue as the elected Member for Vancouver South.

The Speaker's most visible role is to preside over debate in the House and to apply the rules from time to time in the interest of order and decorum. But the task is much more than just a rigid adherence to the rules of the place. It is important to sense and measure the mood of the House, to know when to intervene effectively and when to let something go.

Ultimately, the maintenance of order depends on the collective self-discipline of the Members because the authority of the Speaker derives from the support and cooperation of the whole House. As much as possible, I try to anticipate what issues are likely to cause intense differences or, at times, disorder. I try to maintain reasonable order in the Chamber because, without that, there can be no freedom of speech.

The House of Commons has never been a tea-party. It consists of strong-minded, often very idealistic people, who are trying to accomplish something for our country. We are the inheritors of an adversarial system and that, in itself, fosters conflict. Thus, it is the Speaker's task to contain vigorous differences within the bounds of civility, and at the same time to permit the often emotional expression of feelings which reflect the intensity of some issues.

While the accumulation of well over one hundred years of traditions, rules and practices provide a solid base of jurisprudence upon which the Speaker can rely, there are many grey areas. The application of rules according to a strict compliance with precedent is not always appropriate. There are times to be firm, and other times to be flexible. Of course, there are times when there is very little by way of guidance for the Speaker.

The modern Speaker must abstain from party politics. I do not attend caucus. I cannot speak on partisan issues in the House, nor do I attend committee meetings. Outside the House, I do not comment on issues that divide the Members. It has been said that the Speaker's task is a lonely one, and that he must withdraw into a state of splendid isolation whence he observes from a distance the tumult of the political fray. This may have been true in the past. However, while I cannot be partisan, my role remains intensely political because the House is a political arena. It is my practice to be in daily contact with the House leaders of all parties, and I maintain an open door policy for all Members.

A Speaker who is in close touch with all parties can achieve things through negotiation and consultation that just can't be accomplished in the Chamber. Since 1986, with the election of the Speaker by secret ballot, there is, I think, a closer relationship of trust and confidentiality between Members and the Speaker. That, inevitably, changes a person from a partisan to something akin to a judge. While the role is judicial in many respects, I find that I am a combination of parish priest and social worker, advisor and conciliator and, often, a friend and confidant.

What makes a good Speaker? Many things, I suppose, and they are not all learned from a textbook. Experience, patience, understanding and humour all play a part. Suffice it to say that I have had the privilege of serving the House, with the cooperation and understanding support of all the Members and, I hope, my electors in Vancouver South.

Hence this book — let it be clear at the outset — is intended to be a practical handbook, not a book of memoirs or a theoretical treatise. After all, just prior to putting my name forward to be re-elected as Speaker in 1988, I assured my colleagues that I would never write a tell-all book, which is how I got re-elected! Besides, historical truths are rarely the object of unanimity. Recollections differ, opinions differ, even the same facts appear different to different people.

The main focus of this book is the House of Commons. But to understand Canada's parliamentary system, the House must be put in context. Our system of government must be described and the relations between the Government and Parliament must be defined. Equally, it is impossible to talk about the House without dealing at least briefly with the Senate. It is impossible to talk about the House of Commons without saying a few words about the Senate. I will offer some explanations to clarify its role within our Government.

Taking as a guide the questions the public have asked, I have tended to go into details and clarifications that some readers may be surprised to find in a book of this type. I have taken this approach because I think it is the best way of responding to what people want. There is no detailed bibliography: only the works specifically referred to or quoted from are listed.

Finally, I wish to acknowledge the substantial participation of Henriette Immarigeon in the preparation of this text, and to extend sincere thanks to her for undertaking the necessary research and editorial work. I also want to thank all the other members of the House of Commons staff who have cooperated, and add a particular word of thanks to the Library of Parliament for its kind cooperation.

I have undertaken the writing of this book on the occasion of the 125th anniversary of Confederation; it will be my modest contribution to its celebration. I hope it will prove useful.

The System of
Government

1

Canada is a liberal democracy, characterized by a system of parliamentary government. To understand its political system and institutions, we have to trace its evolution from colony to independent state, through a gradual process of detaching itself from Britain's influence. Canada is a young country, but nonetheless bears the marks of its past: a government, like an individual, is shaped by heredity.

REPRESENTATIVE GOVERNMENT

If everyone lived in isolation, and needed nothing from anyone else, we could each do whatever we chose, with no need for laws.

Representative government requires an elected assembly.

But this is not the case. We are all interdependent, part of a community. No one lives in complete isolation, or is completely self-sufficient. We all need transportation, health care, and other social services — and an organization that regulates life in the community. The country's security, well-being, and development must also be safeguarded.

To put it in the simplest terms, the institution that provides these services within a society is its government. Governments may take a variety of forms, ranging from despotism to government by referendum. In the first form, all powers are concentrated in the hands of a dictator; in the second, each and every decision is voted on by all the people. The first is disappearing gradually as democracy gains ground. The second, it must be admitted, seems impractical.

Between these two extremes are a wide variety of forms of government that have been shaped by historical forces. Over the centuries, absolute monarchs were progressively obliged to accept both legal and political limitations to their authority to the benefit of democratic institutions. The result has been the constitutional monarchy in which the head of state is a monarch whose functions are hereditary. The monarch acts on the advice of ministers who are willing to assume responsibility for their actions. In a constitutional monarchy, the real power is in the hands of an elected body from the majority of which the government is selected.

In Canada the Queen, represented by the Governor General, is the Chief of State; the Prime Minister is the Head of Government.

The monarchy has at times been replaced by a republican system where the head of state is a president rather than a monarch. In some countries, such as the United States, the president is head of the government as well as head of state. In others, India for example, the functions of the president are similar to those of a constitutional monarch. A monarchy is usually hereditary, whereas a president may be elected or appointed, depending on the system of government.

While it is practically impossible for each of us to play a personal part in considering and passing laws, and in making the decisions that affect our lives every day, it is on the contrary quite easy for a single person to represent a group of citizens. Then decisions are not made directly by the citizenry, but by the representatives to whom they have delegated their authority by electing them to speak and act on behalf of the group. If citizens are not satisfied with their representative's performance, they need only vote for someone else in the next election.

This is what is meant by "representative government": it is government by the elected representatives of the people. Canada achieved representative government only through a long series of developments that date back to the time when it was a collection of British colonies. In those days, each colony was administered on the sovereign's behalf by a governor, assisted by a council whom he chose and appointed himself. The orders came directly from London.

Very early on, the courts ruled that British subjects in the New World retained the laws and liberties they had enjoyed in the mother country. The right of a British subject to play a part in the making of the law of the land was an inalienable one, and could not be lost merely by crossing an ocean.[1]

In Great Britain the citizenry had had this right for a long time. Consequently, laws could not be passed in the colonies without the consent of the inhabitants or their representatives. Representative institutions were an inherent right in the British North American colonies.

Political authorities have undoubtedly been influenced by the judicial interpretation of the Constitution by the courts.

In the northern half of the North American continent, the colonial administration was not accepted meekly. Protests and demands were made, increasing in vehemence with the arrival of the Loyalists, the American colonists who were opposed to the revolutionaries during the

---

1.   R. MacGregor Dawson, *The Government of Canada*, 7th ed., revised by Norman Ward, (Toronto: University of Toronto Press, 1987), pp. 15-16. (For more details, see the 5th ed., p. 5.)

War of Independence. The latter already had experience with representative institutions and had every intention of continuing to enjoy their right to a representative system.

Under the pressure of the colonists, and propelled by events, the Governor of Nova Scotia summoned the first elected assembly in 1758. That date marks the first step in establishing representative government in what was to become Canada. In 1773, Prince Edward Island obtained its assembly, and in 1784, when New Brunswick separated from Nova Scotia, the Governor was authorized by the Crown to summon a representative assembly. The elected assemblies of Upper Canada and Lower Canada were provided for by the *Constitutional Act of 1791.*[2]

RESPONSIBLE GOVERNMENT

Progress had certainly been made, but the resulting mechanisms did not function smoothly. The governor of each colony was assisted by a council, chosen from among the colony's influential residents, its churchmen, the educated and cultivated elite. Such people were not really representative of the population as a whole. Many disagreements and disputes between the governor and the assembly turned into real conflicts, complicated and aggravated by economic, social, religious and cultural problems.

The concept of responsible government originated in Britain.

Gradually the colonists who wanted to see reforms introduced began calling for the right to control the governor's advisers. They demanded that he choose his council members from among men who had the representative assembly's confidence. They also wanted the council members to be changed when the assembly so wished. Representative government would thus be transformed into responsible government, which had by then been in existence in Great Britain for a long time.

The rebellions that erupted in Upper and Lower Canada in 1837 and the agitation in the other provinces led the British government to dispatch Lord Durham as Governor General and High Commissioner to British North America. His mission was to restore order and recommend measures for the future. Among his recommendations, two were of particular importance: the union of the two Canadas and the establishment of responsible government. As he explained in his report, implementing such a system of government would not involve radical changes, or even the passage of special legislation. All that would be required would be to apply the same rules and conventions in effect at Westminster, where responsible government had grown up informally. The only thing that

2.   According to the Statutes of United Kingdom adopted in the 31st year of the reign of George III.

needed to be done was to instruct the governor to consult the elected assembly and entrust responsibility for forming the government to the leader of the party with the majority.

Lord Durham was certainly describing responsible government, where the leader of the party with the most seats in the legislature is called upon to form a government. However, there is no reference to responsible government in the *Union Act, 1840*. As Lord Durham had suggested, the Act instructs governors to choose their councils from among the people who had the confidence of the electorate. However, true responsible government, where a government that loses the confidence of the legislature must resign, had still not quite arrived.

Once again it was in Nova Scotia that interesting developments occurred: this was the first province to see representative government replaced by responsible government. On January 25, 1848, the assembly passed a vote of no confidence in the administration. The administration resigned, and a new premier formed a government. The following March, the same thing happened in the Province of Canada. At almost the same time, the principle of responsible government was recognized in New Brunswick, three years later in Prince Edward Island, and in 1855 in Newfoundland.

In 1867, at the time of Confederation, the system of responsible government had been in effect for some two decades in the provinces that came together to make up the new country of Canada. The system had functioned well and needed only to be retained.

There is no provision in the Canadian Constitution that speaks of "responsible government," the system whereby the executive is accountable to the legislature and must, to remain in power, keep the confidence of the elected house. Yet, from the mid-nineteenth century on, this principle was the driving force behind political developments in Canada. It was the goal toward which the politicians of the day were heading. When they had attained that goal, they had taken the most important step toward independence for Canada.

The establishment of responsible government was without a doubt a major achievement in the struggle to make political institutions democratic. However, the understanding that democracy must include universal suffrage, and the achievement of that goal, were still far in the future.

PARLIAMENTARY DEMOCRACY

In the long and dogged crusade that the human race has fought in favour of democracy, the ideal of liberty, of freedom, has always been the goal. The freedom to speak and write, to think, to choose one's religion, to assemble, to develop one's talents, to disagree, to make choices — all these and more are aspects of liberty in a democracy. Liberty cannot be dissociated from equality, which is itself a kind of freedom: the freedom to be treated fairly, to receive the same treatment as every other citizen. In concrete political terms, equality means one person, one vote.

The Canadian system of parliamentary democracy is founded on the ideal of freedom.

Democracy is not a form of government. It is a political philosophy that can be embodied in various systems of government. Where the ideal of democracy is found, suffrage, or the right to vote, is universal and the government is controlled by the people. Canada is a classic liberal parliamentary democracy, in other words, a democracy in which freedom is regarded as fundamental. All the fundamental values in which Canadians believe are guaranteed by our Constitution.

In a parliamentary democracy, government "by the people" is understood in the sense of government "for the people." In such a system, the people do not govern directly, but they do choose their government. In a democracy, the majority rules. This can mean a number of things. First of all, when there is an election under Canada's electoral system, the candidate who wins the most votes is elected. At the party level, it means that the party that gets the most candidates elected is the winner. At the legislative level, it means that when our elected representatives do not all agree on a piece of legislation, the opinion that is shared by the largest number of legislators decides the issue for everyone. In a democratic system, the opinion of the majority must prevail; minorities must recognize this rule and accept it. At the same time, however, the majority must recognize that minorities have their rights and that these must be respected.

Sovereignty is the property of the citizens in a democratic state.

In a liberal democracy there must be respect for the opinions of others. Discussion must be free, criticism accepted, differing beliefs tolerated. There must be respect for the law and for the decisions reached by the majority, as well as recognition of the rights of minorities. If the minority were to deny the majority's right to decide, the system would cease to be democratic. The same thing would happen if the majority were to use its weight to deprive the minority of a legitimate right.

THE CONSTITUTION

Canada has been shaped by a history closely linked with that of the United Kingdom, but it has also been profoundly marked by constitutional thinking in the United States. Canada and her southern neighbour have in common a tradition of liberty, equality, and respect for the law. Both were created from groups of communities that only a federal regime could unite. But while the American Constitution was the child of war, ours grew out of discussion, bargaining and negotiation. Like the United States, Canada is a federation. Both countries have written constitutions, essential in a federal system. The characteristic of such a system is that powers are divided between the central government and the members of the federation; this is why it is indispensable to have a written document that clarifies all power-sharing arrangements. The *Constitution Act, 1867* states in its preamble that the provinces "have expressed their desire to be federally united . . . with a Constitution similar in principle to that of the United Kingdom."

As far as the form of government was concerned, that meant a system incorporating responsible government, with a Cabinet accountable to the House, which in turn was answerable to the people. In this regard, the applicable principles are based on convention, custom, and usage, or the unwritten part of the Constitution.

With respect to the federal system, the *Constitution Act, 1867* divides powers between the federal and provincial levels of government. "Level" should not be understood as involving any idea of subordination since in a federal system each legislature is supreme in those areas that come under its jurisdiction.[3]

The courts have the function of ruling on any encroachment by either level of government. There are many federal systems in the world, each encompassing a variety of ethnic groups and a number of regional and territorial disparities. Federalism is generally a marriage of convenience between groups who share common interests but nevertheless want to preserve a certain independence. It is a form of government that tries to reconcile unity with diversity.

Sections 91 and 92 of the *Constitution Act, 1867* enumerate the powers devolving upon the federal government and the provincial governments. Some are held in common. Some are not listed at all: issues relating to the natural environment, for example. Local and municipal governments are not mentioned because, unlike the federal and provincial governments, they do not derive their authority from the Constitution. Rather they are subordinate governments, created by statute by the provinces. Without this legal basis, cities, towns, counties and villages would not exist.

It is not the purpose of this work to examine in detail the provisions of the Constitution, which is not limited to the *Constitution Act, 1867*. As we have already noted, Canada's written Constitution is complemented

3.   K. C. Wheare, *Federal Government*, 4th ed. (New York: Oxford University Press, 1964), p. 10.

by unwritten practices and traditions, and by British and Canadian orders-in-council, as well as by a large body of case law in which the courts have interpreted the Constitution. The constitutional proposals which were rejected by the Canadian voters in October 1992 would have introduced important changes in the Constitution. It should be noted that discussions on the Constitution are not a recent phenomenon. For decades Canada tried to bring its Constitution home, and as late as 1982 we were still obliged to apply to the British Parliament every time a constitutional amendment became necessary. This situation was due to a simple question of procedure. Since it was the British Parliament that passed the *British North America Act* in 1867, that Parliament remained the only body that could amend the Act, for it contained no amending formula. It should be noted that before 1982 all Canada's proposed amendments were passed in London without the slightest interference. Nonetheless, Canadians were eager to free themselves from their dependency on Britain and find an amending formula that would make it possible to introduce constitutional changes at home. The term "patriation" came into common parlance to designate the procedure that would make it possible to amend the Constitution in Canada. Solving the problem took as long as it did because a procedure had to be found that would be acceptable to all the provinces.

In the 1980s the federal government took the initiative and proposed an amending formula, although quite a complex one, it must be admitted. After much discussion, an agreement was signed in 1981 by all the provinces except Quebec. Despite this lack of unanimity the federal government decided to go ahead. It presented a bill to the British government which was, after some debate, enacted by the British Parliament and became law in 1982. The *Constitution Act, 1982* contains the amending formula and the *Canadian Charter of Rights and Freedoms*. Since 1982, then, it has no longer been necessary to appeal to Westminster to amend our Constitution.

It wasn't until 1982 that efforts to patriate the Constitution met with success.

The government took advantage of the occasion to bring the *Constitution Act, 1867*, together with all its amendments, into what is known as the *Constitution Acts, 1867 to 1982*.

THE GOVERNOR GENERAL

Canada is a constitutional monarchy whose fundamental characteristic resides in the fact that the powers of the executive are divided: the official functions of Head of State are carried out by a person who has no party affiliation, while the powers of Head of Government are exercised by the Prime Minister, who is normally the leader of the party with the most seats in the House of Commons. Canada's Head of State is the Sovereign, represented by the Governor General.

The role and duties of the Governor General have their origins in those of the governors of the former colonies. They have evolved with our system of government and with Canada's status. First in Great Britain, then in Canada, the powers of the Sovereign diminished gradually and are now exercised only on the recommendation of his advisers, chosen from among the elected members of the majority party in the House of Commons. Nowadays it is safe to say that the Head of State can do very little without Cabinet's recommendation.

The *Constitution Act, 1867* defines some of the functions of the Governor General, but it is in the Letters Patent of 1947 that all the details are to be found. Under this document, the then King, George VI, delegated his powers to the Governor General, who was to exercise "with the advice of Our Privy Council of Canada . . . all powers and authorities belonging to Us in respect of Canada."

By this delegation of authority the Governor General ceased to be under the control of the United Kingdom. Later developments loosened the connection with the royal authority still further. In 1952, when Elizabeth II came to the throne, it was decided to modify her title to reflect more accurately the political realities of the Commonwealth. Since then, the Sovereign has been designated the Queen of the United Kingdom, of Canada and of some of the other countries of the Commonwealth. It should be noted that, although the two titles — Queen of the United Kingdom and Queen of Canada — are borne by the same person, Canada's monarchy is distinct from that of the United Kingdom. A further loosening of ties occurred in 1977 when it was decided that the Governor General, and not the Sovereign, would officially appoint and recall ambassadors accredited to foreign countries.

The Right Honourable Jeanne Sauvé was the first woman to be Governor General of Canada.

The Governor General is appointed by the Sovereign on the advice of the Prime Minister. The appointment is generally for a period of five years, but this may be shortened or extended. Since 1952, only Canadians have been appointed, and in 1984, for the first time in the country's history, a woman was appointed. The Right Honourable Jeanne Sauvé held office until 1990.

The official duties of the Governor General are many, both in Canada and abroad. They include representing Canada at international events as long as these are non-political in nature, for example, at the opening of world's fairs or the coronation of a monarch. They also include receiving dignitaries, heads of state, or other important personages invited by the Prime Minister and the awarding of civilian or military medals, honours and decorations, recognizing the merits of citizens who have distinguished themselves. As representative of the Head of State, the Governor General is also Commander-in-Chief of the armed forces, although this title is purely ceremonial. Further duties include providing a State presence at a variety of artistic, scientific, and sports events, and making many appointments. However, when the Governor General summons, prorogues or dissolves Parliament, issues proclamations and signs orders-in-council, appoints judges and diplomats or pardons criminals, it is only on the advice of the Prime Minister.

There is one function, however, that does lie exclusively with the Governor General, and that is without a doubt the most important one: the choosing of the Prime Minister. In a great many cases the choice is easy to make, because under the conventions that obtain in a parliamentary democracy, the leader of the party that holds a majority of the seats in the House of Commons must be called upon to form the government. The decision becomes much trickier, however, when no party has a majority. In such a situation the Governor General must display considerable discernment, and call upon the leader who seems most likely to be able to obtain and keep the confidence of the House. The Governor General is also responsible for ensuring that the country always has a legitimate government. If, for example, the Prime Minister were to die suddenly, a replacement would have to be selected quickly. Previous Governors General have sometimes found themselves in an awkward position. In 1891, when Prime Minister Sir John A. Macdonald died in office, the country remained without a Prime Minister for ten days.[4]

Another important power belonging to the Governor General is that of dissolving Parliament. Once again, in most cases it is sufficient to follow the advice of the Prime Minister. But in certain special circumstances the question may arise: may the Governor General refuse to dissolve Parliament when requested to do so by the Prime Minister? What if, for instance, a Prime Minister who had been defeated in the House did not wish to resign, but asked the Governor General to dissolve Parliament instead? This difficulty arose in 1926, when the Governor General, Lord Byng, refused the dissolution as requested by Prime Minister Mackenzie King. Lord Byng considered that it would be better to give the Leader of the Opposition an opportunity to form a government than to call an election, since there had just been an election and the Opposition held more seats than did the governing minority Liberals. The results proved the Governor General wrong, since Arthur Meighen was unable to retain the confidence of the House and in his turn requested dissolution. The election that followed was won by King. This example illustrates vividly the important role that the Governor General can be called upon to play in some circumstances and the good judgement he must be able to exercise.

Sir John A. Macdonald was Prime Minister from 1867 to 1873 and from 1878 until his death in 1891.

4.   J. R. Mallory, *The Structure of Canadian Government*, Rev. ed. (Toronto: Gage Publishing, 1984), p. 79.

Each Governor General has his own personality. However, all must exhibit only the most perfect neutrality, without the slightest hint of political partisanship. Complete objectivity must be displayed and personal opinions set aside, whatever the circumstances in the cause of the public good.

THE PRIME MINISTER AND THE CABINET

In Canada, the Queen, represented by the Governor General, is the Head of State and the Prime Minister is the Head of Government.

If the Governor General is the official representative of the Head of State, the Prime Minister is the Head of Government. It is the Prime Minister who exercises the power. It is the Prime Minister who provides the link between the Cabinet and the Governor General and advises the latter to summon, prorogue or dissolve Parliament. The powers that accompany the office are considerable. And yet, though the holder of this position is the most important person in the government, the position is mentioned only incidentally in one single constitutional document.[5] It is alluded to in a few very specific texts, for instance in the section on parliamentarians' remuneration in the *Parliament of Canada Act*, and in the *Official Residences Act*. But the role and functions are described nowhere. As we have seen, the Prime Minister is chosen by the Governor General, who requests that a government be formed; the choice is usually dictated by the result of an election.

All measures taken in the name of the Sovereign or the Governor General in fact result from initiatives and decisions made by the Prime Minister and the Cabinet. The Cabinet is not mentioned anywhere in the Constitution either. The *Constitution Act, 1867* refers to the Privy Council, but this is not the same thing. The Privy Council is made up of a certain number of people, appointed for life by the Governor General, on the advice of the Prime Minister. Generally, these people include past and present members of the Cabinet; past and present chief justices of the Supreme Court; past and present Speakers of the Senate and the House of Commons; often, past and present leaders of the Opposition; and other distinguished persons whom the government wishes to honour. The Privy Council does not meet except in the most exceptional circumstances, such as the accession to the throne of a new Sovereign or the investiture of a new Governor General.

Former Privy Council meeting room

The active part of the Privy Council is the Cabinet, technically a committee of the Privy Council, which acts and speaks on behalf of the Privy Council. The Governor General acts on the recommendations of the Cabinet, and the instruments by which this is done are called orders-in-council and minutes of council. These are adopted by the

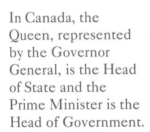

5.   *Constitution Act, 1982*, s. 37(1).

Cabinet and sent for approval and signature to the Governor General, who does not attend Cabinet meetings.

The centre of gravity of government activity is the Cabinet, which holds all the powers of government, and is the true executive. Under the direction of the Prime Minister it formulates policies and proposes the measures required for those policies to be implemented. It is responsible for the administration of the various government departments. It is Cabinet that prepares most of the legislative program and exercises a virtually absolute control over the country's finances.

The Prime Minister chooses the members of Cabinet, who become members of the Privy Council.

The Cabinet consists of members of the party in power chosen largely from members of the House of Commons. However, the Prime Minister may decide to appoint a Senator, or may choose someone who is not a parliamentarian. In the latter case, the new Minister, according to convention, must seek election to the House of Commons. However, this method of appointing Ministers is not well regarded by the electorate. For example, in 1974 Prime Minister Trudeau appointed Pierre Juneau, former chairman of the Canadian Radio Television Commission, as Minister of Communications. He tried to win a seat which had been held by the Liberals since 1921. He lost the by-election and resigned as Minister.

In appointing a Cabinet the Prime Minister follows a convention by which the provinces are fairly represented. As far as is practicable, Cabinet should reflect the country's multicultural character, and the Prime Minister must thus take gender, religion, linguistic, and ethnic considerations into account, to make sure that the Cabinet is really representative of all Canadians.

The great majority of Cabinet Ministers are Members of the House of Commons, although a few Senators may be included. There is normally one Senator who represents the government in the Upper House. Since 1969, the Government Leader in the Senate has had the status of a Minister. In the early years of Confederation, Senators played quite an important part in Canada's governments, indeed the first Canadian Cabinet included five of them. Two Prime Ministers have been Senators: Sir John Abbott in 1891 and Sir Mackenzie Bowell in 1894. But since 1911 it has been unusual to include more than one Senator in Cabinet. Following the elections of 1979 and 1980, however, because of the geographical polarization of seats in the House of Commons, more Senators were appointed to the Cabinets of the day. It must be borne in mind that a Senator may not sit in the House, any more than an MP may sit in the Senate, which makes the exercise of power difficult when the Prime Minister is a Senator. Ministers from the Commons may, however, be invited to speak in the Senate, although they may not vote.

When the Prime Minister assigns a portfolio to someone, there are a number of considerations to be taken into account, apart from the ones that have already been listed, including the person's competence, training and experience, and role in the party.

To ensure continuity, the Prime Minister designates a Minister who will act as Deputy Prime Minister if and when necessary. The first Deputy Prime Minister was appointed by Pierre Elliott Trudeau in September 1977 when he chose Allan MacEachen to fill that new position.

Custom dictates that where possible each province is represented in Cabinet.

Nowadays the Cabinet consists of from 35 to 40 Ministers. The number can vary according to need and political circumstances — which may also at times make it expedient that one Minister hold two portfolios. Ministers remain in office at the pleasure of the Prime Minister who chooses them and recommends their appointment to the Governor General, in whose presence they are sworn in. It is also the Prime Minister who recommends to the Governor General that a Minister's resignation be accepted. In the course of a term in office, a Prime Minister may make and remake ("shuffle") Cabinet many times, and for many reasons, among them political considerations, the need for change, the opportunity to broaden experience and exceptional circumstances. But the Prime Minister's powerful role does not remove the necessity of seeking ministerial co-operation, without which governing would be impossible.

The Prime Minister, named by the Governor General, plays a key role in Cabinet.

Obviously the Prime Minister is the dominant figure in Cabinet. The Prime Ministerial role and the exact way in which it is carried out will vary with the personality, gifts, and experience of the individual. Each Prime Minister has a unique style. The duties of the office include deciding on the agenda for Cabinet meetings, chairing the meetings, and playing a leading role in the House. In Cabinet, decisions are reached by consensus, and achieving consensus depends to a great extent on the Prime Minister's leadership capabilities. Persuasiveness, an ability to reconcile different ministers' viewpoints, flexibility but also moral authority, are all assets for a Prime Minister.

Ministers may be divided into two groups: those with departmental responsibilities and those without. The larger group is that of Ministers who are the political heads of departments, such as the Ministers of Finance, Agriculture, Transport, etc. There are Ministers whose titles do not indicate their responsibilities, such as the Secretary of State, who is in effect the minister for the arts, and the Solicitor General, who is responsible for the RCMP, Internal Security and Correctional Services. Another category of Minister is that of Minister of State. Some of these are assistants to the Minister running the department — the Minister of State (Transport), or the Minister of State (Environment). But there are also Ministers of State who are simply attached to a department, for example, the Minister of State (Small Business and Tourism), who is attached to the Department of Industry, Science and Technology Canada. The responsibilities and powers of Ministers of State can vary from one Cabinet to the next, so that the Prime Minister has greater flexibility when making up Cabinet. There are many reasons for bringing into Cabinet MPs who do not run a department, one being the opportunity for the MP concerned to gain experience.

Each Minister with a portfolio is the political head of a department and is responsible for its activities. He must be willing to answer for any shortcomings of subordinates, and to have the final word in all important decisions. If necessary, the Minister must resign in the event of a serious failing: this is what we call "ministerial responsibility." This rule is not always rigorously applied, however. There are many cases where a Minister has not resigned after having demonstrated he was not aware of the situation, or having shown that the necessary steps were taken to rectify matters as soon a the situation became known.

To this individual responsibility incumbent upon each Minister is added the Cabinet's collective responsibility. Ministers who disagree with the Cabinet's policies must either concede their objections or resign. This principle is known as Cabinet solidarity. The Cabinet's collective responsibility is the essence of the system of responsible government, and an accountable government was the innovation that transformed representative government into responsible government. If the House withdraws its confidence, the Cabinet must resign. In the British tradition, the defeat of a bill involving a matter of policy or a money bill is usually regarded as a vote of no confidence and thus results in the fall of the government. This tradition is not rigorously applied, however, since the government is free to interpret a vote as it sees fit. In 1968, for example, a money bill introduced by the Pearson government was defeated in the House (because there were not enough MPs of the government party present at the time). If the principle of responsibility had been applied to the letter, the government would have had to resign. It did nothing of the kind. Instead it introduced a motion asking the House not to interpret the vote as a vote of no confidence. By then the government MPs were back in force, the House expressed its confidence, and the government remained in office with the support of a minor party.[6]

> Responsible government is characterized by collective responsibility.

---

6. For details in this matter see: Philip Norton, "Government Defeats in the House of Commons: Three Restraints Overcome," *The Parliamentarian*, Oct. 1978, Vol. LIX, No. 4, p. 231.

It should be noted that the Government cannot be defeated in the Senate. It is responsible only to the elected chamber.

The relationship between the executive and the legislature changes significantly when the government is in a minority situation. This occurs when the government does not have a majority of seats in the House. To stay in power, it must continually seek the support of the members of other parties, who then hold the balance of power and can defeat government initiatives or even defeat the government itself by voting against measures brought in by it.

The minority Liberal government did not have undue difficulty remaining in power from 1963 to 1968, because they were short only a few votes and they easily found supporters among the NDP, the Ralliement des Créditistes or the Social Credit Party. From 1972 to 1974, the Liberals governed with the support of the NDP, but they remained in power only as long as the NDP was willing to co-operate.

Minority governments have to struggle to survive, and are obliged to make many compromises to hang on to power. The short life of the 1979-80 Conservative minority government demonstrates how difficult it is for a government in this position to stay in office.

THE ELECTORAL SYSTEM

Elections give Canadians the chance to re-elect their representatives or to replace them with new ones.

Elections are a very important political event. The citizens are being called upon to elect their representatives, so that in practical terms they choose the government. This gives them an opportunity to evaluate the outgoing government and decide whether it should stay in power or be replaced.

During the eight weeks of campaigning, the country's focus is entirely on the election. The media concentrate on it — saturating newspaper headlines and television news lead stories with election coverage. The political parties are mobilized. The opposition parties attack the government, hoping to gain ground, and every party proclaims the policies it would implement if it were to take office. Millions of dollars are spent on advertising.

General elections take place when the Prime Minister asks the Governor General to dissolve Parliament and call an election. This generally happens every four years. The Constitution stipulates that a Parliament cannot go on for more than five years from the day selected for the writs of election to be returned, although Parliament sat for six years at the time of the First World War thanks to a constitutional amendment. Shorter parliaments have included those of the governments in power in 1957-58 and in 1979 (nine months in both cases) and in 1962-63 (ten months). Nowadays the maximum duration of a Parliament may be prolonged "in time of real or apprehended war, invasion or insurrection" if such an extension "is not opposed by the votes of more than one-third of the members."[7] The government must of course be able to justify its claim that a state of emergency exists.

When the government has a majority, the Prime Minister generally opts for an election at a time when the party is seen to have the best chance of being returned to power. Waiting for the five years to run out leaves no room to manoeuvre, and only three governments have gone the full five years: two lost the subsequent election (in 1896 and 1935) and the third squeaked back in with a slim majority in 1945. After holding power for four years, the Prime Minister starts, in close collaboration with the party's leading thinkers, or *éminences grises*, to determine when the most favourable period for a general election would be.

In the case of a minority government, the life of the Parliament tends to be shorter, since the government can only survive with the support of certain members of the opposition. In such a situation, it is not the government that controls the duration of the Parliament. The moment it loses the co-operation of the opposition Members who have hitherto supported it, the government may be defeated and in most cases a general election follows. This has happened several times in Canadian history, most recently in 1974 and 1979.

The election is announced by means of a proclamation by the Governor General, which sets out not only the date of the polling day but also the date the returns must be reported (see Document 1). An election must be held on a Monday, unless that particular Monday happens to be a statutory holiday, in which case the election is held the next day.[8]

General elections are always held on a Monday, unless that day is a statutory holiday.

A by-election is held in a riding when a seat in the House of Commons becomes vacant through the death or resignation of the sitting Member. The government can choose the date of a by-election, but it must do so within six months of the day when the Chief Electoral Officer is officially informed of the vacancy.[9] The rules applicable to by-elections are analogous to those that govern general elections.

Elections are run under the direction and supervision of the Chief Electoral Officer, who is an independent senior official appointed by resolution of the House. The Chief Electoral Officer acts as ombudsman with

7. *Canadian Charter of Rights and Freedoms (1982)*, s. 4(2).
8. *Canada Elections Act*, R.S. (1985) c. E-2 am. R.S. (1985) c. 27 (2nd. supp.), 1989, c. 28. (For more details concerning the laws see the list of the Canadian laws at the end of the book.)
9. *Canada Parliament Act*, R.S. (1985) c. P-1 am. (1985) c. 31 (1st supp.), c. 38 (2nd. supp.), 1991 c. 20.

DOCUMENT 1

PROCLAMATION

of which all persons are asked to take notice and to govern themselves accordingly and in obedience to Her Majesty's writ of election directed to me for the electoral district of

dont chacun est requis de prendre connaissance et d'agir en conséquence. En conformité avec le bref de Sa Majesté m'ordonnant de tenir une élection pour la circonscription de

for the purpose of electing a person to serve in the House of Commons of Canada, public notice is hereby given of the following.

d'un député pour siéger à la Chambre des communes du Canada, un avis public est par les présentes donné de ce qui suit:

NOMINATIONS OF CANDIDATES WILL BE RECEIVED BY ME AT

JE RECEVRAI LES PRÉSENTATIONS DES CANDIDATS À

ADDRESS
DATE
TIME

ADRESSE
DATE
HEURE

IF A POLL IS GRANTED
POLLING DAY WILL BE

SI UN SCRUTIN EST OCTROYÉ
LE SCRUTIN SE TIENDRA

MONDAY

LUNDI

DATE
HOURS

DATE
HEURES

AT LOCATIONS TO BE PUBLISHED BY ME AT A LATER DATE

AUX ENDROITS DONT JE DONNERAI SUBSÉQUEMMENT AVIS

I HAVE ESTABLISHED MY OFFICE for the conduct of the election at the following location, where I shall add up the votes cast for each candidate as taken from the statements of the poll and declare the name of the person who obtained the largest number of votes as noted.

J'AI ÉTABLI MON BUREAU pour la conduite de l'élection à l'endroit suivant où j'additionnerai les votes déposés en faveur de chaque candidat d'après les relevés du scrutin et déclarerai le nom du candidat ayant obtenu le plus grand nombre de votes.

ADDRESS
DATE
TIME

ADRESSE
DATE
HEURE

DESCRIPTION OF URBAN OR RURAL AREAS

INDIQUER LES ENDROITS URBAINS OU RURAUX

GIVEN UNDER MY HAND

DONNÉ SOUS MON SEING

AT À	DATE	RETURNING OFFICER/PRÉSIDENT D'ÉLECTION

OFFENCE: It is an offence with severe penalties to take, deface or otherwise tamper, with any publicly posted election notice.

INFRACTION: Quiconque enlève, détériore ou altère de quelque façon un avis d'élection affiché publiquement commet une infraction entraînant des peines sévères.

Source: *Canada Elections Act*, c. E-2.

respect to the application of the *Canada Elections Act*, and keeps a register of political parties, as required by the Act. To remain in the register, a party must field at least fifty candidates. The Chief Electoral Officer has an assistant and a permanent staff that is augmented by temporary employees at election time. In each riding a Returning Officer and a Deputy Returning Officer see that the election proceeds as stipulated in the Act.

As soon as the date of the general election has been announced by proclamation of the Governor General, the Chief Electoral Officer sends a writ to each of the Returning Officers (see Document 2). They must return these immediately after the election bearing the name of the candidate who has received the most votes, although the latter does not actually become a Member of Parliament until he is sworn before the Clerk of the House. However, MPs do receive their salaries as of election day.

All Canadian citizens aged 18 and over may vote in the riding in which they live. A very few Canadians are disqualified from voting: the Chief Electoral Officer and his assistant, the Returning Officers, judges appointed by the federal government, inmates in federal penitentiaries, persons confined to institutions for the mentally ill, and persons who have been found guilty of an offence against the election laws. As we go to press, Bill C–114 has just been passed by the House of Commons. It proposes some amendments to the Electoral Act. Among other things it proposes to repeal the provision depriving judges appointed by order-in-council and people with mental disease of the right to vote. With regard to inmates, it proposes to remove the right to vote from those who are imprisoned in a correctional institution, serving a sentence of two years or more. Today the right to vote is guaranteed by the *Canadian Charter of Rights and Freedoms*, which is entrenched in the *Constitution Act, 1982*, and it is fair to say that suffrage is now universal for adults in Canada. But this was not always so. Women obtained the vote in a federal election in 1918 and the right to run as candidates in 1919,[10] the Inuit in 1950, and aboriginal people living on reserves in 1960.

Women achieved the right to vote in 1918.

Only citizens whose names appear on a list of electors may cast ballots. These lists are drawn up following a procedure known as enumeration. As soon as an election has been called, each returning officer appoints enumerators, whose role is to call on voters at their place of residence and get their names for the voters' list. Lists are prepared from scratch in this way for each election. The system has the advantage of removing

---

10. C.L. Cleverdon, *The Women Suffrage Movement in Canada*, 2nd. ed. (Toronto: University of Toronto Press, 1974), p. 135.

DOCUMENT 2

WRIT OF ELECTION

. . . .

Deputy of the Governor General

ELIZABETH THE SECOND, by the Grace of God of the United Kingdom, Canada and Her other Realms and Territories, QUEEN, Head of the Commonwealth, Defender of the Faith

To . . . .

of . . . .

GREETING:

WHEREAS, by and with the advice of OUR PRIME MINISTER OF CANADA, We have ordered a PARLIAMENT TO BE HELD AT OTTAWA, on the . . . . day of . . . . next. (*Omit the foregoing preamble in case of a by-election*.)

WE COMMAND YOU, that notice of the time and place of election being duly given,

YOU DO CAUSE election to be made according to law of a member to serve in the House of Commons of Canada for the said electoral district in the Province aforesaid (*in case of a by-election: in the place of* . . . . .);

AND YOU DO CAUSE the nomination of candidates to be held on . . . . ;

And if a poll becomes necessary, that the poll be held on . . . . ;

AND YOU DO CAUSE the name of such member when so elected, whether present or absent, to be certified to Our Chief Officer, as by law directed (*in case of a by-election, omit the following*) as soon as possible and not later than the . . . . day of . . . . 19. . . .

Witness: . . . . , Deputy of Our Right Trusty and Well-beloved . . . . , Chancellor and Principal Companion of Our Order of Canada, Chancellor and Commander of Our Order of Military Merit upon whom We have conferred Our Canadian Forces' Decoration, GOVERNOR GENERAL AND COMMANDER-IN-CHIEF OF CANADA.

At Our City of Ottawa, on . . . . and in the . . . year of Our Reign.

BY COMMAND,

Chief Electoral Officer

Source: *Canada Elections Act*, c. E-2.

from the citizenry the responsibility of registering to vote, and of ensuring that the lists are as up-to-date as possible. Provisions exist to enable members of the Armed Forces, and ordinary Canadians who find themselves outside the country, to cast their ballots.

For the purpose of representation in the House of Commons the country is divided into constituencies, or ridings, each of which sends one MP to the House. The ideal would be for each MP to represent exactly the same number of voters, but in a country like Canada this is not easy to achieve since our territory is vast, our population is densely concentrated in a few cities, and people move around a great deal within the country. Moreover, there are legislative safeguards for the less populated provinces, to ensure them equitable representation. The Constitution stipulates that no province may have fewer MPs than it has Senators.[11]

Parliament has also passed legislation in this area: the *Representation Act, 1985*, provides that constituencies must be redistributed, that is, the boundaries must be redrawn, after each decennial census. Under the *Constitution Act, 1867*, a major census must be held every ten years and a less detailed one every five years. In each province a commission chaired by a judge, who is assisted by two other commissioners designated by the Speaker of the House, is responsible for the redistribution. A similar commission is set up for the two Territories. Commissioners apply a complex formula designed to ensure that the smaller provinces, large but underpopulated regions, and densely populated urban concentrations are all fairly represented. The commissioners' reports are sent to the Chief Electoral Officer and then to the Speaker of the House, who sees that they are tabled in the House.

To run for the House of Commons, would-be candidates need certain qualifications, which are spelled out in the *Canada Elections Act*. These are virtually identical to the requirements for being able to vote. But there are two additional categories of person who are excluded from running: people who are under contract to the Crown, and people who are already members of a provincial legislature or territorial council. Until recently, employees of the federal public service were not authorized to participate in political activity, effectively barring them from running for public office; but the law now allows them to take leave without pay for the period of an election campaign. If leave is granted they can return to their jobs with the public service afterwards if they are not elected.

11. *Constitution Act, 1867*, s. 51a.

A sample ballot

To run under the banner of a particular party, a candidate usually must be nominated by that party's local riding association. Nominations generally take place before the campaign begins, and different riding associations have different rules and procedures for nominating candidates.

Every candidate must be nominated and supported by 25 people who have the right to vote. The nomination must be approved and signed by the candidate and accompanied by a deposit of $200, required to discourage frivolous candidates. The winning candidate, and candidates who win at least 15 percent of the total of valid votes cast in the riding, are entitled to get their deposits back. Some candidates can also be partly reimbursed for their expenses during the campaign.[12] Independent candidates can run for election if they meet the same conditions, that is, if they have the declared support of 25 eligible voters and they pay a deposit of $200. Candidates need not necessarily live in the ridings or even the provinces where they are running.

Voting is by secret ballot. A voter may cast only one ballot, and may vote for only one of the candidates who appear on the list.

Returning officers gather the votes of the electors at polling stations. The Chief Electoral Officer is responsible for the election in one riding.

When the polls close, the counting of the ballots begins in the presence of scrutineers. Although this creates a lot of excitement and generally does produce an accurate count, the results are not official. The ballot boxes are sent to the Returning Officer for the official count. A recount is provided for in case there are irregularities or a candidate requests one. When the counting is finally over, the Returning Officer returns the writ of election, with the name of the elected candidate entered, to the Chief Electoral Officer. To be elected, a candidate must simply receive more votes than anyone else, a relative, but not necessarily an absolute, majority.

The secret ballot guarantees that the vote remains completely confidential.

Canada's electoral system is democratic. It is universal, and the results depend on a single-ballot, first-past-the-post majority or plurality. It is democratic in that everyone can vote and vote freely. Citizens can vote without fearing pressure or intimidation. Each riding will elect only one MP. There is only one round of balloting.

This type of electoral system is open to certain criticisms. Because a candidate does not need an absolute majority, he may be elected with very few of the votes indeed, perhaps only a handful more than the runner-up. The result may be that the number of MPs a party elects does not really reflect the proportion of votes it received at the national

12. *Canada Elections Act*, R.S. (1985) c. E-2 am. R.S. (1985) c. 27 (2nd. supp.), 1989, c. 28.

level.[13] The response to these criticisms is that our system has the merit of being simple and avoiding dilution of the vote. We can count on a certain stability, with our governments remaining in office for a reasonable term. Although these remarks hold true in a two-party system, or one where third parties are not really contenders, matters could change if the votes were to become more evenly distributed among a number of parties.

POLITICAL PARTIES

Political parties are an important element in the parliamentary system, indeed there would be no parliamentary system without them. It is the party that fights and wins an election that places a government in power. Despite this, there is no mention of parties in our constitutional texts. In a democratic system, parties play an essential role since without competing opinions there can be no democracy. Often the opposition parties succeed in modifying the government's position. In addition, they offer the electorate an alternative when they become dissatisfied with the party in power.

Political parties as we know them today are a relatively recent phenomenon in Canada. Coalitions of loosely structured groups gave way to nationally-organized parties only at the end of the last century.

Although at the federal level just two parties have shared power between them since 1867, Canadian parliamentary history teaches us that since 1921 Canada has had a multi-party system, with more than two, and sometimes as many as five, parties represented in the House at all times.[14]

The origins of the Conservative Party may be traced to about 1854, when two groups joined forces under the paradoxical title of the Liberal-Conservative Party. However, it was not until the early days of Confederation that Sir John A. Macdonald transformed his electoral faction into a true party.[15] In 1942, the party replaced the word "Liberal" in its name with "Progressive" and became the Progressive Conservative Party, to

13. C. Alan Cairns, "The Electoral System and the Party System in Canada, 1921-1965," *Canadian Journal of Political Science*, Vol. 1 (March 1968), pp. 55-80.

   J.A.A. Lovink, "On Analysing the Impact of the Electoral System on the Party System in Canada," *Canadian Journal of Political Science*, Vol. 3 (December 1970), pp. 497-516.

14. C.E.S. Franks, *The Parliament of Canada* (Toronto: University of Toronto Press, 1987), p. 36.

15. W. Christian and C. Campbell, *Political Parties and Ideologies in Canada: Liberals, Conservatives, Socialists, Nationalists*, 2nd. ed. (Toronto: McGraw-Hill Ryerson, 1990), p. 106.

reflect more accurately the evolution that had taken place in its ideology (see Appendix A).

The origins of the Liberal Party are a little harder to pin down. It may be said to have originated with the reformers who called for responsible government. The first Liberal government came to power in 1873, however, it was Sir Wilfrid Laurier, when he became leader in 1887, who created the Liberal Party on a national scale as we know it today.

The first Liberal government was lead by the Honourable Alexander Mackenzie.

The Great Depression saw the founding of the Co-operative Commonwealth Federation, or CCF, whose roots were in the West. The CCF united a number of labour, farm, and reform movements. It ceased to exist in 1961, when it was transformed into the New Democratic Party (NDP).

Social Credit too originated in the West, in Alberta and British Columbia, where it won many provincial elections; it reached its peak at the federal level in 1963 when the largest number of its members was elected. Its Québec wing, the Ralliement des Créditistes, broke away in 1963. By 1980, both had ceased to be represented in the House of Commons.

In 1993, there are two political movements represented in the House in addition to the Conservatives, the Liberals and the New Democrats: the Bloc Québécois and the Reform Party. Neither is officially recognized by the House as a party. Members from these parties are treated as independents.

What about the political ideologies of Canada's parties? It is difficult to be hard and fast in defining them. It is said, for example, that the Conservatives are further to the right than the Liberals, but within each party there is a wide range of opinions, and as a result it is sometimes difficult to distinguish a liberal Conservative from a conservative Liberal. This situation can be explained in part by our electoral system, which favours the existence of large, broadly-based parties which share much common ground. Nor is Canada the only country where ideologies are becoming eroded and blurred.[16]

Political parties contribute to the proper functioning of government.

The reality of modern government is that circumstances, more often than political doctrine, dictate a course of action.

It is a little easier to define where the NDP stands because it is a social democratic party. The Bloc Québécois is basically dedicated to achieving

16. Meisel, J. "The Decline of Party in Canada," in *Party Politics in Canada*, 6th ed., H.G. Thorburn, 1991, pp. 178-201.

the independence of Québec, while the Reform Party presents itself as a populist political movement.

The success, the failure, the very existence of a party, depends on its organization. The party keeps the members united, maintains contact with them to learn what they think about proposed policies, persuades the electorate to vote one way rather than another and stimulates voters' interest. Each party has its own organization, methods and techniques, but all have the same goal: success at the polls.

Every two years, each party regularly organizes a huge national gathering, called a convention. The membership comes together for this mass meeting, at which they discuss existing policies and propose new ones, develop strategies, attract wide media coverage, and sing the party's praises in the hope of attracting new recruits. Resolutions are adopted that may eventually become part of an election platform. The convention organized when a party needs to choose a new leader is called a leadership convention. A party leader must thus be elected twice: once by fellow party members (voting for the leader is limited to party members only) and once by universal suffrage of the qualified electors of the leader's riding. A leadership convention is always a noisy, lively event that takes place under the gaze of the news cameras. The parties take the greatest possible advantage of the media coverage to arouse voter interest.

Each party has a national executive that meets regularly under the chairmanship of a national director or party president. The executive is largely responsible for running election campaigns. There is a permanent office with a limited staff that increases when campaign time arrives.

Another party activity is the holding of small-scale think tanks. These gatherings were introduced in the 1960s and are usually held in relatively isolated locations such as resort hotels. Well away from their offices, participants can discuss the country's problems and come up with policies and strategies free from interruption. Participants are few in number, all dominant figures within the party, whether parliamentarians or not; experts and advisers are there to assist.

The members of the party in power occupy a number of positions. First of all there are the Prime Minister and the Cabinet Ministers. Then there are the Parliamentary Secretaries, the Speaker of the Senate, the Deputy Speaker of the House, and the Deputy-Chairman and Assistant Deputy-Chairman of Committees of the Whole. Until recently the Speaker of the House was a member of the party in power as well, but now that the latter is elected by secret ballot it is not impossible that in the future a Speaker might belong to an opposition party (see, however, Chapter 4 where it is mentioned that in 1979 Speaker Jerome remained in Office when a minority government came into power).

In all parties the leaders play decisive roles. Their personalities, their political sense, and leadership capabilities, are vital to the success of the parties they personify. They have enormous power within the party. For example, the approval of the leader is needed for the nomination of every candidate who wants to run for the party in an election. The leader dominates, but there are other influential party members as well, who are not necessarily parliamentarians. The party must please the electorate, whether to gain power or to retain it. It must also find the financial resources required for its own needs and activities.

In addition to a leader, each party has a "House Leader," who represents it in discussions on organizing the work of the House of Commons. When the House is sitting, the House Leaders meet every week in the office of the Government House Leader to discuss the business of the House. Additional emergency meetings are held when necessary. It should be noted that it is the prerogative of the Government House Leader to proceed with any Government Order he chooses. The prestige enjoyed by the House Leaders and the fact that they are chosen by their party leaders give them the authority they need to handle the legislative burden of the House.

The Whip is responsible for party discipline.

Another important figure on each party's team is the Whip, who wields considerable authority among fellow party members. The Whips of the two main parties are chosen by their leaders, while the NDP caucus elects its Whip.

The Whips have very important functions. First, they are responsible for party discipline. This means they have to make sure that the MPs who ought to be in the House are in fact there. They do the same for committee meetings. This is a responsibility that requires a great deal of diligence, because MPs often arrange replacements for themselves, and it is up to the Whip to check that these arrangements have been clearly understood and that the party is appropriately represented in the House and in committees. Party Whips keep records of participation by their parties' MPs in parliamentary activities. Party discipline is also exercised when the time comes for a vote in the House. Under our party system it is expected that each MP will vote the party line; in other words, all MPs belonging to the same party normally vote the same way. Very exceptionally the party leader may relax this rule and authorize a free vote, where each MP may vote as he or she chooses. These rare cases generally occur when the vote is on an issue with moral implications, such as the death penalty or abortion. In general, however, a party votes as a block. It is the Whip's job to make sure that MPs respect the party line. Whips have many other duties, all more or less related to discipline. Whips allocate office space. They designate the MPs who will participate in Question Period, and often in debates as well. They play an essential role in communication and liaison among MPs, leaders and the caucus. At the present time, they sit on the Standing Committee on House Management, whose mandate includes establishing the list of MPs on each standing and legislative committee.

The Whips have different ways of establishing their authority. They rarely encounter any difficulties because the considerable powers at their disposal give them a great many levers for exerting influence.

Another of the Whips' duties, though one that is not often mentioned, is that of mediator. They share this responsibility with the House Leaders. In the course of the proceedings, it can happen that incidents occur in an atmosphere so charged with tension that there seems to be no way out of the situation. Informal meetings among some or all of the House Leaders and Whips are then held. Most of the time, in that calmer atmosphere, the incident can be settled outside the House through negotiation and compromise. Effective, harmonious parliamentary activities depend a great deal on the Whips.

The caucus is an essential organ of the party, and each of the three parties has one. It consists of all the parliamentarians — MPs and Senators both — who are party members. The caucuses meet once a week on Wednesday mornings, while Parliament is sitting, and additional meetings are held if circumstances dictate. In addition to the full caucus, there are regional caucuses, made up, as the word indicates, of parliamentarians from a particular province or region.

The structure and activities of a caucus will vary from one party to another. Major changes occur within an opposition party caucus if the party comes to power. The Government party caucus has the advantage of knowing what legislation the Government is going to propose before it is presented in the House, so that a component of caucus meetings are briefing sessions on upcoming legislation.

There are, however, certain similarities among caucus meetings. For one thing, only rarely does anyone attend who is not a parliamentarian, though a representative of the Canadian Labour Congress and certain staff members regularly attend the NDP caucus. The atmosphere is informal and relaxed. People speak frankly. In a caucus meeting ordinary backbenchers can raise special problems in their ridings and if necessary ask for help.

During caucus meetings the parliamentarians discuss all the issues that concern the party, initiate strategies, and develop policies. The caucus is also educational for MPs who often arrive in Ottawa very familiar with local problems for which they want solutions — but unaware that these solutions may not fit in with their party's national policies. Discussions in caucus shed light on all aspects of the problem and present issues in the national context. Needless to say, caucus meetings are strictly confidential. Reports are presented orally, there is no agenda, and no minutes are written.

LOBBY GROUPS

Pressure groups (lobbyists) defend common interests and attempt to influence Government decisions.

It is not possible to study the way Parliament works without looking at special interest pressure groups, commonly called "lobby groups" or "lobbies."

There are many lobby groups in Canada: for business and financial interests, manufacturers, farmers, consumers, lawyers, supporters and opponents of particular ideologies, etc. There are so many special interest groups that it would be impossible to list them all. The word "interest" should be understood in the broad sense — it is not restricted to a financial interest. The expression refers to organized groups whose aim is to influence the policies of the federal government in favour of protecting and encouraging their particular interests.

The terms "lobby," "lobby group," and "lobbyist" derive from the antechambers to which MPs withdraw when they leave the House proper. These are known as the lobbies, and it was here that representatives of special interest groups used to wait in an effort to buttonhole MPs and try to influence them in the exercise of their legislative functions.

How do lobby groups exert pressure? Because their aim is to persuade the Government, they use all the means at their disposal to press their point of view: repeated contact with senior departmental officials, meetings with Ministers and MPs, presentation of briefs and studies. Sometimes they mobilize the media, which can be of great help to them. They may organize demonstrations in the streets or on Parliament Hill. They do everything they can to bring public opinion around to their point of view. Their goal is either to influence legislation, whether it has yet to be introduced or is already under consideration, or to induce the Government to take action of some kind. In either case they use persuasion and persistence, and can be very effective indeed.

Lobby groups generally have to be well organized and well informed, so that they can intervene at just the right time. Some, it must be admitted, are in a more advantageous position than others: an association of manufacturers or bankers will have more financial resources than certain environmental groups or groups that are for or against access to abortion. On the other hand, though these groups do not always have big budgets, they often succeed in attracting the attention of the media.

Of course, lobby groups cannot be described as objective as their role is to defend a point of view and bring forward only the arguments that support it. Nonetheless, the Government lends them an attentive ear, and in some cases asks for their co-operation. When a major tax reform is undertaken, for example, the Government consults the special interest groups concerned, whether they represent business or labour. If law reform is envisaged, the Canadian Bar Association is automatically asked to participate. Consultations between the Government and special interest groups occur frequently.

Even though the opinions expressed to the Government are subjective, they can still be very helpful. First of all, they tell the Government exactly what a particular segment of Canadians is thinking. Second, the groups often retain experts who know the subject under discussion thoroughly and can point out aspects that might well have been missed. The Government has its own experts who can clarify matters and restore some balance to the arguments presented by a lobby group. In the same way, special interests are often asked to appear before committees studying legislation that involves them. They send representatives to speak at hearings, and they present briefs that are often valuable sources of information.

Intervention by lobby groups is part of a representative system. Such groups bring together people with common concerns and communicate those concerns directly to the decision makers. Some may wonder whether this process does not reduce the role of the MP. This is not the case. For one thing, MPs are not equipped for this role, and for another, the lobby groups often appeal to parliamentarians, whether MPs or Senators, for help in achieving their objectives. The groups leave no stone unturned, and would never fail to approach parliamentarians likely to be able to help them in some way. In many cases an MP can open doors for them, for example when the issue involves more than one level of government. In that case an MP is in an especially good position to communicate with all the appropriate authorities.

Lobby groups play an important role in the formulation of policies and the passing of legislation. They are officially recognized by the *"Lobbyists Registration Act."*[17]

---

17. *Lobbyists Registration Act*, R.S. (1985) c. L-12.

2 The Parliament Buildings

One of the many bas-reliefs that adorn the Parliament Buildings.

Does anyone have an image of Ottawa, the nation's capital, that does not include the Parliament Buildings? Parliament Hill's location, on a cliff overlooking the Ottawa River, makes this complex of Buildings unique.

Although this book deals mainly with the activities of Parliament, it is worth pausing here to take a look at the Parliament Buildings themselves because they are rich in history. The very structures, the corridors, the rooms and offices, are eloquent testimony to our past. The walls are covered with carvings, and virtually everywhere you look there are historic paintings, commemorative plaques, scenes from the past, not to mention the portraits of our Prime Ministers and of the Speakers of the two Houses.

Queen Victoria chose Ottawa as the capital of the Province of Canada (formed from the union of Upper and Lower Canada) on December 31, 1857. At that date, the Hill was the site of a military barracks, and the soldiers tended vegetable patches along the edge of Wellington Street.

CONSTRUCTION

The preparing of the ground was done in 1859 and construction began the same year on all three Buildings — the Centre Block and the East and West Blocks — simultaneously. On June 8, 1866, the Buildings were ready for the last session of the Parliament of the Province of Canada. The first Parliament of Canada met there on November 6, 1867. The *Constitution Act, 1867* confirmed Ottawa as the capital of Canada.

It was thought that the Buildings were fireproof, because their basements and ground floors were built of concrete and all the towers contained water reservoirs. But on February 3, 1916, a fire broke out in the reading room and the Centre Block was razed to the ground in 24 hours. Only the Library was spared, thanks to the presence of mind of an employee who shut the iron doors from the Library to the main part of the building. The cornerstone of the main building survived the fire

The Parliament Buildings at the turn of the century

and was incorporated into the new building, the only link between the old Centre Block and the new. While work went on in haste to reconstruct Gothic Revival buildings that would closely resemble what had been destroyed, Parliament sat in the Victoria Museum at the far end of Metcalfe Street, today the Canadian Museum of Nature.

On September 1, 1919, the Prince of Wales laid a cornerstone inscribed in his honour. The work was completed in 1920, and on February 20 of that year the Senators and MPs moved into the new building.

Approaching Parliament Hill, the Centre Block can be seen directly in front, flanked to the right by the East Block and to the left by the West Block. In the foreground is a fountain in the centre of which burns the Centennial flame, erected in 1967 to celebrate the first hundred years of Confederation.

The new Centre Block, the work of John Pearson and Jean Omer Marchand, was completed in 1920.

THE PEACE TOWER

Dominating the Parliament Hill complex is the Peace Tower, part of the main entrance to the Centre Block. It commemorates Canada's human and material contribution to the First World War. The Peace Tower also houses the Memorial Chamber, which in turn houses the Books of Remembrance that commemorate the sacrifice of those Canadians who perished in all the wars in which Canada has been involved. The Tower houses a carillon, first rung on July 1, 1927, in honour of the Diamond Jubilee of Confederation. It comprises 53 bells, on which the Dominion Carillonneur performs for the pleasure of visitors to the Hill.

The Peace Tower

The Parliamentary
Library

Sculpted woodwork in
the Library

The main entrance to the Houses of Parliament is through the base of the Tower, where the centre door opens onto the circular Confederation Hall. The Hall of Honour leads to the Library from Confederation Hall. In the centre of the Hall stands an imposing stone column, inscribed in memory of the Canadian soldiers "who in the Great War fought for the liberties of Canada, of the Empire and of Humanity."

THE LIBRARY

Opposite the main entrance, at the far end of the Hall of Honour, is the Library of Parliament. Near the door to the Library, on both walls of the corridor, are various commemorative plaques, one of them to the memories of the nurses killed during the First World War. The stone walls are especially rich in fossils, as are many of the other interior walls, because of the material used, Tyndall limestone.

Gothic in inspiration, circular in form, and decorated with magnificent carved wood, the Library is one of the jewels of the Houses of Parliament. While it survived the fire of 1916, it was not so lucky in 1952, when major damage was caused both by a fire and by the water used to put it out. The Library contains more than 650 000 volumes and is equipped with the most modern technology. It provides reference, documentation, and research services to parliamentarians and their staffs, the committees, parliamentary associations and delegations, and senior officials of the Senate and the House. In addition to the Main Library, there are three branches in various Buildings used by Parliament off the Hill.

The Hall of Honour

THE SENATE

The two Houses of Parliament, the Senate chamber and the House of Commons chamber, are symmetrically positioned one on each side of the main door in the Centre Block. The Senate is to the right, the House to the left. Each has its own door to the outside, on the eastern and western ends of the Block respectively (see Figure 1).

The Senate is often referred to as the "Red Chamber," because the upholstery, carpeting, and decor are all crimson. In this respect, the Senate is simply following the example of the House of Lords. It would seem that the colour was chosen because it is the colour of royalty: peers of the realm wore red robes to court.

The Senate chamber is an elongated rectangle, with galleries at both ends in which a total of 350 people can be accommodated. The walls are decorated with striking paintings representing scenes from the First World War. At the north end of the chamber, on a dais, are the two thrones occupied by the Sovereign and her spouse, or the Governor General and his spouse when they attend the opening of Parliament, and from which the Sovereign or the Governor General reads the Throne Speech. The chair placed just in front of the throne is for the Speaker, but when the Governor General is in the Chamber, the Speaker sits in a chair to the right of the thrones, aligned with the Senators' benches. In front of the Speaker's Chair is the Senate Table, where the Clerk of the Senate sits with the Clerk Assistant and the other Table Officers. The Senate Mace rests on the Table while the Senate is sitting; it is carried in and out of the Chamber on the shoulder of the Mace-bearer who, together with the Gentleman Usher of the Black Rod, precedes the Speaker in the procession which opens a sitting of the Senate.

Access to the Senate chamber is via an antechamber on whose west wall is a plaque in memory of the five Alberta women who by their courage and tenacity succeeded in opening the Senate to women. At the outer entry to the Senate precincts is a handsome foyer hung with paintings.

High on the Senate walls vivid paintings illustrate scenes from the First World War.

The Senators have their offices in the east end of the Centre Block, on the floors above the Senate chamber, in the East Block, and in the Victoria Building on Wellington Street, just across from the Hill. The increase in the number of MPs, the improved facilities provided for parliamentarians, and the evolution of administrative and support services for the two Houses has meant that space has had to be found off the Hill.

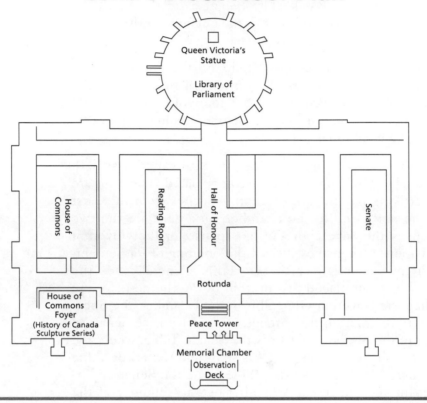

FIGURE 1

Centre Block Floor Plan

Source: Public Information Office, House of Commons.

THE HOUSE OF COMMONS

Canada's House of Commons, like that of Westminster, is decorated in green. No record exists of why this colour became traditional. Perhaps it was simply that a colour had to be chosen and red was already the preserve of the House of Lords.[1] The Commons chamber too is an elongated rectangle, larger than that of the Senate (see Figure 2, page 37). It has galleries, not only at both ends but also along the sides, that can accommodate a total of 581 people. In the gallery that faces the Speaker, the front rows are reserved for the diplomatic corps and other rows for distinguished guests. At the opposite end of the chamber, above the Speaker's chair, is the press gallery, with the front rows reserved for journalists; the rest is open to the public. The south end of the gallery

1.   J.M. Davies, "Red and Green," *The Table*, v. 37, 1968, pp. 33-40.

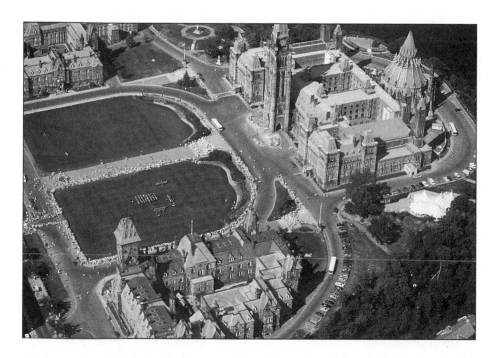

Aerial view of the
Parliament Buildings

facing the Government side is for guests of Government MPs, the north end for Senators and their guests, and the centre for guests of the Governor General, the Prime Minister and the Speaker. This is where Heads of State, Heads of Government, and members of parliamentary delegations invited to Canada are recognized and introduced by the Speaker to the House of Commons following Question Period. The gallery on the opposite wall, facing the opposition benches, is reserved for the guests of opposition leaders and MPs.

The Speaker's chair is placed at the north end of the chamber. It is a reproduction of the Speaker's chair at Westminster that was destroyed in the bombing of the House of Commons in 1941. The Canadian chair arrived as a gift in 1921 from the British branch of what is now the Commonwealth Parliamentary Association, to replace the one lost in the fire of 1916.

The use of the word "chair" in parliamentary practice should perhaps be clarified at this point. It designates the presiding officer, whether this is the Speaker in person or some other parliamentarian replacing the Speaker: the Deputy Speaker, the Deputy Chairman of Committees of the Whole, the Assistant Deputy Chairman of Committees of the Whole, or an ordinary MP acting as Speaker. It is quite common for the word "Chair" to be used in the House to refer to the occupant of the Speaker's chair or the chairman of a parliamentary committee.

Behind the Speaker's chair there is a door opening on a corridor that leads directly to the Speaker's office. This is very convenient if the Speaker has to leave the House or must be reached with an urgent message.

In the Chamber itself, Government MPs sit to the Speaker's right, opposition MPs to the left. On the Government side, the Prime Minister and Cabinet sit in the front row, surrounded by the other members of the party in power. Opposite, across the floor, sit the Leader of the Official Opposition and party members. The second-ranked opposition party, with its leader, is seated to the left of the Official Opposition. Sometimes there are more government MPs than can be accommodated on the benches to the Speaker's right; they are then allocated places on the left. The assigning of seats is the Speaker's responsibility, carried out in collaboration with the Whips. Placing may vary somewhat depending on election results, but the Prime Minister, the Leader of the Official Opposition and their respective entourages are always seated in the same places.

A short distance from the Speaker is the Table where the Clerk of the House sits with the Deputy Clerk and other Table Officers. The Clerk must be seated close to the Speaker so as to be able to offer advice, and to be on hand for consultation at all times. In the years after Confederation it was the custom for the Clerk, like the Speaker, to take his chair with him when his term was over, but this custom ceased when the family of the distinguished Clerk, Sir John Bourinot, donated his chair to the House after his death.

The Parliament Buildings house works of art and irreplaceable treasures.

When the House is sitting, the Mace rests on the Table; when the House meets as Committee of the Whole, the Mace is placed on special brackets below the Table. When Parliament sat in the Victoria Museum after the 1916 fire, the Senate Mace was used until a replacement could be found. A temporary Mace was made out of wood and that temporary Mace is now displayed under glass in the House foyer. A careful search through the ashes in the aftermath of the fire turned up nothing but small pieces of debris with traces of gold and silver on them. The current Mace was a gift from the Lord Mayor of London, who wanted to offer it from the moment he heard about the fire. It is a replica of the lost Mace, and the small pieces found in the ashes were incorporated into it.

The Sergeant-at-Arms is the guardian of the Mace, which is carried on the right shoulder. It is the Sergeant-at-Arms who places the Mace on the Table and removes it again. During the sitting, the Sergeant-at-Arms is seated near the Bar of the House, at the far end of the Chamber from the Speaker.

The centre Block
after 1880

At the entrance to the House chamber is an antechamber. Beyond the antechamber is a large foyer where journalists with both the print and electronic media frequently wait to question MPs and request interviews. Onlookers often gather there too, hoping to catch a glimpse of the Prime Minister and members of the Cabinet as they come from the Prime Minister's office in time for Question Period. The Prime Minister has a parliamentary office, at the south-west corner of the Centre Block, but the ministerial offices are located in the Langevin Block, on the other side of Wellington Street opposite the East Block.

Running the length of each side of the chamber is a room commonly known as a "lobby." The one behind the government benches is reserved for members of the party in power while the one on the opposite side is for opposition MPs. The lobbies are equipped with tables, armchairs, and telephones, and are connected to the chamber by four doors. Parliamentarians can withdraw here to converse, make telephone calls, discuss certain matters, or simply relax without interrupting the debates, and still be close enough to the chamber to be able to return at a moment's notice.

Offices for Members of Parliament are located in the Centre Block, the East Block, the West Block, the Wellington Building and the Confederation Building. The latter two are located close to Parliament Hill, at two corners of Wellington and Bank streets. The Hill has its own bus service running among the various buildings used by parliamentarians, committees, and parliamentary services. It should be noted that there is not room on the Hill for all the many services that support Parliament's work, and so they have had to be installed in several nearby buildings: the Committees Directorate, Parliamentary Publications and administrative services are quartered in the Wellington Building, sometimes referred to as the South Block; still others are in buildings along Sparks Street, one block south of Wellington, including the two services in charge of inter-parliamentary relations, the office of the legal advisers, the Table Research Branch and the Research Branch of the Library of Parliament.

At the time of Confederation, the Government could house every single department in only two Buildings, the East and West Blocks. Since then the functions of Government have multiplied, and the needs of Parliament as well. Today the East and West Blocks are occupied by MPs' offices and administrative and support services for the two Houses, and the demand for space is, it must be admitted, a perpetual problem for the officials in charge of planning.

The Parliament of Canada owns many paintings, works of art and historic treasures that until very recently were not even inventoried. Not only was this difficult from a purely practical standpoint, but it also made it impossible to determine which collections ought to be added to and which pieces were in need of maintenance. To rectify this situation, a curator was appointed in 1989 to oversee the collections, establish the location of each work of art, draw up an inventory and compile a catalogue.

Parliament: architectural details

FIGURE 2

House of Commons

1. Speaker
2. Pages
3. Government Members
4. Opposition Members
5. Prime Minister
6. Leader of the Official Opposition
7. Leader of second largest party in opposition
8. Clerk and Table Officers
9. Mace
10. Hansard Reporters
11. Sergeant-at-Arms
12. Interpreters
13. Press Gallery
14. Public Gallery
15. Official Gallery
16. Reserved Gallery
17. MPs' Gallery
18. Special Gallery
19. MPs' Gallery
20. Speaker's Gallery
21. Senate Gallery

Source: Public Information Office, House of Commons.

3 The Senate

The Senate

Canada has a bicameral system, that is, a political structure that includes two assemblies.

Section 17 of the *Constitution Act, 1867* provides that the Parliament of Canada shall consist of the Queen, the Senate, and the House of Commons. All three must consent to legislation before it can become law. In Canada we do not, properly speaking, have what is known as separation of powers, of which the American system is an example. Here the head of the executive and the Ministers sit in the legislature, and Cabinet carries out both legislative and executive functions.

With respect to the business of Parliament, the Governor General, representing the Sovereign, follows the Cabinet's advice, which in turn is expected to reflect the decisions of the House. In practice, we can say that the Senate and the House are responsible for the passing of legislation. By custom, if a member of one House refers to the other in debate, the term employed is "the other place." Thus in the Senate, the Commons should not be called the Commons but always "the other place," and in the House the same will apply to the Senate.

Because Canada's Parliament has two Houses, or Chambers, it is what is known as a "bicameral" legislature. The provincial legislatures are today all unicameral, Québec being the last province to abolish its Upper House in 1968.

MEMBERSHIP

The Senate is what is called an Upper House. Its role and functions are to a great extent modelled on those of the House of Lords, and it is regarded as the senior House: in the Canadian order of precedence, Senators come ahead of MPs.

The Constitution stipulates that there shall be 104 Senators, a number that can be changed only by a constitutional amendment. Distribution of Senate seats is by region, with 24 seats each for Ontario and Québec, 24 for the Maritimes (10 for Nova Scotia, 10 for New Brunswick and 4 for Prince Edward Island), 24 for the West (6 for Manitoba, 6 for Saskatchewan, 6 for Alberta and 6 for British Columbia), 6 for Newfoundland, and 1 each for the Territories.

Section 26 of the *Constitution Act, 1867*, provides that in exceptional circumstances an additional four or eight Senators may be appointed. This provision was invoked for the first time only recently.

In 1873, Prime Minister Alexander Mackenzie attempted to appoint additional Senators but the Colonial Secretary did not consider that circumstances warranted, on the grounds that the provision could only be invoked if there were a serious conflict between the two Houses, and then only if it were probable that the additional appointments would resolve the difficulty. Sir Wilfrid Laurier in 1900 and Sir Robert Borden in 1912 considered invoking the provision but in the end did not do so. Thus the provision was never actually used until December 1990, when the Senate systematically opposed passage of the legislation introducing the goods and services tax, legislation that had been passed after much contentious debate in the Commons. Faced with this impasse, the government decided to resort to Section 26. The necessary procedure was unclear. While Section 24 of the *Constitution Act, 1867* provides that the Governor General appoints Senators on the Sovereign's behalf, Section 26 says that "if . . . the Queen thinks fit" she may appoint additional Senators on the Governor General's recommendation. It was therefore to the Queen that the Canadian Government addressed itself in 1990 to bring about the appointment of eight additional Senators, two for each of the regions. In this way, the governing party became a majority in the Senate and the legislation finally passed after further acrimonious debate. However, under the provisions of the Constitution, it is anticipated that the number will return to normal for each region and for the Senate as a whole before the Government may appoint any additional people to the Senate (s.26). It may, however, appoint a Senator to one of "the four Divisions until such Division is represented by 24 Senators and no more" (s.27).[1]

As just mentioned, Senators are appointed by the Governor in Council, which in practice means by the Prime Minister. Up to 1965 they were appointed for life, but they are now obliged to retire at 75 by virtue of a constitutional amendment adopted in that year. All Senators must live in the province they represent. To be eligible for appointment, a person must be at least 30 years old, which the Fathers of Confederation saw as a safeguard against immaturity, and possess real property valued at $4,000 or more in the province represented. In addition, each Senator from Québec represents one of the 24 former electoral divisions of

Senators are appointed by the Governor in Council on the recommendation of the Prime Minister, and may remain in office until the age of 75.

1. Eugene Forsey, "Alexander Mackenzie's Memorandum on the Appointment of Extra Senators, 1873-4," 27 *Canadian Historical Review* (1946), pp. 189-190, "Appointment of Extra Senators under Section 26 of the British North America Act," *Canadian Journal of Economics and Political Science* Vol. 12 No. 2 (1946), pp. 159-167.

The Fathers of Confederation

Lower Canada. It should be noted here that the concept of democracy has evolved since 1867. In those days suffrage was not universal, and no one saw anything wrong with an upper house made up of appointees whose primary qualification was that they were prosperous land owners. Four thousand dollars was no small sum in 1867, and only a man of a certain maturity could be expected to be worth that much. It was anticipated that an upper house made up of such men would provide a brake on the impulsiveness of the elected House.

Both men and women can become Senators but this was not always the case. The *Constitution Act, 1867* provides that "qualified Persons" may be appointed to the Senate, and it was for a long time argued that a woman was not "a person" within the meaning of the Canadian Constitution. It took the courage and determination of five women, all from Alberta, to bring this issue before the courts. They had to take their case all the way to London and the Judicial Committee of the Privy Council, which was then our court of final appeal, before they won their fight.[2]

Cairine R. Wilson was the first woman to be named Senator in Canada, in 1930.

In February 1930, Cairine R. Wilson became the first woman appointed to the Senate. But the proportion of women Senators has remained low. In the 1992 Senate there were only 14, the highest number so far. Two women in succession have been appointed Speaker of the Senate: Muriel McQueen Fergusson in 1972 and Renaude Lapointe in 1974.

---

2. This case is called "Persons Case." See *Edwards v. The Attorney General for Canada* (1930), *Appeal Case* 124.

It is interesting to note that in 1990 the first "elected" Senator was appointed to the Senate. The Alberta government has for some time favoured an elected Senate, and in pursuit of this goal a provincial "election" was organized to fill a Senate vacancy though the election was not recognized by the federal government. Stan Waters, a member of the Reform Party, won the election and although he was not obliged to do so, Prime Minister Mulroney appointed Mr. Waters to the Alberta vacancy. He has since passed away.

Traditionally, the Prime Minister appoints people to sit in the Upper House who generally have valuable experience. They are often political figures of long standing, at either the provincial or the federal level; successful business people; eminent personalities in a variety of fields; and there is no doubt about the competence and prestige they bring with them.

We have seen that during the early years of Confederation two Prime Ministers were members of the Senate. It is unlikely this will ever happen again. In the modern political context, recognizing that the Cabinet is responsible to the elected House of Commons, it would be impractical for the head of the Government to sit in the Senate. On the other hand, it is always possible that to ensure balanced regional representation, a Prime Minister might make one or more Senators Cabinet Ministers. This occurred in 1979, when Joe Clark appointed Senators to Cabinet to compensate for the lack of Conservative MPs from Québec, and in 1980, when Pierre Trudeau appointed Senators to Cabinet because no Liberal MPs were elected from three western provinces.

THE SPEAKER

Chosen from among fellow Senators, the Speaker of the Senate is appointed by the Governor in Council on the advice of the Prime Minister. The Speaker can be replaced at any time, but in principle is appointed for the life of the Parliament. Speaker Charbonneau, however, was appointed to a second term in 1988. The Speaker of the Senate has the rank of Cabinet Minister and is a member of the Privy Council. The office of Speaker of the Senate occupies a high place in the order of precedence, fourth, in fact, after the Governor General, the Prime Minister and the Chief Justice of the Supreme Court. This is why the holder of this office is sometimes called upon to represent the Government. The Speaker of the Senate, unlike the Speaker of the House of Commons, is not obliged to break off all party ties while in office. The Speaker thus becomes an important political figure, and may be asked by the Prime Minister to represent Canada on official missions or at official functions. Again, the Speaker has the right to vote,

The Speaker of the Senate is appointed by the Governor in Council on the advice of the Prime Minister for the life of the Parliament.

as does every other Senator, although he often chooses the neutrality of abstention.

The Speaker directs proceedings according to the rules and practices of the Senate and chairs debates, ensuring as far as possible that they proceed with calm and dignity. The Rules of the Senate resemble the *Standing Orders of the House of Commons*, although procedure in the Senate is less rigid. For example, during debate the Senators do not address themselves to the Chair, as is the case in the House, but may speak directly to their colleagues. In June 1991, however, the *Rules of the Senate* were amended significantly and the powers of the Speaker were increased at the same time.

In general, the debates in the Senate, and especially Question Period, are calmer than they are in the House of Commons. There are a number of reasons for this: the Government is not responsible to the Senate in the same way it is to the House, there are usually no Ministers who head departments to be questioned, and overall the Senate is less closely involved with the day-to-day incidents that affect the political climate in the House. Although the Government Leader in the Senate is a member of the Cabinet, he cannot stand in for all the Ministers who head departments. The function of the Government Leader in the Senate — as in the House of Commons — is to ensure passage of the Government's legislative program.

The Speaker of the Senate is responsible for decorum during the daily proceedings and official ceremonies. It is in the Senate that the Governor General delivers the Throne Speech marking the opening of a new Parliament or a new session. At the official opening of Parliament, the Speaker of the House of Commons is summoned together with all of the other MPs to the Senate to ask the Sovereign's representative to confirm "all the undoubted rights and privileges" of the House of Commons. (see "Sittings and Sessions," Chapter 10). This is a traditional ceremony inherited from the British Parliament.

Royal Assent to bills that have been passed by both Houses is given in the Senate in the presence of the Speaker and formally signified by the Governor General, or more often by a judge of the Supreme Court on behalf of the Governor General. On all these occasions, and when taking the Chair, the Speaker is robed. The ceremonies that take place in the Senate are a vestige of the past, as the Senate has inherited the mantle of the appointed councils that existed before Confederation, which were modelled on the House of Lords.

The Speaker embodies and represents the Senate both in Canada and abroad. This entails leading parliamentary delegations on official visits to other countries, hosting foreign delegations to Canada, and receiving many visitors, including the members of the diplomatic corps and distinguished guests.

THE SENATE'S FUNCTIONS

In 1980 the Legal and Constitutional Affairs Committee's report on "Certain Aspects of the Canadian Constitution" listed four functions of the Senate: to legislate, to conduct investigations, to represent the regions and to protect linguistic and other minorities. All of these functions are also performed by the House of Commons. The main function of the Senate is to pass legislation. In this area the two Houses have, in principle, the same powers. Although the Senate is modelled on the House of Lords, its powers have never been limited by statute as they have in the United Kingdom. On the other hand, Canada's Constitution does include an important limitation to the Senate's legislative power. Section 53 of the *Constitution Act, 1867* provides that "Bills for appropriating any Part of the Public Revenue, or for imposing any tax or impost, shall originate in the House of Commons." This provision has its roots in British parliamentary history, going back to the era when the Sovereign was obliged to ask the agreement of the elected Commons to raise funds, termed "aids and supplies to the Crown," for the purpose of running the government and fighting wars.

> The Government may introduce any bill in the Senate, with the exception of money bills.

The legacy of this cautious attitude towards the Crown is that money bills can never be introduced in the Senate. The Senate accepts this limitation on its authority, but claims that the limitation does not take away its right to propose amendments to money bills, or even to defeat them. The two Houses are not in agreement on this point: the House of Commons, like its British counterpart, insists that the Upper House has no authority at all in financial matters; the Senate argues that there is nothing in the Constitution forbidding it from amending a bill passed by the Lower House. In the past, the Senate has in fact amended money bills passed by the House. When the House wishes to expedite a bill, it has tended to accept the amendments rather than argue the point, but in such cases it has taken care to specify that this is not to be regarded as a precedent. On other occasions, the House has made a point of insisting on its privilege. In general, differences of opinion end by being settled through consultation, although neither House concedes its position in principle.

Although the House denies the right of the Senate to amend money bills the courts have decided that such amendments, when agreed to by the House, do not affect the validity of the legislation.[3]

---

3.   A. Elmer Driedger, "Money Bills and the Senate," *Ottawa Law Review*, Vol. 3 (Fall 1968), p. 25.

The *Constitution Act, 1982* places a further limitation on the powers of the Senate, giving it only a suspensive veto on constitutional amendments that require the consent of the provinces.[4]

The Senate has three legislative functions: it examines bills passed by the House, it considers bills introduced by the Government in the Senate, and it considers private bills, which are bills promoted by private interests. The legislative function of the Senate will be discussed further on when the legislative process is dealt with in its entirety (see "The Legislative Functions," Chapter 9).

Over the years, the Senate has come to play an especially useful role in inquiries. Inquiries that in the past would have been carried out by a Royal Commission are increasingly being undertaken by Senate committees. Royal commissions disband once their reports have been tabled, whereas the members of a Senate committee continue to be available. Many Senate studies have been quite remarkable both for their content and for their quality: on the mass media (1970), science policy (the report was composed of four volumes, the last one published in 1977), poverty in Canada (1971). In all such cases, the Senate mandates a special committee to make the requisite investigation, summon witnesses, consult experts and produce a report. This does not mean that the Government will necessarily endorse the committee's conclusions, or act on its recommendations. But in these well-documented reports the Government has a source of information that enables it to form an opinion and decide what policy to adopt and what measures to take.

The role of the Senate as protector of the regions and the rights of minorities is less obvious. But the Senate has always seen itself as protector of provincial rights. For example in 1918 the Senate endorsed the assertion of one of its special committees that "the Senate as shown by the *British North America Act* as well as by the discussion in the Canadian legislature in the Québec Resolutions in addition to its general powers and duties is specially empowered to safeguard the rights of provincial organizations." From time to time, the Senate blocks a piece of legislation, as happened in 1977 with the Maritime Code Bill, or undertakes specific regional studies as in the 1976 study of the rural economy of Kent County, New Brunswick. But despite the intentions of the Fathers of Confederation, the Senate has never quite become a Chamber of the provinces or regions. On the contrary, the balance among the country's regions was upset when new provinces were admitted and the territories gained representation.

4. Section 47(1).

It has often been said that the Senate tends to go along with the decisions of the elected House, and that political partisanship is not much in evidence in its proceedings. This may be the case when the two Houses are dominated by the same party, but it does not always hold true when the Senate is dominated by the Opposition.

The Senate sits less frequently than the Commons; it usually sits three days a week, and often has to adjourn while waiting for the House to pass the legislation brought in by the Government. It does not sit when Parliament is prorogued.

THE SENIOR OFFICIALS OF THE SENATE

The Senate has three senior officials, of whom two — the Clerk (whose full title is Clerk of the Senate and Clerk of the Parliaments) and the Gentleman Usher of the Black Rod — are appointed by order-in-council, in other words by the Prime Minister and the Cabinet. The third — the Law Clerk and Parliamentary Counsel — is appointed by resolution of the Senate. The Clerk of the Senate plays a role similar to that of the Clerk of the House: duties include assisting the Speaker when the latter presides over debates, and carrying out administrative responsibilities. The Gentleman Usher of the Black Rod performs duties similar to those of the Sergeant-at-Arms in the House. The Law Clerk and Parliamentary Counsel, as the title indicates, provides legal advice to the Speaker and members of the Senate.

4 The Office of Speaker of the House of Commons

The House of Commons in 1925

The office of Speaker is almost as ancient as Parliament itself. It emerged in the Middle Ages when the Commons — the ordinary people — of England needed a spokesman in their dealings with the King, someone who would voice their grievances and present their petitions. This was by no means a safe or easy thing to do at that time, and potential spokesmen generally had to be pressured into accepting the responsibility. In those days the individual chosen spoke for the whole Commons to the King (hence the name "Speaker"), but today's Speaker takes no part in the debates. It is interesting to note that the first occupant of this quintessentially British office, whose name has come down to us from the thirteenth century, was a certain Peter de Montfort.

The Speaker presides over the deliberations of the House, and is its representative. The dignity of the House, the respect owing to it, the privileges it possesses, all rest with the Speaker. An affront to the Speaker is an affront to the House as a whole and may be punishable as a breach of privilege.

ELECTION

The Speaker is elected by secret ballot. Any MP who is not a party leader may be a candidate for the Speakership.

Until 1986, the Speaker was ostensibly elected by all Members of the House, but for all practical purposes the choice was made by the Government, usually after consultation with the opposition parties. In 1982, the Special Committee on Standing Orders and Procedure proposed that the choice of the Speaker no longer be the sole prerogative of the Prime Minister. It recommended a new Standing Order that set out the steps to be followed in electing a Speaker by secret ballot. A general election and a change of Government made it impossible to follow up on this recommendation immediately. A subsequent committee on reform of the House revived the proposal, and it was agreed to in June 1985. The Standing Order went into effect on a provisional basis in September of that year and since February 1986 the Standing Orders of the House have provided for the election of the Speaker by secret ballot. The first time these Standing Orders were invoked was in September 1986.

When the election takes place at the beginning of a new Parliament, it is presided over by the MP with the longest period of unbroken service. The same would hold true if a Speaker died while in office. Normally a Speaker remains in office for the term of the Parliament; but it can happen that he resigns. In that case the election of a successor is presided over by the outgoing Speaker. This happened in 1986 when Speaker Bosley resigned. On September 30 of that year I became the first Speaker elected by secret ballot, eleven ballots being necessary to produce a final result. After the general election of 1988 I was re-elected to the speakership on the first ballot (the procedure for electing a Speaker is explained under "The Clerk," Chapter 6). The prestige and authority of the Speaker have definitely been enhanced by the new system of election.

INDEPENDENCE

Until 1935, the convention in Great Britain was to allow an outgoing Speaker to run unopposed in a general election. This practice aimed to ensure continuity in the speakership, and to underline the Speaker's independence. Since 1935, the Speaker has always faced opponents during general elections.

In Canada, there has never been such a convention, although the principles of neutrality and independence of the Speaker are also respected here. A number of outgoing Speakers have been re-elected in their ridings in the normal way, that is, they have had to campaign and defeat candidates from other parties. A Speaker may have to abstain from active partisan politics while in office, but is free to remain a party member and to canvass for votes once Parliament has been dissolved. Speaker Lucien Lamoureux made an interesting attempt to reinforce the Speaker's neutrality. He had become Speaker in 1966 as a Liberal member, and in 1968, when a general election was called, he announced that he would run as an independent, having obtained the agreement of the two major parties that they would not oppose him. He was re-elected in his riding and subsequently to the speakership with the support of all parties. In the 1972 election he again ran as an independent, but this time, far from being unopposed, he faced three opponents. He carried his riding despite this and became Speaker once again. When he retired from political life he was replaced in the Chair by James Jerome, the first Speaker in the history of the Parliament of Canada to remain Speaker through a change of Government (see Appendix B).

Although neither of these initiatives established a precedent, they undoubtedly paved the way for electing the Speaker by secret ballot, a practice that is an expression of democracy and a guarantee of the Speaker's independence.

PRESTIGE

Solemn ceremony characterizes the ritual procession that precedes each sitting.

The Speaker's office carries with it a great deal of prestige. Evidence of this can be found in the ceremony that surrounds parliamentary activities in which the Speaker plays a part. The dignity of the office is underlined by many symbols, including the Speaker's robes, which resemble the courtroom robes of Queen's Counsel and the tricorn hat, worn in procession. Each sitting of the House is preceded by a Speaker's Parade. The Sergeant-at-Arms goes first, bearing the Mace, and the Clerk of the House and other Table Officers bring up the rear. This solemn procession is much admired by visitors to the Hill, who wait every day in the corridors to see it pass. At the opening of a new Parliament or session, the Speaker is again escorted in procession to the Senate, to hear the Throne Speech. At the opening of each day in the House, the Speaker says a prayer before being seated in the magnificent, ornately carved armchair that is further testimony to the dignity of the office. (See Chapter 2 for more history of the Speaker's Chair.) Custom requires that MPs bow to the Speaker when they enter, leave, or cross the Chamber. When they speak in the House, it is always to the Speaker that they address themselves, usually beginning their remarks with the words, "Madam Speaker" or "Mr. Speaker." If the Speaker rises to call the House to order or to hand down a decision, silence must prevail. The Speaker may be censured only on a substantive motion subject to a vote of the House. This happens only rarely, the last time such a motion was debated and voted on being in 1956.[1]

The Speaker's Chair

THE MACE

The Mace is another symbol closely associated with the Speaker. It embodies the ancient authority of the Crown, today exercised by Parliament. In the House it also represents the authority of the Speaker, because "the authority of the Speaker and of the House are indivisible."[2]

In the Middle Ages the Mace was the weapon of the Sergeant-at-Arms, who was then the King's bodyguard. It was heavy enough to smash

1.   Debates of the House of Commons, May 31, 1956, 1956 session, Vol. 5, pp. 4517-34.
2.   Norman Wilding and Philip Laundy, *An Encyclopaedia of Parliament*, 4th rev. ed. (London: Cassell and Co., 1972), p. 451.

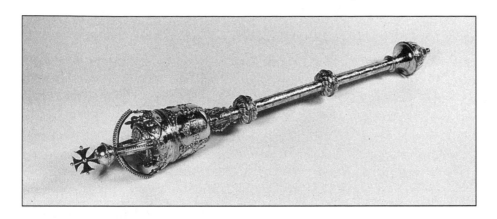

The Mace

In the Middle Ages
the Mace symbolized
the authority of the
House of Commons.
It was used by the
Sergeant-at-Arms to
protect the Speaker
on his way to the
Chamber.

armour and was used to defend the King's person from any attacker. It was also used in summoning accused persons before the King for judgement. In the thirteenth century the Mace began to be ornamented with jewels and precious metals, the origin of the elaborate modern Mace. Its shape has changed over the centuries: it no longer looks like a weapon, but rather an ornamental and purely symbolic object.[3]

Nowadays the Mace is an integral part of parliamentary decorum. Without it the House is not constituted and proceedings cannot begin. It is borne on the shoulder of the Sergeant-at-Arms when the Speaker processes from place to place, and when the Speaker is seated in the Chair, the Mace rests on the Table (see Chapter 2). When the House sits in Committee of the Whole, the Mace is placed below the Table on special brackets.

Recently an incident occurred that is unique in Canadian parliamentary history, and illustrates very clearly the significance of the Mace and the respect due to its symbolic value.

On October 30, 1991, an MP who was dissatisfied with the manner in which a vote was conducted angrily tried to grab the Mace as the Sergeant-at-Arms was carrying it away following the adjournment of the House. This act was considered by the House to be a breach of its privileges. The Speaker, in the name of the whole House, reprimanded the MP, who was called to the Bar of the House having been found guilty of "a breach of privilege and a gross contempt of the House."[4] The Speaker commented, "The Mace is the symbol which embodies not only the authority of the House but its privileges as well . . . The House

3.   Norman Wilding and Philip Laundy, op.cit., p. 456.
4.   Debates of the House of Commons, October 30, 1991, Vol. 55 and 56, p. 4269.

of Commons can only function when its dignity is upheld by all Members and its rules are followed."[5]

DUTIES

Although Sections 44 and 45 of the *Constitution Act, 1867* refer to the Speaker of the House, and Section 46 stipulates that "The Speaker shall preside at all Meetings of the House of Commons," it is in the *Standing Orders of the House of Commons*, and above all in the *conventions and precedents of the House*, that the Speaker's many duties are defined. The *Canada Parliament Act*[6] also contains some relevant provisions.

The responsibilities of the Speaker may be divided into three categories. The first includes presiding in the House and guarding its privileges. The second has to do with representing the House, in its external relationships and at official parliamentary events, both in Canada and abroad. The third encompasses responsibilities for the internal administration of the House, similar to those of a Minister responsible for a department of government.

Presiding in the House

The Speaker has many important duties. He presides over the work of the House, interprets the Standing Orders, and carries out administrative and representational functions.

The Speaker's chief function is to preside over the deliberations of the House and to ensure Members conform to the Standing Orders and parliamentary practice. This demands objectivity and impartiality. This is why as soon as an MP is elected Speaker he must refrain from all political activity, cease to be an active member of a party, and of course cease attending caucus meetings. The neutrality of the office does not permit the incumbent to participate in debates, as Standing Order 9 makes clear: "The Speaker shall not take part in any debate before the House." However, if when a vote is taken, the "yeas" and the "nays" are equal in number, the Speaker casts the deciding vote. Even then, this vote should not express personal convictions, but should maintain the status quo or leave the matter open for further consideration.

The House governs its own proceedings, and the Speaker is there to serve the House, not to rule it — a great principle, always to be respected. However, the course and direction of proceedings in the House, and the orderly flow of debate, are profoundly influenced by the Speaker's decisions. These decisions form the body of precedents that constitute parliamentary case law.

---

5. Debates of the House of Commons, October 31, 1991, Vol. 55 and 56, p. 4309.
6. *Canada Parliament Act*, R.S. 1985 c. P.-1 am. 1985, c. 31 (1st supp.), c. 38 (2nd supp.), 1991, c. 20.

Before the proceedings begin, the Speaker must ensure the House is properly constituted. A quorum, as required by the Constitution, is 20 members, including the Speaker. Except at the beginning of a sitting, it is taken for granted that there is a quorum, unless an MP rises to indicate that there is not. If after a count a quorum is found not to be present, bells are rung for 15 minutes to summon the absent Members. When this time elapses, if a quorum is not found, the Speaker adjourns the House.

The Speaker chairs the proceedings, reads the motions, puts the questions to which the House must respond with a vote; and also enforces the Standing Orders and current practices, decides on points of order and interprets the rules when necessary. When invoking the powers articulated in the Standing Orders, it is provided: "In deciding a point of order or practice, the Speaker shall state the Standing Order or other authority applicable to the case" (Standing Order 10). No debate is permitted on the Speaker's ruling.

When there is a voice vote, the Speaker announces the results by saying "In my opinion the *yeas* (or the *nays*) have it" — a very old parliamentary formula. It is up to the Speaker to interpret the volume of voices. Should five or more MPs rise, the Speaker says "Call in the Members" and a recorded division takes place (see "The Rules of Debate," Chapter 10).

To ensure that the deliberations proceed in accordance with the Standing Orders, the Speaker has the duty of directing the attention of the House to motions or amendments that may be out of order.

A further duty of the Speaker is that of selecting and grouping amendments at the report stage of a bill. This is a responsibility calling for shrewd judgement. Amendments whose objectives are the same are grouped to make judicious use of the time of the House, since an MP can speak only once on the group of amendments and then only for 10 minutes.

Presiding during Question Period is another challenging task. The atmosphere during Question Period is often electric, with the Government and the Opposition confronting each other under the glare of television cameras and in the presence of the public. It is then that the Speaker's impartiality is most sorely tested. Traditionally the Speaker calls on the MP who rises first, but in practice other factors must be considered. Conventions have developed which have had the effect of limiting the Speaker's discretion. Question Period is regarded as largely the prerogative of the opposition parties and their leaders have the right to ask the first questions. In addition, party Whips generally provide lists of Members they wish to be recognized, although the

Speaker also calls on some Members who are not included on these lists. Wisdom, fairness, and common sense are required in order to reconcile the various rules and practices that apply, to decide whom the House would most like to hear, and who should have the chance to be heard. Details of the issues involved will be examined in "The House of Commons and the Executive," Chapter 9.

A Member who infringes on the Standing Orders may be "named" (designated by his name) and is usually suspended for the rest of the sitting.

The Speaker has a number of disciplinary powers available for maintaining order in the House. If disorder breaks out, the Speaker will intervene, by calling the House "to order," repeatedly if necessary. If a Member uses improper language, the MP is asked to withdraw the offending remarks. If the MP refuses, the Speaker will usually persist in calling for a withdrawal. If this does not produce the desired effect, the Speaker may "name" the MP, thus forcing the offender to leave the Chamber for the rest of the day. If the MP refuses to leave, the Speaker calls on the Sergeant-at-Arms to escort the Member from the Chamber. Another strategy at the Speaker's disposal is to give such Members time to reflect, refusing to recognize them until they agree to withdraw. But the Speaker is not a policeman and it is only rarely that a Member is named. Order in the House must be maintained, but good sense must come into play to dictate when, if at all, to intervene, and how.

Representation

The Speaker represents the House in all its dealings with the Governor General, the Government, the Senate, the diplomatic corps, the provincial legislatures and foreign parliaments and other bodies outside the House of Commons.

To take the political arena first, it is the Speaker who represents the Commons in its dealings with members of the Government and the Senate. Immediately after being elected at the start of a new Parliament, the Speaker proceeds to the Senate to ask the Governor General to confirm "all the undoubted rights and privileges" of the House of Commons, a tradition inherited from Great Britain. (Details of the formal ceremonies that surround the opening of a Parliament are presented below, under "Opening of Parliament," Chapter 10.)

It is as the representative of the Commons that the Speaker leads the procession of MPs when they are called to the Senate to meet the Sovereign or the Governor General, as, for example, at the opening of a new Parliament or new session. The Speaker officially communicates the text of the Speech from the Throne to the House when a new session or a new Parliament opens and, on the House's behalf, personally presents the Governor General with the Address in Reply to the Speech from the Throne following the debate on the contents of the speech. All messages addressed to the Commons by the Governor General, the Government, or other parliaments or legislatures are communicated to the House by the Speaker.

The Parliament of Canada maintains relations with the provincial legislatures and with most foreign parliaments. Responsibility for maintaining these relations rests with the Speaker. Collaboration between the provinces and Ottawa is excellent in the area of information exchange, and there are some very valuable parliamentary co-operation programs. Within the framework of these programs, parliamentary officials spend time working and training in a parliament or in a legislature other than their own. The Speakers of Canada's Parliament and of provincial and territorial legislatures meet once a year, in a different province or territory each time, to discuss subjects of common interest. Procedure, parliamentary affairs, and the role of the Speaker, are of course perennial items on the agenda. The Speaker of the House of Commons seldom fails to attend. Canada's Speakers also meet every year when the meeting of the regional council of the Commonwealth Parliamentary Association is held. These are the regular occasions on which our Speakers get together.

The Parliament of Canada is active in a number of interparliamentary associations. The Speaker of the House is an honorary president of all of them. In addition to these structured interparliamentary contacts, our Parliament joins in exchanges with many other parliaments throughout the world. Every year the Speaker receives numerous invitations from foreign colleagues. One regular international activity is participation in the Conference of Commonwealth Speakers and Presiding Officers, which meets every two years in a different Commonwealth country. The subjects discussed are always directly linked to Speakers' responsibilities, as they are at the gatherings of Canadian Speakers, which are modelled on the Commonwealth Speakers' Conferences. The meetings are always very productive and valuable for the Speakers, whose parliamentary systems are in many respects similar.

The Speaker represents the House of Commons in all its dealings with the Canadian Government, and in this capacity receives all manner of communications of interest to the MPs. Equally, there are often invitations to attend cultural events, and receptions held by embassies and high commissions on their countries' national days; the Speaker considers it a duty to attend as the representative of the House as often as other duties in the House permit.

Representational functions take up a great deal of time for both the Speaker of the House and the Speaker of the Senate, for there are large

The Speaker is kept extremely busy. Aside from his duties in the House, he carries out numerous protocol and representation functions.

numbers of diplomats and both Canadian and foreign dignitaries to be received. In addition, during and after trips abroad, the Speaker invites parliamentary delegations and other speakers to Canada, and must then receive and host them. When the Prime Minister receives heads of state or other foreign dignitaries, the Speaker is often called upon to receive them on behalf of the House of Commons. Occasionally a foreign head of state addresses the Houses of Parliament jointly: when that happens, the ceremony takes place in the Commons and the Speaker is, of course, the host. Parliamentarians and other important visitors passing through Ottawa generally attend Question Period. Other parliaments send a great many communications to the Speaker, for example, notices of the election of a new Speaker or the death of a well-known parliamentarian, or copies of resolutions passed in favour of establishing parliamentary relations with Canada. The Speaker must reply in writing to all this correspondence, which represents an immense volume of mail every day.

Administration

In addition to the other duties that have been described, the Speaker has extensive administrative duties that involve a heavy burden of responsibility and take up a great deal of time.

The House of Commons employs about 2000 people on staff and has a budget in the neighbourhood of $240 million. The *Canada Parliament Act* entrusts the financial and administrative management of both employees and budget to the Board of Internal Economy.[7]

The Speaker chairs the Board, which usually meets every other Wednesday evening when the House is sitting. The administration of the House will be examined in greater detail later on (see Chapter 11) but the important point here is the involvement of the Speaker in yet another set of heavy administrative and management responsibilities.

The Speaker also chairs the meetings of the Executive Committee, which is an essential element in the administrative structure. This committee is responsible for management and for important decisions affecting the general administration of the finances and personnel of the House. The Executive Committee meets in order to prepare for the meetings of the Board of Internal Economy.

The *Parliament of Canada Act* provides that the Speaker and the Deputy Speaker continue to carry out their responsibilities even after Parliament has been dissolved — in fact, until a new Speaker and a new Deputy

7. *Canada Parliament Act*, R.S. 1985 c. P.-1 am. 1985, c. 31 (1st supp.), c. 38 (2nd supp.), 1991, c. 20.

Speaker are elected. In this way, there is no interruption in the management and administration of the House, for the outgoing Speaker remains in office through the election campaign and until the new Parliament meets.

QUALIFICATIONS

As has been shown, the Speaker's duties are many and varied. They demand the skills of a shrewd politician (though the Speaker must be above politics), a judge, a diplomat, a man or woman of the world. Sound common sense must be combined with tolerance and firmness. It has been said that a Speaker does not require rare qualities, but rather common qualities in a rare degree.

A thorough knowledge of the rules of procedure and of the parliamentary environment are essential to the Speaker's role.

The Speaker makes many decisions that are genuine judgements, which raises the question: is legal training a necessary prerequisite? Most Speakers have in fact been lawyers. Others have come from a variety of backgrounds including medicine, journalism, business, newspaper publishing, farming and dentistry. Certainly training in the law is extremely useful, but the primary requirement for a Speaker in the House of Commons is knowledge of the parliamentary environment. Nothing can replace extensive experience in the House. That is what enables the Speaker to assess correctly the mood of the House, its possible reactions, and its Members' behaviour.

The essential quality in a Speaker is impartiality, which must be evident in everything he does. Thus, it is important to be seen to be impartial, to treat all Members with equal fairness and to win their trust.

A careful and sympathetic sense of humour can also be a great asset when there is a need to get out of difficult situations gracefully. It is important to know how to turn a blind eye at the right moment. It may also be better to let a deliberately offensive remark fall on deaf ears rather than plunge into disciplinary action that might do more harm than good. The fact that the Speaker is now freely elected by all Members has helped to reinforce the authority of the position, and makes it easier to demand the co-operation of the House when necessary.

OTHER CHAIR OCCUPANTS

The Speaker has three colleagues who share the duty of presiding over the proceedings of the House. Standing Order 7 states that "at the commencement of every Parliament . . . [the House shall elect] a Deputy Speaker . . . [who] shall be required to possess the full and practical knowledge of the official language which is not that of the Speaker for the time being." The Deputy Speaker also chairs the Committees of the Whole and is appointed for the life of a Parliament. There are also a Deputy Chairman and an Assistant Deputy Chairman of Committees of the Whole, who are appointed not for the duration of the Parliament but for the session only. They are nominated by the Government, normally after consultation with the opposition parties.

A Deputy Speaker and two Assistants support the Speaker in his duties. In 1993, a woman, the Honourable Andrée Champagne, was Deputy Speaker.

The time spent in the Chair is divided among the Speaker, the Deputy Speaker, and the latter's two assistants. But it is almost always the Speaker who presides during Question Period, and whenever important decisions have to be handed down — during major debates, for example, and during the presentation of the Budget. The Deputy Speaker is at this time, and for the first time, a woman, the Honourable Andrée Champagne. The Deputy Speaker is a member of the Board of Internal Economy. In addition, because of the importance of the Speaker's representational duties and the number of social events they entail, the Deputy Speaker is often called on to represent the Speaker in receiving guests or attending functions.

Whoever sits in the Chair has the same powers as the Speaker in presiding over the deliberations of the House. Clearly, all Chair occupants must have the same qualities: impartiality, objectivity, and sound judgement. Like the Speaker, they must refrain from partisan activities in order to keep their neutrality beyond question, although, unlike the Speaker, they may vote in divisions unless they are occupying the Chair.

THE SPEAKER AS AN MP

No description of the Speaker's role would be complete without a discussion of certain other difficulties that arise due to the requirement of impartiality. If, for instance, the Speaker wishes at election time to run once again for a seat in the House, an awkward situation may present itself. The lack of any involvement in political life for several years may present a disadvantage with respect to the other parties' candidates. If there is a desire to return to the speakership, the campaign must be non-partisan, leaving opponents free to use the political issues of the day to their advantage.

Although a Speaker must be non-partisan and cannot debate, there is a long-standing tradition that is very much alive. It is simply this: the Speaker accepts limitations in the interests of all Members. In view of this, Cabinet Ministers, Private Members and, to a remarkable degree, senior civil servants, go out of their way to assist the Speaker in resolving his constituents' problems. It is an unusual, but very effective, relationship which affords the Speaker full access to those in positions of influence and power. Notwithstanding all the duties of the office, a Speaker must still serve his constituents, his community, and be re-elected.[8]

8.   Philip Laundy, *The Office of Speaker in the Parliaments of the Commonwealth* (London: Quiller Press Ltd., 1984), pp. 71 and 73.

5 The Members of the House of Commons

The House of Commons has 295 seats, divided as follows: 26 for Alberta, 32 for British Columbia, 14 for Manitoba, 10 for New Brunswick, 7 for Newfoundland, 2 for the Northwest Territories, 11 for Nova Scotia, 99 for Ontario, 4 for Prince Edward Island, 75 for Québec, 14 for Saskatchewan and 1 for the Yukon.

PROFILE

In 1993, 295 Members sit in the House.

Who are the people who hold these seats in the House of Commons?

C.E.S. Franks, in his 1987 work *The Parliament of Canada*, describes the typical MP as being from "one of the two founding ethnic groups, middle-aged, and a success in a profession or career before entering Parliament."[1] Members of Parliament do indeed, as a general rule, come from a higher social stratum than most of the electorate: 70 percent have attended university while in the population at large the proportion is only 10 percent.[2] This means that, while MPs may represent all the geographical regions of the country, they are less representative of all its social classes. Nowadays issues of representativeness are of increasing concern.

Members represent diverse professions, notably lawyers and businessmen.

The make-up of the House has scarcely changed since Confederation. Professional men have always dominated, with lawyers the leading group and businessmen a close second. Farmers, administrators, and teachers come next. The remainder are not sufficiently numerous to be categorized. These groups have not always been represented in exactly this order. There have been variations from one Parliament to the next, but overall, this has been Parliament's image for 125 years.

1. C.E.S. Franks, *The Parliament of Canada* (Toronto: University of Toronto Press, 1987), p. 66.
2. Richard J. Van Loon and Michael S. Whittington, *The Canadian Political System: Environment, Structure and Process*, 3rd rev. ed. (Toronto: McGraw-Hill Ryerson Ltd., 1987), p. 459.

Changes both in our social life and mores and in our laws have had an impact on the kinds of people who sit in the House. Women, for example, could not be present in the days before they had the right to vote. Clergy too are more frequently found in the House now than they used to be. Nor is it surprising that MPs who previously worked in radio or television appeared in the House only in 1966, or that by 1993 there were ten of them.

The average age of MPs is between 35 and 50. Many are elected without previous experience in political life, although they may have worked in their parties' organizational ranks. Often they come from political backgrounds in which family members or close connections are, or have been, active in politics. In the 1984 elections, more than half the MPs were elected for the first time. Few MPs stay in office for very long, with six or seven years being the average and barely 10 percent remaining for more than 12 or 15 years.[3] Because of their lack of experience and the complexity of their functions, MPs must work very hard to adapt when they first come to Ottawa.

ROLE

Two theories tend to be put forward in discussions of the role of the MP. The first view says that the MP represents constituents, the second that he is their agent. In the latter view, the MP is a spokesman, relaying constituents' views and preferences. The mandate from the electorate is very clearly defined. If on the other hand, the MP simply represents constituents, the mandate is much looser. The voters have chosen their representative based on party membership, on ideas, and on personal qualities. Having made their choice for all these reasons, the electorate then trusts their candidate to use sound judgement and to defend their interests as well as possible. In Canada, it would seem that this representative role is the one generally conceded to an MP, although the distinction between the two roles is not always very clear. If we have opted for representation, however, it is for practical reasons. How could an MP possibly ascertain constituents' views every time a vote or an expression of opinion was called for? Many ridings are economically and socially very diverse — how would it be possible to arrive at a stand that satisfied all the voters all the time? Given the multitude of questions with which MPs must deal, often urgently, it is impossible for them to consult their constituents every time on every topic. More realistically, we assume that MPs are elected because they have the confidence of their constituents. The MPs must then prove that this confidence has been

3.   C.E.S. Franks, op. cit., p. 74.

well placed by staying in close contact with their ridings. Overall, MPs must take a number of factors into account, including party loyalty, loyalty to the electorate, duty to the country, and the desire to be re-elected. These considerations are sometimes difficult to reconcile.

Members of Parliament are referred to in the House by the names of their ridings. When they are addressed collectively, for example, by the Speaker, they are called "Honourable Members." In the House, one member is expected to refer to another as "the Honourable Member" or "my Honourable Friend." Outside the House, however, only Cabinet ministers, other members of the Privy Council, and Senators are entitled to the prefix "the Honourable" and Prime Ministers to the prefix "the Right Honourable."

A parliamentarian's life is a very busy one. It must be borne in mind that for many of them, home is thousands of kilometres from Ottawa, and they are obliged to shuttle back and forth between the capital and their ridings, with the added complication of jet lag from the different time zones. Nor is the MP's role limited to being present in the House. Certainly participation in the business of the House is a vitally important responsibility, but there are many others.

Although the main function of Parliament is to make laws, the role of MPs in this area is much less than one might think. The legislative process is dominated by the Government, that is to say the Cabinet, as we will see later when we explore the legislative functions of the House of Commons. Government Members are told about proposed legislation in caucus but Opposition Members do not have the opportunity to hear about upcoming bills. Backbenchers on both sides do have a chance to debate the principle of a bill at second reading and to intervene when a bill reaches committee stage, where it is discussed by a much smaller group of MPs. The procedural rules in committee are much more flexible than in the House, so that MPs can question witnesses, move amendments, and do everything in their power to influence the Government's policy. The position of a Government MP is clearly different from that of an Opposition MP, since only Opposition MPs want to embarrass the Government. Party discipline hampers MPs who might want to display some initiative in the area of legislation, and when the time comes to vote on a bill, MPs almost invariably support their party in the final analysis.

Even though MPs may not play a major role in formulating legislation, they can still make a contribution. For example, they serve their parties by advocating and interpreting party policy. Especially on controversial subjects like free trade or the goods and services tax, MPs serve as a conduit between the people and the policy-makers, facilitating communication and comprehension. They are close to their constituents, and can explain their parties' positions. At the same time they can make recommendations back to their party about how these positions are being received. It often happens, however, that MPs find themselves having to justify unpopular measures to the voters.

As we will see when we look at the rules of debate, five hours a week are set aside for Private Members' Business. During this time, MPs may introduce their own bills. Certain limitations are imposed here, for example, they may not commit the Government to any expenditure or taxation (see "The Rules of Debate," Chapter 10).

In addition to being able to introduce bills, MPs may move their own motions during the hours provided for Private Members' Business. Neither of these options, however, gives MPs much real voice or influence. Private Members' bills have little chance of proceeding beyond first reading stage, especially as the Standing Orders provide that once debate ends on a non-votable bill or motion, it is withdrawn and cannot be voted on except with the unanimous consent of the House.

Another avenue open to MPs is to present petitions. These are written requests signed by ordinary Canadians, asking the House to take certain action to resolve a problem or respond to a particular situation. A petition must be endorsed by an MP and then examined as to form and content and certified by the Clerk of Petitions. A petition may be either filed with the Clerk of the House or introduced orally by an MP during Routine Proceedings. An MP who wants to be heard will naturally choose the second method, which provides the opportunity to make a short statement. A maximum of 15 minutes every day from Monday to Friday is reserved for the presentation of petitions.

Another opportunity to be heard is during the 15-minute period every day just before Question Period, when MPs may make a statement on any subject they deem to be of interest or importance. Although this statement may not last more than 60 seconds, MPs have the chance to be heard and if necessary to draw the Government's attention to a problem of local, national, or international, interest. The opportunity to speak is allocated proportionately to private Members of all parties.

There are other ways that private Members can express their views and draw the Government's attention to problems of concern to their constituents. They can request emergency debates, ask the Government to produce papers, speak in an adjournment debate, or ask questions either orally or in writing. Opposition MPs take full advantage all of these options to call the Government to account, as we will see more

> Bills originating in Parliament may not entail public expenditure or the raising of taxes.

> Recent changes have made it easier for Members to bring their bills to a vote.

fully in the chapter on Parliament's role as a critic of the Government (see "The House of Commons and the Executive," Chapter 9).

Even though they do not all rise to speak, MPs make a point of attending Question Period. It is vital that they know what issues are being discussed in Parliament, both at the national and at the international levels. During Question Period all the issues of the day may be raised, and very few current events escape exposure.

Members must stay in touch with the electorate.

Members of Parliament must be in constant touch with their constituents in order to stay on top of local problems and also to keep abreast of people's reactions to current issues in public life. By being active in their ridings, MPs prove that they have their voters' interests at heart. They also increase their chances of being returned in the next election. Experience has shown that even good MPs, however active and hard-working, have little chance of being re-elected if they neglect to maintain regular contact with their constituents. It is particularly hard for Cabinet Ministers to carry out their duties in the riding consistently because they are so busy with their Government responsibilities. The situation is complicated further for those who live far from Ottawa.

Virtually all parliamentarians maintain offices in their ridings, and try to organize their time so that they can spend time there on a regular basis. One of the major changes introduced by the parliamentary reforms of April 1991 was a re-arrangement of the calendar to provide longer Christmas and summer recesses, and to set aside entire weeks when the House does not sit. The purpose of the changes was to enable MPs to spend more time in their ridings and to plan their work schedules well in advance. Members are in constant contact with their riding offices so as to keep abreast of requests, complaints, and claims, and to be able to take appropriate action.

Members act as ombudsmen in the interest of their electors.

One of an MP's most important roles is to act as an ombudsman for his constituents. The latter may not always know just how to tackle the bureaucracy or indeed which level of the bureaucracy to address. Queries addressed to a department or government agency may have received no response. Constituents can then appeal to their MP who is well placed to help. The MP knows the ins and outs of the administration, knows whom to approach, and stands a better chance of being heard than does an ordinary citizen. Members of Parliament handle appeals from people on social assistance who are in difficulty, requests from people who do not know how to apply for an old-age pension, requests for visas for relatives abroad, and many others. Often the MP's staff can provide the necessary information, but in many cases the Member will have to intervene personally. A telephone call may suffice in some cases, while in others a whole series of steps may be required.

Complaints and requests come in from both individuals and groups. For example, if the possibility is raised of closing a post office or a rail line, the people affected will object vociferously and will do their best to involve their MP. The MP is also a source of information to his constituents, giving them the facts and finding the documentation they need.

Members of Parliament pass a considerable amount of time looking after their constituents' affairs. They are channels for information, and this responsibility is expanding steadily. People appeal to them, and they have to try to find a remedy. The ombudsman role is important, because without it many people would feel they had no access to their Government at all. The MP offers a means of communication with a monolithic bureaucracy. There is nothing partisan about this assistance, as MPs work to represent every person in their ridings, not just those who voted for them or who belong to their party.

Party obligations are also important, as the party organization will be key to success at the next election. Regular attendance at caucus meetings is called for, as all matters of interest to the party are discussed there. The caucus is a forum where MPs can speak freely about everything of concern to them, their constituents and the party, as we noted earlier in our discussion of political parties (see Chapter 1). An MP must maintain close contact with the party Whip, who provides instructions for participating in the business of Parliament, the committees, voting in the House, and other such matters.

In addition to parliamentary obligations, an MP has what might be called social obligations, both at home in the riding and in Ottawa. Having received a mandate from the electorate, the Member must be seen to be carrying it out. There are all kinds of local events to be attended: inaugurations, meetings with special interest groups, cultural and sports activities, and even such entirely private affairs as funerals and weddings. In Ottawa, as in the riding, the MP must be available to meet the press and give interviews. Although this latter activity makes additional demands on an already overburdened schedule, MPs are generally happy to agree to requests for interviews, since in politics a little publicity is rarely a bad thing. It would be impossible to list all the requests, invitations and appeals that flood into an MP's office — certainly many more than can be accommodated. They come from just about every sector of activity, including constituents, business people, unions, associations, ethnic and religious groups, diplomats, journalists, and other MPs.

In addition to parliamentary duties, MPs are involved in numerous activities, especially in their ridings.

WORKING CONDITIONS

Many foreign
countries envy the
working conditions of
Canadian MPs.

Canadian parliamentarians enjoy working conditions that are the envy
of many of their foreign counterparts. Normally their salaries and
expense allowances are adjusted upward every year, although under
Government policy remuneration in 1992 was frozen at the 1991 level.
On January 1, 1993, remuneration was increased by 0.636 percent,
bringing the sessional allowance to $64 800, plus an expense allowance
in most cases of $21 400. Members from remote or very large ridings
receive a somewhat higher allowance. The expense allowance is tax
free. Remuneration begins as of election day and stops only when the
MP fails to be re-elected or resigns.

Senior positions entitle MPs to additional allowances. In decreasing order
of amount, these allowances go to the Prime Minister, the Members of
Cabinet, the Speaker, the Leader of the Official Opposition, the other
party leaders, the Deputy Speaker, the Opposition House Leader, the
Chief Government and Opposition Whips, the Parliamentary Secretaries,
the Deputy Chairman and Assistant Deputy Chairman of Committees of
the Whole, the other House Leaders, the Deputy Government and
Opposition Whips, and the Whips of other recognized parties.

Parliamentarians are required to submit a statement of attendance every
month. For every day beyond 21 days that an MP does not attend a sitting, $60 are deducted from both sessional and expense allowances.
Travel allowances enable MPs to visit their ridings regularly in order to
keep in touch with their electors and to do their constituency work.

The House of Commons allows each MP an operating budget, which
must be administered in accordance with guidelines issued by the
Board of Internal Economy. Most of the budget is used to pay secre-
tarial, research, administrative and support staff working in either the
Ottawa or the riding office, and to defray other related expenditures.
Nowadays, MPs enjoy comfortable, well-designed, well-equipped
offices. These offices are a necessity, given the way the MP's role has
evolved. There must be enough space to receive many visitors and for
staff to work. Moreover, computers, photocopiers and other equipment
now occupy a considerable amount of space.

Parliamentarians may use other services provided by the House, such as
printing and copying, translation, messenger service, health care and
child care. They "frank" their mail, i.e. it does not require postage. The
integrated office communication system called OASIS, gives MPs
access to a variety of video programs and information services from their
offices on the Hill, and to certain services in their riding offices as well.
The Broadcasting Service produces live television coverage of the daily
House of Commons proceedings in English and French, enabling MPs

The Parliamentary Library at the end of the 19th century

to follow the debates from their offices in Ottawa or in their ridings when they cannot attend in person. Some committee proceedings are also being televised on an experimental basis.

In addition to the research staff that parliamentarians can hire and pay for out of their operating budgets, there are other resources they can call on for assistance in carrying out their functions. The three official parties currently represented in the House receive funding every year to finance their own research services. The money allocated for research goes mainly to pay salaries for research officers and secretaries, as the House assumes office expenses. Party research services are at the disposal of their respective caucuses, MPs and Senators.

The Library of Parliament, which serves both the Senate and the Commons, offers parliamentarians all the services of a well-equipped library. In addition, it employs a research staff that has expanded considerably under the pressure of demand. The Research Branch has many specialists in fields such as law, economics, the sciences, history and sociology. Both individual MPs and committees make frequent use of this expertise, with research officers often being assigned to assist a committee. The main difference between the Library's Research Branch and the party research services is that the former is completely non-political. Studies are objective and non-partisan, even though they

The highly qualified staff of the Parliamentary Library provide information and research services to MPs.

may be carried out at an MP's request, and may subsequently be given a partisan slant. Frequent queries to the Research Branch include requests for technical studies and arguments for or against a given proposal or policy.

The working conditions of MPs are frequently the object of criticism, especially by the press. However, MPs' salaries are comparable with those earned by civil servants, teachers, or private-sector managers, in fact with almost any job that entails a certain level of responsibility. It is legitimate to treat our elected representatives comparably with other citizens who do similar work. If MPs were poorly paid, only the wealthy could afford to go into politics. Moreover, MPs are part of one of the most widely representative institutions in the entire country, and it is only fair that they should receive a salary commensurate with the dignity of their position.

WOMEN MPs

For a fuller understanding of the contemporary situation, it is worthwhile looking at the history of women's involvement in Parliament.

At the time of Confederation, the provincial legislatures defined the qualifications for voting in a federal election. When women won the right to vote provincially in Alberta, Manitoba and Saskatchewan in 1916, and in British Columbia and Ontario in 1917,[4] they automatically won the right to vote federally as well.

In 1917, a federal Government that assumed women would be likely to vote in favour of conscription, and wanted those votes, passed two pieces of legislation: one extended the right to vote to anyone serving in the armed forces,[5] the other to the wives, widows, mothers, sisters and daughters of men on active service.[6] In 1918, a bill giving the vote to all women was introduced and passed with little opposition.[7] A year later the *Dominion By-Elections Act* of July 1919 gave women the right to run in federal elections. Finally, in 1920, the provisions of the two Acts were incorporated in the *Dominion Elections Act*[8] and its provisions put women on an equal footing with men. All Canadian citizens could now vote at the age of 21, and stand for election as well. In 1970, the voting age was reduced to 18.

4. Janine Brodie and Jill McCallan Vickers, *Canadian Women in Politics: An Overview* (Ottawa: Canadian Research Institute for the Advancement of Women, 1982).
5. *Military Voters Act, 1917*, 7-8 Geo. V, c. 34.
6. *War Time Elections Act, 1917*, 7-8 Geo. V, c. 39.
7. *Act to Confer the Electoral Franchise upon Women, 1918*, 8-9 Geo. V, c. 20.
8. *Dominion Elections Act, 1920*, 10-11 Geo. V, c. 46.

We saw in the chapter on the Senate that women were recognized as "persons" only in 1929 and that in 1930 the first woman was appointed to the Senate.[9] The federal election of 1921 was the first after women were given the right to vote and stand for election. Four women ran but only one was elected. Agnes Campbell MacPhail sat as an independent for the riding of Grey South East in Ontario, and was re-elected four times. During the first quarter century following extension of suffrage to women (1920-1945), only five women sat in the House. On March 13, 1944, Cora Casselman occupied the Chair for several hours. She was applauded heartily and for the first time in Canadian history the expression "Madam Speaker" rang through the House.

The entry of women into the House continued to be limited. In 1945, only one woman was elected, Gladys Strum of Saskatchewan. In 1950, Ellen Louks Fairclough of Ontario was elected in a by-election and for three years was the only woman in the House. She was the first to join Cabinet, holding posts successively as Secretary of State, Minister of Citizenship and Immigration and Postmaster General. She was also acting Prime Minister for two days. Progress has been slow: 10 women were elected in 1970, 9 in 1974, 14 in 1980, 27 in 1984. In 1988, 39 women won seats in the House and in 1992 there were 40, another woman having won in a by-election. This is certainly progress, but the proportion of women MPs is still only 13.5 percent, while they comprise more than half of the population at large.

Over the years, women have begun to hold parliamentary secretaryships and Cabinet posts. The 1992 Cabinet included seven women, an unprecedented number.

Three women have held positions that involved presiding over the House. In 1974, Albanie Morin became the first woman to be named Assistant Deputy Chairman of Committees of the Whole. This position was also held from September 1986 to May 1990 by the Honourable Andrée Champagne, who subsequently became the first female Deputy Speaker. The first woman to be appointed Speaker of the House was the Honourable Jeanne Sauvé, in April 1980. The first woman to act as Deputy Conservative Party Whip (November 1984-October 1986) was Claudy Mailly. At the summit of the political hierarchy, the Honourable Audrey McLaughlin is the first woman to lead a federal political party, having been elected Leader of the NDP in December 1989. We saw in the chapter on the Senate that two women have been appointed Speaker of that House, in 1972 and 1974.

The presence of women is increasingly felt in politics. In 1992, the Cabinet included seven women as Ministers.

9. *Canada Elections Act*, S.C. 1970 c. 49.

Senior Officers of the House of Commons

The Speaker and the Members are assisted by a number of senior officers, several of whom are appointed by the Governor General by order-in-council, on the advice of the Prime Minister. The appointments are confirmed by commissions under the Great Seal. Another senior officer of the House, the Administrator, is appointed by the Board of Internal Economy. His functions will be examined in Chapter 11.

THE CLERK

The office of Clerk goes back to the first British Parliaments.

This office is as ancient as Parliament itself. The earliest English parliamentary records that have come down to us mention a Clerk of the House of Commons.

As the main procedural adviser and senior officer of the House, the Clerk holds the rank of a Deputy Minister under the authority of the Speaker, who acts in effect as Minister (see Figure 3). In the Canadian order of precedence, the Clerk ranks ahead of departmental Deputy Ministers. For many years a purely political appointment, the position has now been depoliticized, although the Clerk is still appointed by order-in-council and serves "at pleasure." Robert Marleau, the current Clerk, was appointed in 1987 and is the first Clerk to have spent his entire career in the procedural services of the House.

Profile

The varied and complex duties that the Clerk must perform demand not only very specific qualifications but also uncommon personal qualities.

When Richard D. Barlas, himself a lawyer, was Clerk Assistant at Westminster, he speculated on why there was a tendency to think that the Clerk of the House had to have legal training.[1] In his view, knowledge of parliamentary affairs and procedure was much more important

---

1. Richard D. Barlas, "The Role and Qualifications of a Clerk in the 1970s," *The Parliamentarian*, Vol. 49, No. 4 (October 1968), p. 222.

FIGURE 3

Chart of the House of Commons

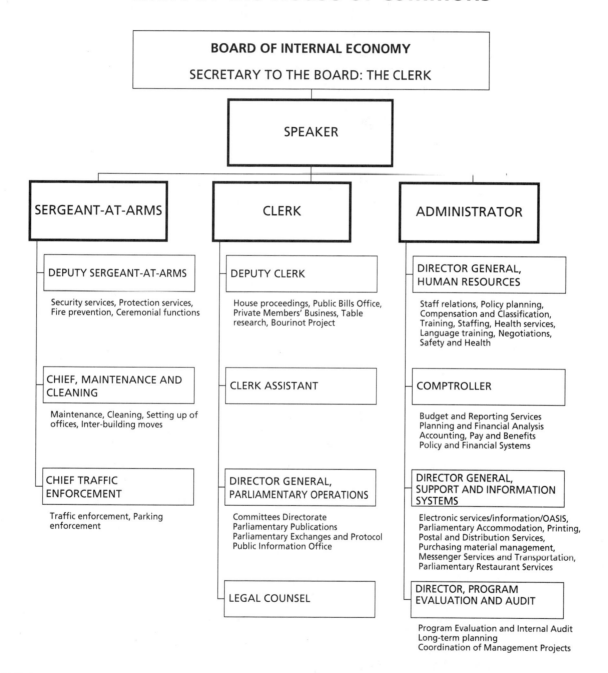

BOARD OF INTERNAL ECONOMY

SECRETARY TO THE BOARD: THE CLERK

SPEAKER

SERGEANT-AT-ARMS

DEPUTY SERGEANT-AT-ARMS

Security services, Protection services, Fire prevention, Ceremonial functions

CHIEF, MAINTENANCE AND CLEANING

Maintenance, Cleaning, Setting up of offices, Inter-building moves

CHIEF TRAFFIC ENFORCEMENT

Traffic enforcement, Parking enforcement

CLERK

DEPUTY CLERK

House proceedings, Public Bills Office, Private Members' Business, Table research, Bourinot Project

CLERK ASSISTANT

DIRECTOR GENERAL, PARLIAMENTARY OPERATIONS

Committees Directorate
Parliamentary Publications
Parliamentary Exchanges and Protocol
Public Information Office

LEGAL COUNSEL

ADMINISTRATOR

DIRECTOR GENERAL, HUMAN RESOURCES

Staff relations, Policy planning, Compensation and Classification, Training, Staffing, Health services, Language training, Negotiations, Safety and Health

COMPTROLLER

Budget and Reporting Services
Planning and Financial Analysis
Accounting, Pay and Benefits
Policy and Financial Systems

DIRECTOR GENERAL, SUPPORT AND INFORMATION SYSTEMS

Electronic services/information/OASIS, Parliamentary Accommodation, Printing, Postal and Distribution Services, Purchasing material management, Messenger Services and Transportation, Parliamentary Restaurant Services

DIRECTOR, PROGRAM EVALUATION AND AUDIT

Program Evaluation and Internal Audit
Long-term planning
Coordination of Management Projects

Source: Administrator's Sector, House of Commons.

to a Clerk than knowledge of the law. The Clerk's primary challenge is to find a way through the maze of Standing Orders, conventions, precedents and usages. How is this skill to be acquired, except in the service of the House? The Clerk must, then, have experience in the House, and be thoroughly familiar with parliamentary procedure; but a full knowledge of the duties involved can only be acquired on the job.

The Clerk is at the service of the Commons, in other words, of all MPs regardless of affiliation. All must be listened to, advised, and counselled with utter objectivity and without any partisanship. Just like the Speaker, the Clerk must accord equal treatment to every MP in order to preserve a reputation for impartiality.

The Clerk must always be courteous, pleasant, patient, able to joke, while keeping a distance compatible with the role of servant of the House. A good memory makes the Clerk's work easier, and in fact is an essential tool in a milieu where constant appeals are made to precedent, to parliamentary history, indeed to history generally. Wide experience in management and financial affairs are also a must, given the heavy administrative responsibilities attached to the role.

Duties

In addition to advising the Speaker and the Members on procedure in the House, the Clerk is the custodian of the Commons official documents.

The Clerk advises the Speaker and the MPs on all procedural questions. It is the Clerk who provides all the documentation the Speaker needs to render decisions on House practice. The Clerk is entirely at the service of the Speaker and the MPs on all procedural questions.

The Clerk wears a traditional black gown and, when walking in procession behind the Speaker, a tricorn hat. The holder of this office is associated with the Speaker in all parliamentary functions. In the House the Clerk is seated at the Table, facing the House, in a chair in front of the Speaker's, so as to be able to respond rapidly when the Speaker has questions, or needs information. The Clerk also advises and assists MPs, who often need an opinion on how to interpret a particular standing order, how to participate in a particular debate, what procedure should be used to achieve this or that end. Other duties include helping MPs track down precedents appropriate to a given case, and assisting them whenever possible.

The *Standing Orders of the House of Commons* entrust a great many responsibilities to the Clerk in the purely procedural realm. The Clerk has other responsibilities in the House in addition to the purely procedural. When there is a recorded division, it is the Clerk, with the assistance of the other Table officers, who counts the votes and announces the result. The Clerk also receives and transmits formal messages

The House of Commons

between the two Houses. A further duty is to record what happens at every sitting and to submit the minutes which are used in drawing up the document called the *Votes and Proceedings*.

The Clerk is the custodian of all House papers and documents.[2] This means being responsible for these documents and not allowing anyone to make changes without the express permission of the House, although the Clerk is authorized to amend the form of certain questions on the *Order Paper*.[3]

As guardian of all Commons documents, the Clerk must certify and authenticate many texts. When a bill is read in the House, the Clerk attests it by noting the date and time. The same is done when a bill is passed. Every day a copy of the *Votes and Proceedings*, certified by the Clerk, is delivered to the Governor General. As required by the Canadian Bill of Rights, the Clerk also delivers two copies of every bill to the Minister of Justice. The Clerk receives a variety of official documents. All reports that have to be tabled in the House under the provisions of an Act or resolution can be filed with the Clerk, and are then deemed to have been tabled in the House. The Clerk is responsible for preparing the *Order Paper* for every sitting, and for presenting a copy of it to the Speaker every morning. In fact, all parliamentary publications come under the responsibility of the Clerk.

2. Standing Order 151.
3. Standing Order 39(6).

The Standing Orders require that the Clerk call meetings of the standing committees at the start of every session, so that the committees can elect their chairmen. This must be done within ten sitting days following the adoption of the report of the Standing Committee on House Management, specifying the membership of the various committees.

The Clerk is responsible for ensuring the regularity of the vote during the election of a Speaker.

With the new procedure for electing the Speaker, the Clerk has taken on the further duty of guaranteeing the vote's regularity. It is the Clerk who receives the names of the MPs who do not wish to stand for election to the speakership (the practice is that all MPs, apart from party leaders and Ministers, are considered to be candidates unless they inform the Clerk in writing that they do not wish their names to stand). The Clerk draws up a list of the non-candidates: MPs who have declined, Ministers, and party leaders. This list is then given to the Member presiding over the election, together with a list of the candidates standing in the first ballot. When the MPs have voted, the Clerk takes the ballot papers from the box in which they have been placed and counts them in private. If there is more than one round of voting, the candidate(s) who received the smallest number of votes, those who received less than 5 percent of the total, and those who no longer wish their names to stand are eliminated. The Clerk then presents the Member presiding over the election with a new list. Once one candidate has received a majority, the Clerk informs the presiding Member, who then announces the new Speaker. The ballots must be destroyed once the Clerk is satisfied of the accuracy of each count and the number of votes cast for any candidate may not be revealed.

After either a general election or a by-election, the Clerk administers the Oath of Allegiance to every elected Member, including those who have been re-elected. They must swear the oath or make affirmation and sign the Test Roll or they cannot take their seats in the House.

Standing Order 22 makes the Clerk responsible for keeping a registry of all trips abroad taken by MPs in their capacity as MPs, if these trips are not sponsored by public funds. When MPs travel in an official or quasi-official capacity, there must be complete openness about the activity. The registry is open to the public.

The Clerk keeps another registry as well, in which the Whips enter the names of pairs of Government and Opposition MPs who have agreed not to vote on a given date. This method of neutralizing a vote, called "pairing," will be explained in greater detail when we examine the rules of debate in Chapter 10.

The Clerk has extensive administrative and financial duties covering a large, well-structured sector. Like a departmental Deputy Minister, the

Clerk is the final authority in matters of personnel management for everyone in his sector. The following officers and the services they direct report directly to the Clerk: the Deputy Clerk, the Legal Counsel, the Clerk Assistant and the Director General of Parliamentary Operations.

Another of the Clerk's management-related duties is the secretaryship of the Board of Internal Economy. As we have seen, the Board is the final authority in matters of the internal administration of the House of Commons. The Clerk sits on the House's Executive Committee and chairs its Administrative Committee (see Chapter 11).

In fact, the Clerk of the House of Commons has so many responsibilities that it would be impossible to list them all. The Clerk is an essential part of the life of the House, and the life of the House goes on in a political climate that is often tense. The Clerk's role demands awareness of even the most minor events, as they may contribute to an understanding of how a situation is developing and make it easier to make recommendations and give advice. Through informal meetings and intelligent and carefully thought-out interventions, the Clerk can help to maintain good relations among all participants in the political arena. This kind of service to the House is the Clerk's primary role and objective. Success in this role, as for all the officers we will consider in this section, depends to a very great extent on personality.

The Clerk is supported not only by the senior officers described in the following paragraphs but also by other collaborators whose role will be examined in Chapter 8.

THE SERGEANT-AT-ARMS

Normally it is a former senior officer of the Canadian Forces who is chosen as Sergeant-at-Arms. This office too is very ancient, going back to Parliament's earliest days. Originally appointed by the Crown as a bodyguard for the Speaker, the Sergeant-at-Arms dresses in a cocked hat and black tailcoat, and wears a sword to symbolize authority. Assistance, and replacement in case of absence, are provided by a Deputy Sergeant-at-Arms, who wears an identical uniform.

Under the authority of the Speaker, the Sergeant-at-Arms carries out two categories of duty. The first category includes House ceremonial activities, while the second encompasses administrative responsibilities primarily related to security.

The ceremonial role involves shouldering the Mace and walking at the head of the parade that escorts the Speaker into and out of the House. It also includes accompanying the Speaker, as Mace bearer, to all official parliamentary functions, for example, when the Speaker goes to the Senate to hear the Throne Speech read. The only occasion on which the Sergeant-at-Arms does not carry the Mace is when, prior to the election of a new Speaker, the Commons is called to the Bar of the Senate at the opening of a new Parliament and instructed to choose a Speaker.

The Sergeant-at-Arms is the guardian of the Mace and ensures that it is properly placed on the Table when the House sits, or on brackets below the Table when the House sits in Committee of the Whole. In the House, the Sergeant-at-Arms sits in a chair near the Bar of the House, facing the Speaker and, upon instruction from the Speaker, will conduct MPs and others who are called to appear at the Bar. This happens only rarely and is usually for disciplinary purposes. Again carrying the Mace, the Sergeant-at-Arms escorts the Senate's messengers into the House. Another ceremonial task of this office is to announce the Gentleman Usher of the Black Rod when the latter comes at the opening of Parliament to summon the Commons to the Bar of the Senate (see "Sessions and Sittings," Chapter 10). When a recorded division is being held, the Sergeant-at-Arms ensures that the doors to the House are locked. In addition to these ceremonial functions the position entails a number of security-related administrative duties.

The Sergeant-at-Arms is responsible for protecting the Prime Minister and the Members while they are within the precincts of Parliament. Another security-related task is to ensure that order is maintained whether the House is sitting or not, and if necessary to expel strangers who are guilty of misconduct, creating a disturbance, or entering a building improperly. In addition, when the Speaker so orders, it may be necessary to carry out disciplinary measures against MPs (though this, as we have seen, is rare). The Sergeant-at-Arms has powers in the area of security, and authority over the security staff. Together they control admission to the galleries and to all other parts of the buildings occupied by the House. It is important that the holder of this office remain in contact with the Royal Canadian Mounted Police (RCMP), the Ottawa police, and the Canadian Security Intelligence Service (CSIS).

The Sergeant-at-Arms is further responsible for controlling traffic on the Hill, including enforcement of the parking regulations, and for ensuring that the buildings are maintained and kept clean and tidy. This includes the preparation of rooms for committee meetings and social events. The maintenance service is concerned about the environment, and is actively involved in both paper recycling and a program to eliminate toxic wastes.

The Sergeant-at-Arms hires and supervises the personnel necessary to carry out the functions coming under the authority of this office. He is a

The Sergeant-at-Arms, garbed in black robes and a cocked hat, carries the Mace on his shoulder to escort the Speaker in parliamentary processions.

member of the Administrative Committee and the Executive Committee, and attends the meetings of the Board of Internal Economy.

THE DEPUTY CLERK

This position as the Clerk's first and foremost deputy was created recently, as part of an administrative reorganization of the House. Similar offices exist in a number of Commonwealth parliaments, but in Canada the position was created in 1987 and a woman, Mary Anne Griffith, was appointed to fill it.

The description of the Clerk's qualifications and responsibilities can also be applied to the Deputy Clerk, whose role is to assist the Clerk in all duties and to stand in, in case of absence. The Deputy Clerk is also responsible for directing and supervising the Table Research Branch, the Legislative Counsel Office and the House Proceedings Directorate, all of which will be discussed later under "Sessions and Sittings," Chapter 10.

The Deputy Clerk assists the Clerk in his duties.

THE CLERK ASSISTANT

A former Clerk-at-the-Table, this officer has been given the special responsibility of directing a parliamentary co-operation program for the benefit of parliamentarians and parliamentary staff from the countries of Central and Eastern Europe, sometimes referred to as the newly-emerging democracies. Following the collapse of the former communist regimes and the end of the cold war, Western countries have been eager to help their former adversaries adjust to a democratic system and cope with their many problems. The contribution of the Canadian Parliament has been to offer training programs and hold seminars for parliamentarians and staff with a view to introducing them to the operation of our system of government in general and our Parliament in particular.

The Canadian Parliament has been operating parliamentary co-operation programs for decades and many other parliaments, from both the developed and the third world, have taken advantage of them. During the cold war, although parliamentary exchanges did take place with the Soviet Union and its satellites, there were no training programs and the exchanges were conducted in a very formal manner. Since 1990, when the special program was inaugurated, the parliamentarians from these countries have been only too eager to inform themselves of the requirements of a democratic system, to study the workings of a democratic parliament, and to give their staff the opportunity of studying the procedures and administration of such parliaments and the services required by their members.

All the former satellite countries, together with Russia and other republics of the former Soviet Union, have participated in these programs and greatly benefited from them. Organizing these activities, together with other inter-parliamentary responsibilities, constitute the mandate of the Clerk Assistant at the time of writing (1993), but it is the Parliamentary Exchanges and Protocol Directorate that is responsible for executing the programs.

Committees

The committees of the House of Commons are made up of MPs. They are created by the House and have only those powers it decides to give them. The vast extent and complexity of parliamentary business, and the large number of MPs, make it impossible for the House to examine legislation and other matters in detail during normal sittings. Some of the duties of the House are therefore divided up among the parliamentary committees, which are given specific mandates and required to report back to the House. There are many advantages to the system. A matter can be considered in greater depth than would be possible in the House, and the views, explanations, and testimony of interested parties who are not parliamentarians can be heard more easily. Discussions between parliamentarians can be more direct and more profitable. In addition, the system allows the House to deal with more business while both government and opposition backbenchers can have a chance to put questions to ministers, officials, and other witnesses.

The House delegates work to a committee by passing a motion asking it to study a bill or a pressing issue. Alternatively, it may provide for the appointment of specific committees in the Standing Orders which define their mandates. The committee is then said to have received an "order of reference." Under the Standing Orders, most standing committees have a permanent order of reference authorizing them to study and report on the mandate, management, and operations of certain government departments, in addition to the items which may from time to time be sent to them for examination. Before looking at the various categories of committee and their roles, let us look at what are known as "Committees of the Whole."

Committees play an important role in the work of Parliament; without them, the House could not deal with all the matters submitted to it.

COMMITTEES OF THE WHOLE

A Committee of the Whole consists of the whole House of Commons, sitting not as the House of Commons but as a committee. At such times it is chaired by the Chairman of Committees of the Whole House who is also the Deputy Speaker, or by the Deputy Chairman or Assistant Deputy Chairman of Committees of the Whole. Whoever is presiding sits at the Table, in the Clerk's chair, while the Speaker's chair remains vacant. One, or more usually two, of the Clerks-at-the-Table act as committee clerks. At such times, the Mace is placed on the brackets below the Table. Of course, the Members of a Committee of the Whole are still the Members of the House of Commons, but there are certain procedural differences between the sittings of a Committee of the Whole and those of the House of Commons. The quorum remains the same (20), but Members are not obliged to sit in their usual places, and can speak from wherever they are sitting. They can speak more than once, as long as they stick to the topic under consideration. Debate tends to be less formal and speeches shorter than during a sitting of the House. And though in theory all remarks are addressed to the Chair, practice is more informal, and Members often address one another and witnesses directly. The appropriate Cabinet Ministers can be questioned about legislation, and reply with the assistance of their senior departmental officials, who may be seated beside them.

There was a time when the House met frequently in Committee of the Whole. Committees of the Whole were called to examine estimates, appropriation bills and in fact all money bills at committee stage. In addition, nearly all bills that had passed second reading were referred to Committee of the Whole for consideration and review. In 1968, a major reform of the committee system was carried out, restructuring the committees and giving them greater powers. This reform took consideration of estimates and detailed consideration of bills away from Committees of the Whole, so that smaller parliamentary committees had more work to do and Committees of the Whole less.

Since the 1968 reform, Committees of the Whole have studied any matter the House decides to refer to them, including certain public bills. Particularly when the Government wants to expedite passage of a bill, and when it has the agreement of the other parties, the House will refer the bill to Committee of the Whole. Nevertheless, the Committee's chief function remains financial, and any bill based on a supply motion goes before Committee of the Whole at its committee stage.

When a Committee of the Whole is seized with a matter, it can neither adjourn nor defer the matter to another sitting unless its Chair reports on the Committee's progress, at which time he may request leave to sit again. In Committee of the Whole, the MPs stand in order to vote for or against motions. The Clerk-at-the-Table counts the votes and announces the results but, unlike a division in the House, the names of the members voting are not recorded. Nothing in the Standing Orders prevents the Speaker from participating in the deliberations of Committees of the Whole, though by custom he refrains from doing so.

STANDING COMMITTEES

Standing Order 104(1) provides for the existence of 20 standing committees, grouped in five envelopes:

(a) Management (House Management; Public Accounts);

(b) Human Resources (Aboriginal Affairs; Health and Welfare, Social Affairs, Seniors and the Status of Women; Human Rights and the Status of Disabled Persons; Labour, Employment and Immigration; Multiculturalism and Citizenship);

(c) Natural Resources (Agriculture; Energy, Mines and Resources);

(d) Economics (External Affairs and International Trade; Finance; Industry, Science and Technology, and Regional and Northern Development); and

(e) Departmental (Communications and Culture; Consumer and Corporate Affairs and Government Operations; Justice and Solicitor General; National Defence and Veterans Affairs; Official Languages).

> Members of standing committees are chosen at the beginning of the first session of each Parliament.

The standing committees are struck at the beginning of the first session of each Parliament and last for the life of the Parliament. Not all are equally busy. Some may not meet at all, while others may be overwhelmed with work — it all depends on the volume and complexity of the matters that are referred to them. As we have seen, each committee has its own name, describing its particular area of concern, and is in addition grouped in an "envelope" of similar committees (e.g. the Finance Committee comes within the "Economics" envelope).

LEGISLATIVE COMMITTEES

As the result of a recent reform, legislative committees are now appointed as needed to deal with specific bills.[1] The Standing Committee on House Management meets within five days of the start of the second reading debate on a bill. It then prepares a list of not more than fourteen members to form a legislative committee to consider the bill clause by clause. The committee is organized only if the House adopts the motion for second reading and reference to a legislative committee. The committee ceases to exist once it has reported the bill back to the House.

> Legislative committees examine the bills that are submitted to them after adoption on second reading.

---

1. Twenty-Eighth Report of the Standing Committee on House Management, presented and concurred in by the House on April 29, 1992.

SPECIAL COMMITTEES

These are set up by the House as required for reviews or investigations of specific topics or issues. A special committee is created by a motion describing its mandate, and it ceases to exist as soon as its mandate has been carried out and it has presented a final report to the House.

JOINT COMMITTEES

With the agreement of the Senate, the House can set up special joint committees to examine specific questions.

Joint committees, which may be standing or special, are made up of both MPs and Senators. The Standing Orders of the House of Commons provide for only one standing joint committee, the Standing Joint Committee for the Scrutiny of Regulations. The creation of a special joint committee may be proposed by either House, with the two Houses being represented proportionately. Usually a special joint committee will be mandated to carry out an inquiry. A number of them, most recently the Special Joint Committee on a Renewed Canada (the Beaudoin-Dobbie Committee), have tackled constitutional reform. From time to time joint committees are asked to review legislation. In 1966, for instance, three bills on labour relations within the Federal Public Service and their impact in other areas had been introduced with a view to allowing collective bargaining in the Public Service. All three bills underwent detailed review by a joint committee.[2]

COMMITTEE MEMBERSHIP

Membership on standing committees can vary from 7 to 14, while membership on joint committees is usually 8.

Under the Standing Orders, the House Management Committee is responsible for drawing up a list of the MPs who will sit on the various standing and legislative committees. Each standing committee must have not less than seven and not more than 14 members; a legislative committee may have a maximum of 14 members; and the Standing Joint Committee for the Scrutiny of Regulations has eight members from the House, although this number may be changed to maintain the correct numerical balance between MPs and Senators.

In drawing up the lists of proposed committee members, the House Management Committee takes into account recommendations from the Whips, who in turn have taken into account the qualifications and interests of the MPs under consideration. Insofar as practicable, the political parties are represented on each committee in the same proportions as they are represented in the House. It follows that a government that has a majority in the House will also have a majority in each committee.

2. J.R. Mallory and B.A. Smith, "The Legislative Role of Parliamentary Committees in Canada: the Case of the Joint Committee on the Public Service Bills," *Canadian Public Administration* 15 (Spring 1972), pp. 1-23.

When the House decides to set up a special committee, the number of members is specified in the motion establishing it and defining its mandate. The Standing Orders do however stipulate that it must consist of not more than 15 members.

Standing committees are authorized to create their own sub-committees, while special committees cannot unless the mandate given them by the House specifically empowers them to do so. Legislative committees can create only one type of sub-committee, on agenda and procedure.

Within ten sitting days of its appointment and at certain times after that, the House Management Committee must table a report containing the names of the MPs who can sit on each standing committee and represent the House on standing joint committees. Within ten sitting days of the adoption of this report by the House, the Clerk of the House calls meetings of the members of the Standing Committees so that they can elect a chairman and two vice-chairmen. Of these three, two must belong to the party in power and one to the opposition. The same applies to special committees. The chairmen of legislative committees are not elected, but designated by the Speaker from a group of parliamentarians of all parties known as the Panel of Chairmen chosen for this purpose at the start of each session. The chairmen of legislative committees are neutral and impartial. They do not participate in discussions of the bill before the committee, and they have not usually been active during the second reading debate. Joint committees elect joint chairmen, one Senator and one MP.

Committee chairmen direct and preside over the whole body of work done by their committees. They must make sure that the business of the committee is carried out in a fair and orderly manner, as the Speaker does in the House. They must also ensure that the committee works efficiently. When the chairmanship of a standing or special committee becomes vacant, it cannot simply be filled by a vice-chairman. Instead, the committee must proceed to the election of a new chairman immediately.

Any MP may take part in the public meetings of any committee, whether he belongs to it or not, but only committee members may vote, move a motion, or present an amendment. The Standing Orders allow MPs to arrange replacements when they cannot attend a committee meeting. Within five sitting days of the organization of any standing or standing joint committee, and from time to time thereafter, every committee member may file a list of approved substitutes. This list must comprise not more than seven fellow party members who are prepared to act as substitutes if necessary, though they do not become committee members. All the formalities regarding substitutes are carried out under the authority of the whips.

In committee, a quorum is a majority of the members. A committee may pass a motion authorizing the chairman to hear witnesses and print the evidence taken even without a quorum, but a quorum is required before the committee can debate a motion or vote.

COMMITTEE FUNCTIONS

The committee system has been modified a number of times since the reform of 1968. Even the legislative committee system, established in 1985, has already been altered. There is nothing too surprising about this, however, since experience alone can reveal the strong and weak points in the system. As our MPs learn, they introduce changes designed to improve the efficiency of the system, and it is quite possible that further changes will be made in the future. No matter what envelopes committees are divided into, no matter how many members they have, no matter what method is used to select those members, our objective here remains a clear presentation of the role of committees. For this reason, committee functions have been grouped under one heading, so that their contribution to the business of Parliament can be explained in general.

House committees perform five major functions. They review legislation, examine estimates, carry out inquiries, examine order-in-council appointments and may have a monitoring role as well. Their legislative function is the most important, as it is indispensable for the passage of legislation.

Both legislative and standing committees are called upon to conduct a clause-by-clause study of bills referred to them by the House. As a general principle, every bill is studied by a legislative committee. However, the Standing Orders provide that the Minister responsible for a bill may, in proposing the second reading, give notice of intention to move that the bill be referred to a standing or special committee.[3] A variation might occur when a bill deals with a very specialized area coming directly within the purview of a given standing committee. Banking legislation would probably go to the Standing Committee on Finance, for example.

A committee entrusted with consideration of a bill studies it in detail. It calls as witnesses officials, experts, and technical witnesses, and may propose amendments designed to refine and improve the proposed leg-

---

3.   Standing Order 73(3)(*a*).

islation. The underlying principle of a bill has already been approved by the House at second reading, and any amendment proposed must be consistent with that principle. The committee's job is to make sure that the form of the bill is the best possible.

No amendment that would result in changes to the substance of the bill is receivable. Although opposition MPs will try to bring in amendments that reflect their parties' policies, they do not take the same attitude they do in the House when debating a controversial bill at second reading. If they oppose a bill in the House they will challenge it on principle, whereas in committee they address the specific provisions of a bill and often propose amendments. Opposition amendments can always be rejected by the committee's government majority, but it is not uncommon for suggestions made by opposition Members to be accepted because they improve the quality of the bill. For this reason it is often claimed that discussions in committee are less partisan than debate in the House. This does not mean, however, that we can dismiss political considerations, for their influence is as present in committee as on the floor of the House.

Committees can travel within Canada and abroad as long as the House has given its authorization and a budget has been allocated. When they travel within Canada they hold public hearings; abroad they do not sit officially and the proceedings are not published.

The 1968 reform made standing committees responsible for reviewing departmental estimates for the upcoming fiscal year. Under Standing Order 81(4), the main estimates for each department are referred to the appropriate standing committee no later than March 1 of the current fiscal year. The nature of the department's mandate determines which standing committee will be responsible for this review: the Agriculture Committee examines Agriculture Canada's estimates, the Committee on Justice and the Solicitor General examines those budgets and so on. The committees go through the departmental estimates with as much scrutiny as possible given the time available. The Minister responsible for each department appears before the committee to justify the estimates publicly, bringing along senior departmental officials so that the committee members can ask for clarifications. The opposition MPs on the committees take advantage of the opportunity to question the department's programs and policies.

Standing committees study ministerial budgetary forecasts for the coming year.

It must be admitted that it is not easy for committee members to discuss the details of departmental estimates. The form in which these estimates are presented is so complex that it would take an expert to understand them fully. However, notwithstanding the complexity of the estimates, their review by committee enables Parliament to perform one of its traditional functions, that of keeping an eye on public expenditure. It has the further benefit of forcing the departments to be more rigorous in preparing their estimates.

Another function of parliamentary committees is to hold inquiries either into questions of general policy or on specific subjects. Often such inquiries are made to lay the groundwork for new legislation, and they are usually entrusted to a special committee, perhaps a joint committee of both Houses, hand-picked for the job. There is nothing, however, to stop the House entrusting such a mission to a standing committee. The External Affairs and International Trade Committee, for one, has already undertaken inquiries of this kind. As a matter of fact, under the Standing Orders all standing committees are authorized to "examine and enquire into all such matters as may be referred to them by the House." The Standing Orders even go on to spell out all the initiatives that standing committees may take.[4] Among other things, the standing committees that oversee government departments are empowered to initiate their own investigations into matters relating to these departments.

Having a committee consider a given topic is an excellent way for the Government to glean opinions, suggestions, and criticisms. Often committees travel across Canada, receiving briefs and hearing from specialists and the public. The Government uses all this information in reaching decisions. This does not mean the Government always follows the committee's recommendations. The Government may choose to take no action, or to act on certain matters only. On the other hand, the purpose of the committee may be to provide information, and no further action would be indicated beyond taking note of the material gathered. The best example of this information-gathering type of inquiry can be found in the various committees, special or joint, that carried out studies on constitutional reform. The data they gathered informed the Government about the aspirations of Canadians from all across the country.

Another role for parliamentary committees is to review non-judicial appointments made by orders-in-council. Notices of such appointments are tabled in the House, and in the 30 sitting days following each appointment or nomination, a committee can review the candidate's qualifications and report to the House. Committees do not, however, have the power to veto these appointments.

The functions of monitoring and overseeing government behaviour are an important part of committee work. Two examples of this are the

4.   Standing Order 108.

Standing Committee on Public Accounts and the Joint Committee for the Scrutiny of Regulations. Slightly different is the case of the Standing Committee on House Management which, as its name indicates, includes among its responsibilities making recommendations concerning the internal administration of the House of Commons.

Through its committees' review of departmental estimates, the House monitors public expenditures before they are incurred. Through the Standing Committee on Public Accounts, the House can monitor them afterwards as well. The Committee is mandated to study how the Government is spending public moneys. Since 1958, the chairman of the Public Accounts Committee has, following British tradition, been a member of the Official Opposition — an opposition MP is the ideal person to keep a vigilant watch on the Government's activities! The Standing Committee on Public Accounts studies the Auditor General's reports carefully to make sure the sums allocated to various services have been spent as prescribed. Any assistance or expertise it may need to do this work is provided by the Auditor General. The Committee consistently draws attention to cases where it feels that public money has been poorly administered, wasted, or used for purposes other than those for which it was approved. The results of its review are published in a report containing recommendations for improving the Government's financial management practices.

The principle of monitoring the management of public moneys is an excellent one. However, the value of the principle is reduced by the fact that the Standing Committee on Public Accounts only produces its evaluations after money has already been spent. On the one hand, this makes the Committee's comments less effective, and on the other hand, the Government is not obliged to follow the Committee's recommendations.

The Standing Joint Committee for the Scrutiny of Regulations plays a monitoring role with respect to "delegated legislation." This term refers to regulations made by departments, agencies or boards, in accordance with Acts of Parliament empowering them to do so. The Committee consists of Senators as well as MPs, and determines whether regulations have been made in accordance with the provisions and powers spelled out in the Act, that they do not violate the provisions of the *Canadian Charter of Rights and Freedoms*, and that they do not constitute an abuse of power. This is a very big job, given the large number of regulations made by each department. To get an idea of the volume of work involved, we have only to think of the many regulations made every year by departments like Transport Canada, Health and Welfare Canada, Agriculture Canada, Environment Canada, and Fisheries and

Oceans. Not only is the volume of regulations immense but also studying them calls for uncommon expertise. This is why in practice the commendable principle of parliamentary monitoring of government activities does not result in an exhaustive review. The Scrutiny of Regulations Committee cannot claim to review every single piece of delegated legislation. It has to pick and choose, guided by the subject matter of the regulations and the priorities of the day.

The Standing Committee on House Management performs functions quite unlike those of the other standing committees (for further details see Chapter 11). Its mandate includes review of all matters relating to the internal administration of the House of Commons, provision of services and facilities to MPs, and all aspects of operations under the joint control of both Houses. As we have seen, it acts as what is known as the Striking Committee, selecting members for all the other House committees. It looks after technical matters relating to the business of Parliament, including questions relating to elections, parliamentary privilege, or any other relevant items. It studies all procedural questions and from time to time suggests changes in the Standing Orders. The Standing Committee on House Management studies the expenditure estimates of the House of Commons itself. It is responsible for deciding which items of Private Members' Business are "votable" (i.e. will come before the House for a vote) and it considers business related to private bills.

HOW COMMITTEES OPERATE

Every day a list of all committee meetings is sent to every MP. The list is also posted in all the various Parliament Buildings, and can be consulted on one of the House's closed-circuit television channels (OASIS).

The calendar of sittings is planned by the various committees. Two committee rooms are allocated to each of the five "envelopes" of committees (totalling 20 standing committees plus legislative committees). The Standing Orders stipulate that while the House is sitting, legislative committees are to be given priority in reserving committee rooms. Committees can meet even when the House is not sitting.

All committees can summon witnesses and send for papers and records. For standing and legislative committees, this authority is set out in the Standing Orders, while for special committees it is contained in their orders of reference. In the case of legislative committees, the power to summon witnesses is more restricted and is limited to those persons competent to testify on technical matters. Committees can also invite interested parties to submit written briefs. Such documents are distributed to the committee members for their information.

Witnesses before a committee have the right to speak in the official language of their choice. Under the terms of the Standing Orders, documentation must be available to members in both official languages. A committee can authorize the printing of its proceedings by motion, and establish how many copies will be printed. The official record is published as the committee's *Minutes of Proceedings and Evidence*, colloquially known as committee issues. When someone refuses to testify, the committee has the power to issue a summons obliging that person to appear.

Committees make decisions on the basis of a majority vote, usually taken by a show of hands. However, a committee member can demand a recorded vote, and in that case the votes are counted by the committee clerk who calls the Members' names in alphabetical order. A committee can retain the services of specialists and support staff, and is provided with a budget for this purpose drawn from funds allocated globally by the House to support the activities of all the Standing Committees. These funds are divided up by a Liaison Committee composed of the Chairmen of all the Standing Committees, on the basis of guidelines issued by the Board of Internal Economy (for further details see Chapter 11).

PERSONNEL

Each committee is assisted in its work by one or more procedural clerks, who are permanent employees of the House of Commons. The Committee Clerk acts as a procedural adviser and administrative officer to the committee and its chairman. He is an independent official who serves all members of the committee impartially.

If a committee wishes to retain the services of experts, technical advisers, or support staff, it must pass a motion to this effect. Hiring is done via contract, funds are managed by the Comptroller's Office, and fees are paid out of the committee's budget.

Committees can also call upon the Library of Parliament's Research Branch. One or more researchers, often specialists in a pertinent area, will be assigned to work for a particular committee. Usually these researchers work as a team with the committee clerk and any contract employees, and like the clerks, they are neutral and completely impartial.

COMMITTEE REPORTS

Most work undertaken by a committee concludes with a report, which generally includes a description of the committee's activities and a list of the recommendations it is submitting to the House. Not all committee reports are the same. Some may raise routine matters of committee operations, for example, requesting authorization of the House to travel.

> The official record of committee proceedings is published in the *Minutes of Proceedings and Evidence*, known as the "committee issues."

> Most committees present reports to the House.

The report from a committee studying a bill will include any proposed amendments, which must be clearly spelled out. The report from a committee that has been studying estimates usually consists of a brief statement to the effect that the committee has examined the estimates and is returning them to the House unamended or with recommendations to reduce or reject them. A committee cannot propose an increase to any estimate.

A committee that has carried out an inquiry normally presents a detailed report of its conclusions and recommendations. All committee reports are published as part of an issue of the committee's *Minutes of Proceedings and Evidence*. In the case of certain important inquiries, the report may be published separately with a special cover. A report tabled in the House will reflect the views of a majority of the committee's members. However, under a recent reform of the Standing Orders, committee reports may now contain, in an appendix, a brief statement of dissenting or supplementary opinion or recommendations by a minority of the committee's members.[5] The chairman signs the report in the committee's name before presenting it to the House. During Routine Proceedings, when the Speaker calls for committees to present their reports, the chairman or vice-chairman of the committee, or even simply one of its members, presents the report in both official languages. He may comment briefly, and a member of the Official Opposition on the committee may, if a dissenting opinion is appended, comment briefly on the minority's reasons for dissenting.

Under the Standing Orders, the Government must table a comprehensive response to a committee report within 150 days after the report has been submitted, if the committee so requests. Normally such a request is expressed as the final recommendation in the report.

A committee room in the Centre Block

5.   Standing Order 108(1).

The House of Commons Services

The House and its committees carry out their work with the help of a number of procedural support services. They all report ultimately to the Clerk, and all except one, are directed either by the Deputy Clerk or the Director General of Parliamentary Operations.

SERVICES REPORTING TO THE DEPUTY CLERK

The Table Research Branch

A Principal Clerk heads the Branch, assisted by two Deputy Principal Clerks, one of whom is in charge of the Bourinot Project, described below. Established in 1980, the Branch is responsible for co-ordinating all procedural research done for the House and its committees.

The Branch does both short-term and long-term research. It prepares briefing notes and rapidly finds precedents in response to urgent requests on particular procedural points. Long-term, it prepares works that will eventually be published, for example, the *Précis of Procedure*, the *Annotated Standing Orders*, the *Selected Decisions of Speaker Lamoureux*, and the *Selected Decisions of Speaker Jerome*. The Branch publishes regularly, as projects are completed.

The Table Research Branch puts out the weekly *Procedural Review*, which summarizes the important procedural points that arose in the House that week. It also publishes a summary of procedural decisions reached in committee.

In addition to preparing reports, the Branch organizes seminars and briefing sessions. After a general election, it is involved in a seminar for newly elected MPs, consisting of briefing and orientation sessions on House procedures. Similar seminars are organized for MPs' staffs, often themselves new to Parliament Hill and needing to be informed of the various services.

The Branch is also responsible for a vast research project aimed at producing an original reference work on the evolution of parliamentary

The publications of the Table Research Branch deal with parliamentary procedure.

procedure and usage in the House of Commons of Canada. The project is named after a former Clerk of the House, Sir John Bourinot, author of a scholarly procedural text last published in 1916. The team assigned to the Bourinot Project is also designing a computerized data base on procedure.

The Principal Clerk directs research for the Table with the help of two assistants, the Deputy Principal Clerks. The three take it in turns to do duty at the Table while the House is sitting, to assist the Clerk of the House and the Deputy Clerk.

The House Proceedings Directorate

This service is directed by a Principal Clerk House Proceedings, assisted by three Deputy Principal Clerks, one of whom heads the Journals Branch, the second the Private Members' Business Office and the third the Public Bills Office.

THE JOURNALS BRANCH

The Journals Branch acts as a secretariat to the House of Commons. It provides the support required so that the House can go about its business in an orderly fashion; it ensures that the documents needed by the Speaker, the other Chair occupants, and the MPs are always available; it also provides MPs and other interested parties with information on the status of business before the House.

At the end of each session, the *Votes and Proceedings* are published under the title *Journals of the House of Commons*.

Producing an official record of the business dealt with by the House is the first and perhaps the most important function of the Journals Branch. It is responsible for the publication of four essential documents. The *Order Paper and Notice Paper* is the official agenda of the House. The *Projected Order of Business* is a brief daily statement of the business expected to be before the House on a given sitting day. As its name indicates, it is only an unofficial outline, and the House may very well modify it. The *Votes and Proceedings* is a formal daily record of the actions and decisions of the House — what is *done* rather than what is *said*. At the end of every session the *Votes and Proceedings* are revised, corrected, and published in a bound volume entitled the *Journals of the House of Commons*. The *Status of Bills and Motions* is a periodic statement of the progress of each bill and motion introduced in the House.[1] All these publications are indispensable for MPs, enabling them to follow the

---

1. Further details on these publications can be found in the *Users Guide to House of Commons Publications*, available from the Journals Branch.

business of Parliament and keep up-to-date with everything happening in the House.

The Branch also has other functions, particularly in the procedural realm. For example, it provides the Speaker with what are known as "forms." These are standard documents in both official languages setting out the precise wording to be used by the Chair at each stage of the business before the House. A variety of other documents are also prepared. Branch personnel advise MPs on motions they wish to present and on the work of the Charter.

In the section on senior officers of the House of Commons, we saw that the Clerk of the House is responsible for the safekeeping of all parliamentary documents. The Journals Branch carries out this responsibility by producing copies of particular documents on demand.

THE PRIVATE MEMBERS' BUSINESS OFFICE

This Office informs and advises MPs and members of their staffs on all procedures that a private Member can use.

The mandate of the Private Members' Business Office is to advise MPs what avenues are open to them for participating in the legislative process. It advises MPs on how to exercise their rights under the Standing Orders and Practices of the House. It sees to most of the administrative and procedural questions that involve private Members' business. Members consult the Office when they wish to introduce a bill.

If an MP wishes to present a petition signed by riding residents, the petition must be certified by the Office's Clerk of Petitions. This officer is responsible for ensuring that petitions are formulated as required by the Standing Orders and Practices of the House (for further details on petitions, see "Routine Proceedings," Chapter 10).

A Deputy Principal Clerk who directs the Office organizes the draw establishing the priority list for items of Private Members' Business (see "The Legislative Functions," Chapter 9). He also takes turns serving at the Table in the House Chamber.

In addition to these functions, the Office provides assistance to the House Management Committee. The latter has created a subcommittee that deals with Private Members' Business. The Deputy Principal Clerk at the head of the Office, or one of the procedural clerks, acts as Clerk of this subcommittee, advising and assisting it on questions of procedure.

THE PUBLIC BILLS OFFICE

The Public Bills Office was established in 1987 as part of the procedural reforms introduced at that time. Its mandate is to act as a secretariat to legislative committees. It provides expertise on legislative procedure for all aspects of a bill from its presentation in the House to passage at third reading. More specifically, the Office is concerned with legislative committees, the Panel of Chairmen, and preparation of the documentation for the ruling handed down by the Speaker at report stage of each bill.

The Public Bills Office provides services to legislative committees, their chairmen, and other MPs. These services include provision of Clerks to assist with all aspects of the legislative process (see the previous chapter on Committees for details about legislative committees). A Deputy Principal Clerk directs the Public Bills Office and he also takes turns serving at the Table in the House Chamber.

The Legislative Counsel Office

Like the Table Research Branch and the House Proceedings Directorate, the Legislative Counsel Office comes under the authority of the Deputy Clerk of the House. Its personnel consists of the General Legislative Counsel who directs the Office, and several lawyers who are members of either a provincial or territorial bar. They provide services to MPs in all areas related to legislation. They assist MPs in drafting bills. They can draw to an MP's attention constitutional limitations that, if disregarded, could compromise the law's validity — a provision might, for example, encroach on an area of provincial jurisdiction. Although MPs are completely free to draft their own legislative texts, the Legislative Counsel Office reviews all bills to check their form and their conformity with the Constitution and with legislative and parliamentary conventions.

Members of Parliament can call on Office personnel if they are concerned about the form or the substance of a bill or an amendment to a bill, at all stages of the legislative process including consideration in committee. The Office's services are available both to individuals and committees.

The Office is further responsible for certifying private Members' bills before they are presented in the House, and for seeing to their printing after first reading. It also sees to the printing of government bills after first and third reading. In addition, it incorporates amendments at committee stage and after the report has been presented. The General Legislative Counsel also takes turn serving as a Table Officer in the House Chamber.

THE PARLIAMENTARY OPERATIONS DIRECTORATE

At the head of the Directorate is a Director General, assisted by five subordinates whose titles vary depending on the unit they head. The Committees Directorate is headed by a Principal Clerk; the Parliamentary Publications Directorate, the Public Information Office and the Parliamentary Exchanges and Protocol Directorate by Directors; and the Parliamentary Associations Secretariat by a Secretary General.

The Committees Directorate

A Principal Clerk is in charge here, assisted by three Deputy Principal Clerks who co-ordinate and supervise the work of the procedural Clerks. The Committees Directorate provides services to standing committees, special committees, and the MPs who comprise them, just as the Public Bills Office does for legislative committees.

The Committees Directorate furnishes expert procedural and administrative support to standing, special, and joint committees and to House subcommittees. The Clerks draft committee minutes of proceedings, assist in drafting reports, and perform other functions related to committee work. They are responsible for all committee documents and must make sure they are kept secure.

Another duty, and not a slight one, that falls to the Directorate is the preparation of budgets. Every year large sums of money are spent to ensure the smooth functioning of the committees of the House of Commons. The standing committees receive a master budget, which is then divided among them by the Liaison Committee, as explained in the chapter on committees. Throughout the fiscal year the committee clerks also advise the chairmen and members of their committees on budget management.

> The Committees Directorate offers expert professional services with respect to administration and procedure to the standing, special and joint committees.

The assignment of Table duty to the Principal Clerks and Deputy Principal Clerk was introduced only recently. It has the double advantage of ensuring good service at all sittings of the House and of giving the Deputy Principal Clerk and his deputies an opportunity to gain Chamber experience.

The Parliamentary Publications Directorate

At the head of this Directorate is a Director assisted by a subordinate heading each of the following services: the Debates Reporting Service, the Committee Reporting Service, the Centralized Support and Publications Service and the Index and Reference Service.

THE DEBATES REPORTING SERVICE

Hansard, the daily record of the debates of the House, originated with the Hansard family who published the minutes of the British debates from 1812 to 1890.

The mandate of this Service is to prepare a daily transcript of the debates in the House in both official languages. This record is commonly known as *Hansard,* after the family who published the debates of the Parliament at Westminster from 1812 to 1890. In Canada, the current form of our *Hansard* dates back to 1880, when a Debates Reporting Service was added to the personnel of Parliament.

Hansard is a complete record of everything said in the House, with only needless repetitions and grammatical and other obvious errors corrected. No change can be made to the substance, because the record must faithfully reflect the speaker's intention. A rough copy of the relevant portion of the transcript is sent to each MP for verification. These rough copies are called the "blues" because of the colour of the paper on which it was formerly printed. Today the "blues" are printed on white paper or more often sent by fax to Members' offices. The "blues" reach the MP less than an hour and a half after he finishes speaking. It is up to MPs to ensure that the text faithfully reproduces what they said in the House, but they cannot change the content of their remarks even if in the meantime they have changed their minds.

The *Hansard* containing the previous day's debates in both official languages comes out every day, usually by 10:00 a.m.

THE COMMITTEE REPORTING SERVICE

This Service records and transcribes committee proceedings in both official languages and publishes them in what are known as committee "issues." The final issue of a series generally contains the report that the committee is presenting to the House. As can be imagined, committee proceedings represent a considerable volume of text, and their preparation is complicated by the tight deadlines within which these official records must be published.

Committee proceedings are recorded, transcribed, edited, translated and published within two to four working days after the committee meets.

THE INDEX AND REFERENCE SERVICE

This Service prepares indexes that make it easier to consult the *Debates,* the *Journals,* and all the issues of *Committee Minutes of Proceedings and Evidence.* Thanks to its computerized system, the Service can also prepare specialized indexes tailored to the needs of individual MPs.

The Service also prepares a cumulative index with references to *Hansard,* the *Journals,* and the committee issues. An unrevised cumulative index to the *Debates* is published at the end of each quarter. A revised cumulative index is published in a bound volume at the end of each session. The *Journals* index resembles the *Debates* index in form, but it is attached to the last bound volume of the *Journals* for each session. The indexes for the *Journals*, *Debates*, and committee issues are cross-referenced under both subject headings and MPs' names.

The Service also offers a telephone service providing general information, updated daily, about *Hansard* and the *Journals*. Questions about the testimony given in committee can also be answered, if the issues have come out.

THE CENTRALIZED SUPPORT AND PUBLICATIONS SERVICE (CSPS)

The CSPS looks after all the technical aspects of drafting and preparing parliamentary publications. It ensures that all publications are impeccable before they go to printing. Moreover, it provides co-ordination with the Department of the Secretary of State, which is responsible for translating parliamentary publications and the Canada Communications Group Publishing Service which prints House publications.

The Public Information Office

The Office's Director is assisted by a subordinate heading each of the following: the Broadcasting Service, the Communications Service, and the Education and Visitor Services. The main mission of all these units is to provide information. The Office was created in 1987 in response to public demand for more information about the institutions of Parliament.

THE BROADCASTING SERVICE

The Broadcasting Service produces live television coverage of the proceedings of the House and distributes it all across Canada by satellite. This makes it possible for most Canadians to watch the House of Commons debates live, or as part of a daily videotaped replay. The actual satellite distribution of televised House proceedings is performed by the Cable Parliamentary Channel Inc. (CPAC), a non profit corporation funded by a consortium of Canadian cable companies.

Canadians can follow the work of the House on television.

The Service also covers some committee meetings, when such coverage has been requested by the committee and permission granted by the House. Coverage of committee meetings may be increased following a recent decision by the House to act on a recommendation of the House Management Committee and equip a special room for the broadcasting of committee proceedings.[2]

2. Twenty-Third Report of the Standing Committee on House Management, tabled February 14, 1992 and concurred in the House on March 27, 1992.

Each year thousands of tourists from Canada and abroad visit Ottawa.

These proceedings will be televised on the Parliamentary Channel and made available to the media on a trial basis. If the House assesses the results of the experiment to be positive, committee coverage may be expanded.

The Broadcasting Service also sees to the operation of a closed-circuit television network called OASIS. This network carries audiovisual presentations and makes a great deal of information available to MPs and their staffs including regional newscasts from across the country. The dates and times of committee meetings are also indicated.

EDUCATION AND VISITOR SERVICES

The mission of this Service is to inform and provide documentation to teachers and to organize programs for visitors. It acts as liaison with the teaching profession, concerns itself with teachers' needs, and drafts texts specially for them. It prepares guides for students and information kits for teachers. It takes part in programs on Parliament Hill organized for groups of young people, like the Forum for Young Canadians and Encounters with Canada.

This unit is also responsible for organizing programs for people who want to visit the Parliament Buildings — the tourists, whether from Canada or abroad, who flock to Ottawa all year round. Tours are conducted by guides who are recruited annually and who offer visitors information about our parliamentary institutions. As well, the Service handles requests from people who wish to attend Question Period, and makes reservations for them.

The Dominion Carillonneur also comes under this unit. Fifteen-minute recitals are planned and given every day from October to July, at 12:30 p.m. Other hour-long recitals are given on Tuesday and Sunday evenings in June and July. The Carillonneur has the further mission of making Canadians more aware of the historic significance of the carillon and the Peace Tower.

Pages carry messages and documents to the Members in the House and in the lobbies.

This Service is also responsible for the Page Program. The Pages are at the service of the House and are on duty in the Chamber while the House is sitting. Bearing messages or documents, they shuttle back and forth between the Chamber, the lobbies and MPs' offices. Like the Guide Program, the Page Program recruits on a yearly basis, giving young Canadians the opportunity to absorb a unique experience in the parliamentary milieu.

COMMUNICATIONS SERVICE

This Service is composed of the Information Service and the Editorial and Creative Service.

Information Service   Its name is self-explanatory! It makes available information on the House and the Canadian parliamentary system to anyone who requests it. A telephone service staffed by specially trained employees answers about 6000 requests for information every month. The Service also responds to written requests and distributes information kits.

The staff at the Information Office is trained to answer questions from the general public.

The creation of this Service filled a real void, as is evident from the growing number of requests addressed to it. In addition to demanding simple facts, the Canadian public is asking for more complex services. The Public Information Office continues to respond, through the Information Service and the other services it administers.

Editorial and Creative Service   As its name suggests, this Service is dedicated to writing and producing illustrated documents. A number of brochures have been published thanks to the collaboration of the two units in the Service — one drafts the texts, the other illustrates them. Each of the publications produced by this Service comments in simple terms, and with appropriate pictures, on a particular aspect of Parliament. The brochures are designed for visitors, teachers, and the general public.

The Inter-parliamentary Associations Secretariat

Headed by a Secretary General, this unit acts as the secretariat for the eight inter-parliamentary associations with which the Parliament of Canada has ties. Some are international, like the Commonwealth Parliamentary Association, the International French-speaking Parliamentary Association, and the Inter-parliamentary Union. Some are bilateral, such as, Canada-United States and Canada-Japan.

This is one of the few services that works for both Houses of Parliament. Its budget is 30 percent financed by the Senate and 70 percent by the House, and the representation of the two Houses on parliamentary dele gations respects this ratio as well.

The Secretariat provides professional and administrative support to the Canadian sections that represent the Parliament of Canada within the eight different associations. Each Canadian section has an executive secretary who is supplied by the Secretariat. The executive secretaries act as advisers to their section chairman or president and the executive committee. They draw up budgets and act as financial advisers. They co-ordinate research work, organize briefing sessions, and travel with delegations. Bilateral parliamentary associations usually meet alternately in Canada and in the other member countries. The parliaments affiliated with multilateral associations take turns to invite the members to meet in their countries. When it is Canada's turn to host an annual general meeting, the Secretariat does the organizing, but the sheer scale of the event requires participation by other House of Commons services as well. For example, the annual general meeting of the Inter-Parliamentary Union brings together about a thousand delegates, representing a volume of work that the Secretariat's personnel could not possibly cope with unassisted.

The Secretary General acts as secretary to the Inter-parliamentary Advisory Council, consisting of the two Speakers, the presidents or chairmen of the Canadian sections of the parliamentary associations, and the House and Senate whips of the main parties. A Subcommittee on Finance and Budgets of the Advisory Council allocates the master budget among the associations and deals with any question involving them.

The Parliamentary Exchanges and Protocol Directorate

Headed by a Director, this service sees to all inter-parliamentary exchanges that take place outside the framework of an inter-parliamentary association. The Directorate is responsible for protocol related to such exchanges and also provides protocol services to the associations. It also organizes parliamentary co-operation programs.

Like the Secretariat, it serves both Houses of Parliament and its financial situation is analogous to that of the Secretariat. Its budget is provided proportionately by the two Houses (30 percent by the Senate and 70 percent by the House) and delegations are composed on the same ratio.

Exchanges are carried out on the authority of the two Speakers, who may lead a delegation in person or transfer the responsibility to another parliamentarian. Trips abroad are made following an invitation from another country. Visits to Canada come about after the Speakers deliver invitations to their counterparts in other countries. The Directorate is responsible for organizing the programs that occur in Canada, and ensures co-ordination for trips abroad. Parliamentary Exchange Officers prepare briefing sessions, supply the requisite documentation, look after logistics and finances and accompany Canadian delegations abroad and visiting delegations when these travel in Canada outside Ottawa.

The Directorate has other responsibilities, so widely varied that they are difficult to list. It organizes programs for many visitors, for example, provincial parliamentarians visiting Ottawa, senior officers from foreign parliaments, committees from other countries that come to Canada to carry out a special study or learn about Canada's committee system, and so on. When heads of state and heads of government come to Canada on an official visit, the parliamentary portion of the visit is organized and run by the Directorate. The Director advises the Speakers, parliamentarians, and senior officials of both Houses on all questions of protocol.

The Directorate looks after parliamentary co-operation programs. As we have seen, this responsibility was entrusted to the Clerk Assistant (see Chapter 6) but it is the Parliamentary Exchanges and Protocol Directorate that actually provides the personnel to carry out the programs.

SERVICE REPORTING DIRECTLY TO THE CLERK OF THE HOUSE

The Legal Counsel Office

This Office is directed by the General Legal Counsel. It reports directly to the Clerk of the House. Its personnel consists of several lawyers in addition to the General Legal Counsel, and its mandate is to provide legal advice to MPs in their roles as Members and to various House services. It acts, in short, as the House of Commons' legal adviser. Its services are protected by the solicitor-client relationship and all opinions and correspondence are strictly confidential.

Parliamentarians often need legal opinions in areas directly related to their duties — possible conflicts of interest, for example, or questions of privilege. In such an event they can call upon the services of the Legal Counsel Office.

The Office also provides legal services to the Speaker, the Board of Internal Economy, and managers in the Clerk's, Administrator's, and Sergeant-at-Arm's sectors. This includes advice on such matters as the drafting and interpretation of contracts, staff relations, and security of the precincts.

The committees may also use the services of the lawyers who work for the Legal Counsel Office. Opinions may be provided on the rights and obligations of committees, including their power to send for persons and documents, the rights of witnesses who are testifying before a committee and the broadcasting of committee proceedings.

The lawyers at the Legal Counsel Office offer legal advice to Members and to the personnel of the different House services on questions relating to their functions and duties.

The House of Commons: Functions

Parliament, and in particular the House of Commons, has three main functions: it passes legislation; it legislates taxes proposed by the Government and authorizes the Government to use public moneys; and it monitors the actions of the executive branch.

Let us look at these three functions in turn.

THE LEGISLATIVE FUNCTIONS

The power of the House of Commons of Canada to make laws is based on the *Constitution Act, 1867*. The *Act* defines the general organization of the House and in Section 91 describes the areas of jurisdiction within which Parliament has the supreme power to legislate. As we have seen, the Parliament of Canada is bicameral, and except in money matters its two Houses have substantially the same legislative powers. In 1982, an additional difference in powers was introduced when the *Constitution Act* of that year gave the Senate only a suspensive veto over certain constitutional amendments.

Every bill must be adopted by both Houses of Parliament before it can become law.

To become law, a bill must first be introduced in either the Senate or the House of Commons. It must then pass through various stages in each House, including a first, second, and third reading.[1] After that, it must receive Royal Assent. Before we look at the legislative process, here are some definitions that are essential to an understanding of the subject.

Public Bills

These are proposals for laws that will affect the public in general. Their provisions will apply, if not to everyone, then at any rate to a very large

---

1. This term derives from the era before the invention of printing when a bill was actually read out in the House. The practice persisted even after the invention of printing as many Members could neither read nor write.

proportion of the population. Examples are the *Food and Drugs Act*, the *Fisheries Act*, the *Canada Pension Plan*—all pieces of legislation that come within the category of public bills because they affect a large number of Canadians.

Public bills constitute the greater part of all the legislation considered and passed by the House. For each session of Parliament, bills sponsored by the Government are numbered from C-1 to C-200 in order of presentation. If they are introduced first in the Senate, they are numbered starting S-1. Bills preserve their original numbering when they move from one House to the other.

Although most public bills are introduced by Government Ministers, the Standing Orders provide that they may also be introduced by any other MP. Such bills, known as Private Members' Public Bills, are numbered C-201 to C-1000, in order of introduction. In the Senate, there is no distinction made on the basis of who introduces a bill so that bills are numbered as received.

Usually a bill has both a long title, setting out in general terms the purposes of the bill, and a short title, by which the bill will be cited once it has been passed into law. A bill consists of a series of numbered clauses accompanied by descriptive notes printed in the margin.

Bills introduced by ordinary MPs, rather than Government Ministers, must meet certain criteria: they must not duplicate measures already on the Government's legislative program and they must not commit the Government to spending public money. In practice, public bills introduced by ordinary MPs constitute a very tiny proportion of the legislation passed by Parliament. Of the 149 bills introduced by private Members during the second session of the 34th Parliament, only three of broad significance received Royal Assent. These were Bill C-223, *An Act respecting a Day of Mourning for persons killed or injured in the workplace*; Bill C-258, *An Act respecting the establishment of the Centennial Flame Research Award to publicize the contributions to Canadian public life of persons with disabilities*; and Bill C-260, *An Act to amend the Canada Pension Plan*. During the same period, other bills introduced by private Members did get through the whole legislative process, but they dealt with matters of more local concern, such as a new name for an MP's riding.

Money bills are always public bills, and will not be dealt with in this section; the following section will be devoted exclusively to them.

Private Bills

Private bills are limited in scope: they concern an individual or a group of individuals only. They confer a right on some person or group, or relieve them of a responsibility. Often a private bill incorporates a

As their name suggests, Private Members' Bills concern individuals or groups of individuals.

company or a non-profit or professional association. They are passed by Parliament in accordance with the same legislative principles as public bills, but are based on a petition and subject to a different procedure. Legally, it is possible to present private bills in either House. In practice, however, they have been introduced in the Senate on a regular basis since 1934, when the House raised the fees it charged for private bills.

It is important not to confuse a public bill sponsored by a private Member, and thus known as a "Private Member's Bill," with a private bill, which may also be sponsored by a private Member. The distinction lies in the bill's nature and scope, and has nothing to do with the person putting it forward. A Private Member's Bill and a private bill follow different procedures.

The Various Stages of a Bill

Most legislation originates with the Government. Often the winning party in a general election has made promises during the campaign, and is expected to act on these promises. The Government may also bring in legislation on the recommendation of departmental officials who think certain legislation needs to be amended or replaced with something corresponding more closely to current realities. Sometimes special interest groups make suggestions to the Government as well.

It is Cabinet that formulates the legislative program, with a view to bringing into force laws that will implement its policies. The Government makes the choices, sets the priorities, and decides what legislation it is going to bring in. Once Cabinet concludes that a particular legislative measure is required in a particular area, it is up to the Minister responsible for that area to present a memorandum to Cabinet for its formal approval. The memorandum is a policy paper that spells out the objectives sought. It is studied by the appropriate Cabinet committee, and if the committee gives its approval, it is transmitted either back to Cabinet or to Cabinet's Priorities and Planning Committee. Finally, if Cabinet agrees, the Department of Justice's Legislation Section is authorized to draft a bill, in consultation with the department concerned and possibly with others as well. At the drafting stage, the bill is confidential, and its contents cannot be revealed to anyone who is not working on it either at the Department of Justice or in Cabinet. As soon as the bill is ready, in both official languages, and the Minister responsible has approved it, it is submitted to Cabinet (see Figure 4).[2]

2. See *The Legislative Process in Canada* (Ottawa: Department of Justice, 1987).

FIGURE 4

Overview of the Legislative Process

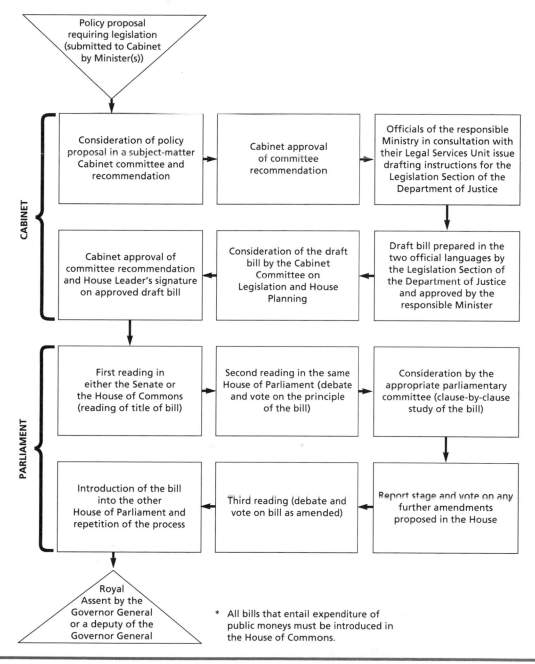

Source: *The Legislative Process in Canada* (Ottawa: Department of Justice, 1987), p. 19.

Cabinet establishes
the legislative agenda
for Parliament.

Once Cabinet approves the bill, it is ready to be introduced in Parliament. Usually the Government House Leader, who is responsible for organizing the business of the House and for advancing legislation, decides on the timing in consultation with the Minister responsible, unless Cabinet has already reached a decision. If the bill is to be introduced in the Senate, the date is set in consultation with the Government Leader in the Senate. The fact that no Ministers responsible for departments normally sit in the Senate explains in part why most Government bills are introduced in the House.

A public bill introduced by an ordinary MP is the personal responsibility of that MP. Having decided on the content of the legislation, the Member turns to the lawyers in the Legislative Counsel Office, who customarily draft bills at the request of MPs, following established criteria. Whether it is a Minister or a private Member who wants to introduce a public bill, a copy of the bill must be submitted and 48 hours' notice of the intention to introduce it must be given. The title of the bill appears in the *Notice Paper* under the heading, "Introduction of Government Bills" or "Introduction of Private Members' Bills," as appropriate. This entry can stay on the *Order Paper* as long as the Minister or MP desires. Once the sponsor is ready to introduce the bill, he informs the Chair or one of the Clerks-at-the-Table.

INTRODUCTION OF A BILL AND FIRST READING

First reading is
preceded by a
formal motion.

This involves the passing of two motions, the first for the leave of the House to introduce the bill, the second for first reading. During Routine Proceedings, the Minister or the Member must propose a motion requesting the leave of the House to introduce the bill. The motion is passed automatically, without debate, amendment or formal vote. A Minister generally does not elaborate on the bill; a private Member may explain its aim very briefly (see "Routine Proceedings," Chapter 10).

The Speaker then asks if it is the pleasure of the House to adopt the motion that "the bill be now read a first time and printed." This motion too passes automatically, without debate, amendment, or formal vote. The Speaker asks the House when the bill is to be read a second time, to which the response is normally, "At the next sitting of the House," although it is not necessarily debated at the next sitting. The bill can now receive its order number and be entered on the *Order Paper*, under "Government Orders," if it is sponsored by a Minister, or under "Private Members' Business," if the sponsor is a private Member. It has now cleared first reading and its subject matter is public knowledge. The bill is printed overnight and distributed to all MPs the next morning. Since the Government decides the order in which its bills come before the House, it can decide at what date the bill will be called in the House for second reading.

Although Government Bills and Private Members' Bills go through basically the same legislative process, there are differences in the way these two types of bill are handled. One important difference is that bills initiated by private Members have to go through a selection process, as there is not enough time to deal with them all. The House considers bills and motions put forward by MPs according to an order of precedence established by random draw. The draw is organized by the Private Members' Business Office on behalf of the Clerk of the House, and is carried out under the aegis of the Deputy Speaker. Each draw establishes a list containing 30 items, and the order in which they will be considered by the House. As soon as the list is down to 15 items, or about every six weeks, a new draw is held.[3]

The type of consideration to be given each item on the order of precedence list is determined by the Standing Committee on House Management, which designates up to five bills and five motions from the list as "votable." Normally the House deals with one item from the list each day, for one hour, although there may be delays or even cancellations due to other business such as the debate that follows the Throne Speech, or an emergency debate. If the item being considered has not been designated as votable, it is dropped from the *Order Paper* following the one-hour debate. Due to the relatively small amount of time allocated to them, and to the weeding-out procedures to which they are subject, few Private Members' Bills actually make it into law.

SECOND READING

Second reading is often described as the most important stage that a bill must go through. The motion for second reading asks that the bill be read a second time and referred to a committee for consideration. The House may decide to refer it to a legislative, a standing or a special committee, or to Committee of the Whole. Debate at second reading is on the principle of the bill, and is usually long and lively. This is the opposition parties' chance to criticize not only the proposed legislation but also the policy it represents. Even if the Government has a considerable majority in the House, its bill will not necessarily move smoothly and rapidly to a vote. Especially in the case of controversial bills, the opposition parties may use every procedural tactic available to delay passage at second reading. Sometimes, when the Government is determined to

During second reading, Members consider the principle of a bill.

---

3. A good source of further detail on the draw is *A Practical Guide to Private Members' Business*, available from the Private Members' Business Office.

push a bill through and finds itself confronted by systematic opposition, it invokes the Standing Order providing for allocation of time and may eventually resort to invoking closure, thus ending the debate. Alternatively, it may negotiate compromises with the opposition parties.

Permissible types of amendment at second reading are the reasoned amendment, that is to say, an amendment that spells out specific reasons for opposing the principle of the bill; discharging of the bill and referral of the subject matter to a committee for further information; and what is known as the "hoist" — delaying a vote for several months, which is a way of having it delayed and perhaps even forgotten. This last type of amendment dates back to an era when the Commons did not, for reasons of courtesy, wish to refuse a request made to them by the Monarch and yet had no intention of carrying it out. To avoid saying "No," they simply deferred consideration of the request indefinitely. It is difficult to imagine this happening nowadays when there is a majority Government.

The procedure followed for a bill introduced by an ordinary MP, as opposed to one introduced by a Minister, is different. To have a chance of reaching a vote at second reading, a Private Members' Bill must, unless the House gives unanimous consent, have been selected as a "votable item." It can then be debated for 2 hours and 45 minutes before a vote is held, and if it is supported by a sufficient number of Members to gain it, a majority it can proceed. If the Government party supports the bill, then it will of course proceed beyond second reading, but such cases are rare. They tend to occur when the bill in question is relatively limited in scope, or when the Government is forced to support it by the pressure of public opinion. One example of the latter is the *Non-Smokers' Health Act*, which received wide support in the House after being introduced in 1986 by the then MP for Broadview-Greenwood, Lynn McDonald.

If a Private Member's Bill is adopted at second reading, it is then subject to the normal legislative process, except that following consideration in committee it will again be listed in the order of precedence and can be debated for no more than two hours at report stage and third reading. However, the Standing Orders provide that the debate can be extended.

CONSIDERATION IN COMMITTEE

Following second reading, bills are sent to committee, where they are studied clause by clause.

After the adoption of the second reading of the bill, it is referred to a legislative or other type of committee. A bill can be referred to a Committee of the Whole, a procedure that normally occurs with the unanimous consent of the House when the bill is urgent, non-controversial, or a Supply bill. In such cases it often passes through several stages at the same sitting. Whatever the type of committee, bills are always considered according to the rules that we looked at in the chapter on Committees.

Once the principle underlying the bill has been affirmed by the House, the committee proceeds to a detailed examination of the bill, studying it clause by clause. As we have seen, a committee can summon the witnesses and experts it thinks most likely to be able to provide it with information and help in improving the bill. Any member of the committee may move amendments, which are generally drafted with the assistance of the Legislative Counsel. Amendments proposed by the Government are drafted by the Department of Justice. It can happen that the committee reports the bill without any amendments at all.

When the committee has completed consideration of the bill, it reports the bill to the House clearly indicating any amendments proposed. It must be borne in mind that no final decisions are taken in committee. A committee can submit all the proposed amendments it likes, but it is up to the House to decide when it votes on the motion to concur in the bill, with or without amendments, at report stage.

REPORT STAGE

Once the committee has made its report to the House, the bill is said to be at report stage. Debate on it will begin when the Speaker calls for "consideration of the report stage of Bill X, as reported from Committee Y." The House has two options. It can either concur in the report as it stands, or move further amendments.

At this stage any MP, and not just the MPs who belong to the committee that considered the bill, can propose amendments. To avoid duplication, the Speaker can select the amendments that will be debated and group similar ones together. He must follow certain criteria, so that all parliamentarians are treated fairly, while ensuring that the time of the House is used efficiently. Amendments to the substance of the bill must not alter the underlying principle in any way, since that was approved by the House at second reading.

Once all the amendments have been reviewed and the House has voted for or against them, the Minister responsible for the bill, or the sponsoring MP, asks the House to concur in the bill, as amended where this is the case. This motion is immediately put to a vote without debate.

When Committee of the Whole completes consideration of a bill, it must also report to the House. In such cases, report stage occurs immediately; there is no debate and no amendments may be moved.

Whether they were on the committee studying the bill or not, Members can propose amendments to bills at report stage.

THIRD READING

The final stage facing a bill is third reading, which begins with the following motion: "That the Bill be now read a third time and do pass." This makes it possible for the House to review the bill in its final form. Third reading is similar to second in that debate must focus on the bill as a whole. Amendments that may be moved are similar to those that may be moved at second reading. Debate tends to be less lengthy than at second reading, but otherwise the process is essentially identical.

THE PASSING OF LEGISLATION IN THE SENATE

Following adoption by the House, bills are sent to Senate, where they undergo a similar adoption process.

Once the bill has been read three times and passed in the House, it is sent to the Senate for its consideration.

By the time a bill is sent to the Upper House, it has already been considered on the floor of the House and in committee, which is to say it has undergone a very thorough examination indeed. The Senate considers it again, with new eyes capable of picking out small defects, weaknesses, contradictions in wording, or technical errors that may have escaped MPs often pressed for time. The Senators, less overburdened than their colleagues in the Commons, can polish and generally improve the legislation. It also happens that the Government, realizing it wishes to make a change to the text, asks that the appropriate amendment be moved in the Senate. Sometimes the Senate makes substantial changes, or even rejects the bill. Sometimes the decision is purely political, a situation that arises most often when the majority party in the Senate is not the same as in the House.[4]

Occasionally, the Government will introduce a bill in the Senate rather than in the House. There again, it all depends on the relations between the Senate and the Government, as the Government would only do such a thing when it knew it could count on the political support of the Upper House. Nor is the procedure made any easier by the fact that Ministers who head departments generally do not sit in the Senate.

Procedural rules in the Senate are more flexible than those in the House. Even if in principle the bill goes through almost identical stages in both Houses, there are certain differences that are worth noting. In the Senate, it is not necessary to request leave to introduce a bill, and consideration in committee is not obligatory. The motion for second reading asks only "that the Bill be now read a second time," and if the motion passes, the Speaker asks when the bill is to be read a third time. At that point any Senator may move that the bill be referred to either a

---

4.   R.A. Mackay, *The Unreformed Senate of Canada* (Toronto: McClelland and Stewart Ltd., 1963), p. 50ff.

standing or a special Senate committee. If no such motion is made, a date is set for third reading. The bill does not then undergo consideration in either committee or report stage.

The Senate, like the House, has its own committee system. The Upper House has 12 standing committees, to which of course must be added special and joint committees. All bills, including those referred from the House of Commons, go through three readings. If the Senate makes no changes, the bill is passed and it moves to the final stage of Royal Assent. If the Senate amends the bill, it must go back to the House for consideration of all the amendments. If the House simply approves the amendments made by the Senate the bill is passed, and lacks nothing but Royal Assent to become law. But the House may reject the Senate amendments and simply disagree that the bill needs amendments. In both cases, a message is sent to the Senate to acquaint it with the House's opinion. At that point, the Senate may reconsider its amendments and/or adopt the amendments proposed by the House. When one House studies amendments proposed by the other, it must confine itself strictly to those amendments.

Communication between the two Houses takes the form of messages conveyed to the respective Speakers. Thus, the Speaker of the House reads out messages from the Senate, informing the House that bills the latter has adopted have been amended in the Senate. The amendments are printed in the sitting's *Votes and Proceedings* and the bill is re-entered on the *Order Paper*. When the House rejects Senate amendments, it passes a motion which may state the reasons for its refusal and sends this motion to the Senate in the form of a message. In this way, the bill may come and go a number of times from one House to the other.

Failing agreement, either House may suggest a conference to discuss and resolve the difference of opinion. A conference of this kind was last held in Canada in 1947. If a conference is not suggested and no compromise can be reached, the bill remains on the *Order Paper* until the end of the session, at which point it "dies." Deadlock between the two Houses is rare, however. The important thing to bear in mind is that all bills must go through three readings in each House and be adopted in exactly the same form by both Houses before they can become law.

The legislative agenda in the House of Commons is usually very crowded, and the business of the House cannot always be dealt with at the pace the Government would like. The result is that bills passed by the House are sometimes sent to the Senate in haste, with little time allowed the Senate for its consideration. On the other hand, at the start of each session, the Senate is hardly busy at all, since it has to wait for the House to start sending it bills. To alleviate this problem, the Senate, in 1971, introduced a new method of proceeding, under which it begins studying the subject matter of certain bills while they are still before the House. This enables the Senate to be better informed when the bill does arrive, particularly in the case of highly complex legislation that demands especially meticulous attention. This previously informal responsibility assumed by the Senate was incorporated into its rules when the latter were reformed in June of 1991. The Senate also undertakes consideration of the estimates while these are still before the standing committees of the House.[5]

ROYAL ASSENT AND PROCLAMATION

Once a bill has been adopted in identical form by the two Houses, it receives Royal Assent and becomes law.

Once a bill, whether public or private, is passed in identical form by both Houses, all it needs to become law is Royal Assent. The provisions governing Royal Assent are set out in the *Constitution Act, 1867*. This final stage in the legislative process is carried out with some ceremony in the Senate Chamber. The Speaker of the House receives a message from the Governor General's Secretary informing him that the Governor General or his Deputy will be in the Senate that day to give Royal Assent to certain bills. It is, in fact, rare for the Governor General to be there in person, and most of the time this role is taken by a justice of the Supreme Court. At the time specified, the Gentleman Usher of the Black Rod comes to the door of the House to inform the Speaker that the Governor General or his Deputy wishes the Commons to come to the Senate. The Speaker or whoever is in the Chair at the time, followed by the MPs, proceed to the Senate where they stand at the Bar. The Speaker bows to the Governor General or his Deputy. The Clerk of the Senate, who also bears the title of Clerk of the Parliaments, reads the title of the bill and the formula of Royal Assent. The Royal Assent is signified by a nod of the head of the Governor General or his Deputy. Usually there are a number of bills, but all are treated separately. The Clerk of the Parliaments enters the date of the assent on each bill, immediately after the title. It is interesting to note that this traditional ceremony, still carried on in Canada, was abolished in Great Britain in 1967.

Although Section 55 of the *Constitution Act, 1867* provides that the Governor General may refuse Royal Assent, in practice this simply does not happen. The last time the Crown refused assent in England was in 1707.

5.   See *The Legislative Process*, 2nd ed. (Ottawa: Parliament of Canada, Table Research Branch, 1992), p. 10.

House of Commons,   **Chambre des Communes,**

Wednesday, June 10, 1992   Le mercredi 10 juin 1992

ORDERED: ORDONNÉ:

That the Clerk do carry this Bill to the   Que le Greffier porte ce projet de loi au
Senate, and desire their concurrence.   Sénat et demande son adhésion.

....
Clerk of the House.   *Greffier de la Chambre.*

PASSED by the Senate, Monday, 22nd   ADOPTÉ par le Sénat le lundi 22
June, 1992, without amendment.   juin 1992, sans amendement.

....
Clerk of the Senate   Greffier du Sénat.

ASSENTED to in Her Majesty's name   SANCTIONNÉ au nom de Sa Majesté
June 23, 1992.   le 23 juin 1992.

....

Royal Assent

When all the bills have received Royal Assent, the Gentleman Usher of
the Black Rod indicates that the ceremony is over. The Speaker once
again bows to the Governor General or his Deputy and returns to the
House followed by the MPs. There he announces that the Governor
General has been pleased to give assent to certain bills in Her Majesty's
name. A list of the enacted bills will appear in *Votes and Proceedings* and
then ultimately in the *Journals*.

After it has received Royal Assent, a bill becomes law. But this does not
mean that it comes into force immediately. Usually, the legislation itself
contains a provision that it shall come into force either once it receives
Royal Assent or on a specified date. Alternatively, the legislation may
provide that it shall come into force only when proclaimed by the
Governor in Council. The Government may want to defer the coming
into force of all or part of a piece of legislation for administrative or political reasons. In that case, the bill is enacted but does not come into
force until the date set by proclamation. When an act contains no provi-

sion as to its coming into force, the *Interpretation Act* provides that it shall come into force on receiving Royal Assent.[6]

THE ROLE OF PARLIAMENT IN FINANCIAL MATTERS

Here we reach the very heart of any parliamentary system based on the British model. In England, Parliament began to gain the upper hand from the moment it was able to insist that the Monarch not levy taxes without the consent of the taxpayers' representatives. This consent they would not give unless they knew why the taxes were needed. By 1407, it was firmly established that all money bills had to be examined first by the Commons. In those days, each separate expenditure was financed by a particular tax. This meant that the link between taxation and expenditure was very close, since a bill providing for the collecting of a tax also authorized the expenditures for which the moneys collected were intended. It was an accepted fact that Parliament did not take the initiative in financial matters. These were the responsibility of the Crown, which governed and thus had to raise the money needed for the expenses of Government. Only the Crown could bring before Parliament bills permitting taxes to be levied and the resulting revenues to be spent. Starting in the 17th century, it became the practice that bills of this kind were studied in the Committee of the Whole House.

Quite early on, it became clear that authorizing an expenditure and its tax at the same time was by no means the ideal procedure. Sometimes not enough money was raised, sometimes more was raised than necessary. Moreover, the Crown was calling for money ("supply") more and more often, which was causing confusion in the allocation of revenues. To resolve this problem, a Consolidated Revenue Fund was created, into which all state revenues were paid and from which the amounts necessary for Government operations could be taken. These rules, established over the years as the British parliamentary system evolved, were incorporated into our *Constitution Act, 1867*.[7]

Our system of public finances is complex and controlled by rigorous rules. A detailed study of this system is beyond the scope of the present work, and in any case it is preferable from a practical point of view to focus on the distinctive features of our public finance system. This

6. *Interpretation Act*, R.S. (1985), c. I-21.
7. Section 53 provides that all financial legislation shall be tabled first in the House of Commons. Section 54 provides that any expenditure for which the Government is seeking Parliament's approval must first have been recommended by the Governor General. Section 102 creates the Consolidated Revenue Fund.

should give enough information to understand how the system functions without burdening the general reader with too many details.[8]

The Budget

The Consolidated Revenue Fund is fed by income taxes and various other kinds of taxes. Out of it come the funds for the operations and needs of the state. As Sir Gilbert Campion, Clerk of the House at Westminster from 1937 to 1948, said of Great Britain's Consolidated Revenue Fund, "It is the reservoir into which all revenue flows and from which all expenditures issue."[9]

First of all, the Government makes its intentions known in the Speech from the Throne, read by the Governor General at the start of each session. The policies the Government intends to implement are announced, and the MPs are requested to allocate the money required to cover the consequent expenditures. The Throne Speech, however, contains only general policy statements, which are not part of the budget process for the very good reason that the budget cycle does not correspond to parliamentary sessions. A session may be of almost any length, but the fiscal year is fixed: from April 1 to March 31 of the following calendar year.

The Government's financial intentions are revealed in detailed form only in the Budget, usually brought down once a year. There is no set date for the presentation of the Budget, although there has been a tendency recently to table it before the main estimates, in other words before March 1. When the Minister of Finance presents the Budget, the business of the House is interrupted and current proceedings are deemed to have been adjourned.[10] It is customary for the Budget Speech to be delivered after the stock markets have closed to prevent possible speculation as new fiscal measures are announced.

Generally, once a year the Minister of Finance brings down the Budget and informs the House of the economic situation and the fiscal measures being proposed.

The Minister's speech is a wide-ranging and complex discussion of economic, social, and financial policies. The Government's intentions are unveiled and the projects it is proposing to undertake are described. The amount of money the state will need is forecast and the ways in which it plans to obtain this money are outlined. This means that any proposed changes in the tax system are announced — any tax increases or reductions, any new taxes, any change in the tax base, etc. The

8. For further details, see the *Précis of Procedure*, 4th ed., published by the Table Research Branch, Ottawa, 1991, p. 103ff; the descriptions in this section are based on this publication.

9. Norman Wilding and Philip Laundy, *An Encyclopaedia of Parliament*, op. cit., p. 611.

10. Standing Order 83.

Minister may then table one or more "ways and means" motions, which are the motions that enable the Government to collect revenue, in other words, that provide for the levying of different kinds of taxes. These motions will be voted on by the House at a future date after the end of the Budget Debate.

When the presentation of the Budget is complete, the Speaker recognizes a representative of the Official Opposition, who makes a brief speech and then proposes that the House adjourn. The debate resumes at a subsequent sitting and lasts for up to four sitting days, although these days need not be consecutive. This is an opportunity for the opposition parties to criticize not only the contents of the Budget but also all the Government's policies. The Finance Minister, the first Speaker from the Official Opposition, the Prime Minister and the Leader of the Opposition, can all speak for as long as they like; other speakers must restrict themselves to 20 minutes followed by 10 minutes of "questions and comments." The rules of debate are relaxed, and the Speaker does not enforce the "relevance" rule (see "The Rules of Debate," Chapter 10). The MPs take full advantage of the debate to make speeches that attract the attention of the voters in their ridings and the public at large. The debate that follows the Budget Speech, like the debates on the main estimates, survives from the days when Parliament insisted on expressing its grievances and reservations before it would vote the Monarch any money. It is now an opportunity for the Members of the Commons to air their own complaints and hold forth on almost any topic of concern to them. This aside, the Budget Speech remains the vehicle through which the Government informs not only Parliament but also the public at large of its needs for revenue, and how it intends to meet those needs.

Financial procedures are designed to meet two fundamental requirements. First, money must be found to feed the Consolidated Revenue Fund (this is known as the business of *ways* and *means*) and second, Parliament must allocate the money collected by the Government so that it can fund its programs and services (this is known as the business of *supply*). All taxation measures and all expenditure authorizations must take the form of bills introduced in the House of Commons. Such legislation goes through a different legislative process from that applicable to ordinary legislation. Any bill proposing expenditure must be preceded by a Royal Recommendation which is transmitted to the House of Commons in the form of a message from the Governor General and read to the House by the Speaker. This is a historic procedure, originating from the days when the King personally requested the Commons of England to supply him with the money needed to run the Government. Its effect today is to restrict the initiation of bills involving expenditure to the

Ministers of the Government. The introduction of bills proposing tax measures is also limited to Government Ministers.

Ways and Means Bills

As we have seen, the Minister of Finance can give notice of one or more ways and means motions at the time he brings down the Budget. The bills based on these motions, however, may well be separate from the Budget. The purpose of all such bills is to raise money through taxation, whether by imposing a new tax, increasing an existing tax, extending a tax that is due to expire, applying a particular tax to a group of citizens hitherto exempt, or other such measure. However, many taxes are collected under continuing statutes such as the *Income Tax Act*, the *Excise Tax Act* and the *Customs Tariff Act*. These statutes provide for taxes that can be collected year after year without new legislation having to be passed, unless of course the Government wishes to amend their provisions in some way. Canada differs in this regard from Great Britain, where an annual finance bill must be reintroduced and re-adopted each year.

A ways and means motion is one which proposes a new tax or an increase in an existing tax.

A ways and means bill is subject to certain conditions prior to its presentation, but once it has gone through first reading stage it follows the same procedure as any other bill. The reforms of 1968 made a number of procedural changes, including doing away with the Committee of Ways and Means. Nowadays, a ways and means bill goes to a legislative or a standing committee after second reading, like any other bill.

Supply

It is not enough for the Government to ensure that revenue is coming in. Once revenue has been collected, Parliament must pass legislation authorizing the Government to spend it. This is done through the Business of Supply, by which Parliament authorizes federal departments and agencies to receive the money they need for each fiscal year. The fiscal year is for this purpose divided into three "supply periods," ending June 23, December 10, and March 26 of the following calendar year respectively.

The Business of Supply allocates the funds necessary to the functioning of the state.

In order to assess the financial requirements of its various services, the Government must be capable of estimating how much money is needed for the coming fiscal year. One of the characteristics of our financial system is that it is based on twelve-month periods, so that everything is evaluated on an annual basis. The budgets of all Government bodies are drawn up for a year that runs from April 1 to March 31 of the following calendar year, and funding cannot overlap two of these fiscal years, or be transferred from one to another. For example, a department that does not use the money allocated to it for a particular fiscal year may not keep the amounts it has saved to use the following year, and money that is not spent returns to the Consolidated Revenue Fund. Preparation of the departmental estimates begins well before the 1st of April on which they will come into effect. It is hardly surprising, then, that they are sometimes inaccurate or incomplete, given the evolution of the economic situation and the changes this may entail in the area of finance, among many other factors.

Government departments and services undertake the preparation of their estimates at the invitation of the President of the Treasury Board who issues guidelines for putting Government policy into practice. When the departments finish drawing up their estimates, they send them to the Treasury Board.

The Treasury Board is a very important body with far-reaching authority in financial matters under the *Financial Administration Act*.[11] It consists of six Ministers: a President (who has no other Cabinet functions), a Vice-President (who usually is the Minister of Finance), and four others chosen for their expertise and their areas of interest. Originally a Cabinet committee, the Treasury Board is now also supported by a department of Government with its own bureaucracy called the Treasury Board Secretariat. The Treasury Board examines the estimates of all Government bodies with great thoroughness. It then discusses the estimates with the department or agency concerned, and usually negotiates cuts. The estimates then go to Cabinet for approval. They are printed up in documents with blue covers, hence the expression "blue books," which is sometimes applied to them.

The estimates come in three parts. The first is the Government Expenditure Plan, which gives an overview of the Government's total spending plans. The second is the Main Estimates, which list the appropriations of each department alphabetically and in summary form. The third comprises the departmental Expenditure Plans, a series of publications each giving details on one department or agency. These publications contain a great deal of detail about the amounts requested, but it must be admitted that reading estimates is not informative for the layperson. Public expenditure is so complex an area that only experts are capable of grasping all its aspects and implications.

The House of Commons focuses on Part II, the Main Estimates, which make financial provision for all the departments and agencies of

---

11. *Financial Administration Act*, R.S. (1985), c. F-11, am. 1991, c. 24.

Government. These include two sorts of estimates, statutory and budgetary. Statutory estimates involve expenditures that have already been approved in legislation on a continuing basis — judges' salaries would be an example. They are included solely for information purposes, because Parliament has already authorized these expenditures. Budgetary estimates, on the other hand, do need Parliament's annual approval. In the fiscal year 1992-93, almost 70 percent of the $160.5 billion set out in the main estimates had been authorized by Parliament in previous years.[12]

To facilitate consideration of the budgetary estimates by MPs, and in particular Opposition MPs, requests for funding for the upcoming fiscal year are presented in a format that includes the preceding year's allocations for purposes of comparison.

The Main Estimates must be tabled in the House not later than March 1 of the expiring fiscal year. They are then referred to standing committees for consideration (this procedure was introduced in 1968; prior to that, it was the Committee of Supply that examined them). Each committee is given the portion of the estimates that relates to its mandate; for example, the Standing Committee on Labour, Employment and Immigration receives the estimates of the departments of Labour and of Employment and Immigration.

The various budget items are known as "votes," and the committees go through them one by one, just as they go through bills clause by clause. A committee may summon witnesses, including the appropriate Minister and senior officials, in order to obtain clarification and perhaps justification of the amounts requested by the department they represent. Each vote is the subject of a separate motion, which can be agreed to, amended or negatived, or in other words approved, reduced or eliminated. A committee cannot amend a vote by increasing the amount, only by reducing it. Committee recommendations must not affect the substance of the estimates but must be restricted to concurring in, reducing or negativing the votes requested by the department or agency.

Committees must report back to the House no later than May 31, which does not leave them a great deal of time, given the complexity of the subject and their many other responsibilities. This time constraint explains why committee consideration of the estimates is not always as detailed as some might wish.

12. *1992-1993 Estimates Part I— The Government Expenditure Plan* (Ottawa: Ministry of Supply and Services, 1992), p. 7.

The Standing Orders provide that each committee shall report, or shall be deemed to have reported to the House not later than May 31.[13] There is only one exception to this ironclad rule: the Standing Orders allow the Leader of the Official Opposition to move a motion extending the time for committee consideration of the estimates for a particular department or agency. In this case, the committee has an extra ten sitting days for consideration. Once the reports have been presented, all the MPs have an opportunity to review them, and to formulate motions proposing amendments to the committee recommendations.

During the 20 "allocated days" the opposition parties may choose the subjects to be debated.

An important aspect of the business of Supply is the recognition of Parliament's ancient right not to approve expenditures without having heard arguments against as well as in favour of doing so. To observe this tradition, 20 days are allotted each fiscal year to the opposition parties on which they may choose the subject for debate. These 20 days may be increased or decreased depending on the amount of time the House sits. The Government designates these supply days, or allotted days. During the debate, motions may be moved on any subject that comes within the jurisdiction of Parliament and the Federal Government. (A closer look at these debates will be taken in the next section, dealing with relations between Parliament and the executive.)

On the last day set aside for consideration of Supply in the period ending June 23, the House considers all motions of opposition to, and concurrence in, the Main Estimates. The Standing Orders provide that on this day, no later than 10:00 p.m., the Speaker shall put all the motions to a vote.

Once the Main Estimates have been approved by the House, the expenditures as such must be authorized. This is effected by passage of an appropriation bill, authorizing the Consolidated Revenue Fund to pay the departments and agencies the amounts requested in the estimates and approved by the House. It goes without saying that the amounts specified in the appropriation bill cannot exceed the limits established by the estimates. The appropriation bill goes through the usual stages of the legislative process but at an accelerated pace, since its provisions have already been approved by the House. No motion for leave to introduce it is required. It is moved, read for the first time, and referred after second reading to Committee of the Whole. The Standing Orders provide that it can be passed in a single day, and because of this time limit, an appropriation bill is not usually debated or amended.

13. Standing Order 81(4).

Supplementary estimates, interim supply, and Governor General's Special Warrants are three additional elements that are part of supply.

Supplementary Estimates

These are essential, because it is virtually impossible to foresee everything at the time the Main Estimates are being prepared. On the one hand, new circumstances often arise; on the other, the preparation of the Main Estimates begins so far in advance that it is hardly surprising if changes are required later. The Supplementary Estimates add amounts for programs that were not anticipated or that turned out to be more costly than expected. They can also be used to fund programs that had been studied but about which no decision had previously been made.

The Government does not always need to request additional moneys, but if it does, this will normally occur well into the fiscal year, usually in November. Some of the items in the Supplementary Estimates may be what are known as "one dollar items," by which the Government asks, not for new money, but for permission to change the way it had originally said it would be allocating funds approved by the House. The Supplementary Estimates are considered by standing committees of the House and go through the same procedures as the Main Estimates.

Interim Supply

As we have seen, a new fiscal year begins on April 1, and the appropriation bill is not passed until the final day of the Supply period ending on June 23. In the almost three months between these two dates, the Government does not have access to the funds it needs to keep operating.

To solve this problem the Government relies on what is known as "interim supply." Using this procedure, the Government can obtain an advance on the amounts set out in the Main Estimates. It does this by moving a motion for Interim Supply close to the end of the expiring fiscal year, usually on the final Supply day of the period ending March 26. In its notice of motion, the Government defines the sums it will need for this period, expressed in twelfths of the amounts given in the Main Estimates, that is on a monthly basis. Since there are three months to get through until the Main Estimates are passed, the sums requested are generally defined as three-twelfths of the amounts in the Main Estimates. Once the House has concurred in the Interim Supply motion, an appropriation bill is passed as described above.

For practical purposes, the Government can obtain "Interim Supply," that is to say, advances on the Main Estimates of the Budget.

Governor General's Special Warrants

In exceptional circumstances — when Parliament is not sitting because of an election campaign, for example — the Governor General may authorize expenditures, although this runs contrary to the principle that only Parliament may grant Supply. The procedure allows the Governor in Council to call for a special warrant to be prepared, which he then signs, authorizing payments out of the Consolidated Revenue Fund. The circumstances must be exceptional indeed to justify recourse to this method. Before 1958, it was the custom to indicate amounts authorized by warrant in the next estimates, so that Parliament would at least have an opportunity to review them after the fact. Since then, this practice has become a statutory requirement. The *Financial Administration Act* provides that all special warrants must be published in the *Canada Gazette* within 30 days of their being issued. Moreover, within 15 days after the commencement of the next sitting, the Government must table a statement in the House of all the warrants that were issued while Parliament was not sitting, and the amounts involved must appear in the next request for Supply.

Borrowing Authority

When the Government's revenues are not sufficient to cover all the expenditures it needs to make, it is sometimes forced to borrow money by issuing treasury bills, Canada Savings Bonds, and marketable bonds on the Canadian and foreign markets. However, the Government needs Parliament's approval before it can borrow. Section 43 of the *Financial Administration Act* stipulates that "No money shall be borrowed or security issued by or on behalf of Her Majesty without the authority of Parliament." Borrowing authority is obtained by passage of a bill that can be debated and amended by the Commons like any other bill.

Characteristics of Financial Procedure

The Budget Debate, like the business of Supply, is specifically provided for in the Standing Orders. The essential purpose of these debates is to give MPs the opportunity to discuss the Government's policies, and, more specifically, the way in which it is spending public money. For this reason, we will examine Budget debates in the next section dealing with relations between Parliament and the Executive.

All financial legislation must be passed by both Houses of Parliament. In the British parliamentary tradition, the Upper House does not reject or amend money bills. As we have seen, however, the Canadian Senate does not accept this principle (see "The Senate's Functions," Chapter 3).

The following points sum up the features characteristic of our financial procedures:

– The House of Commons claims exclusive authority in financial matters, and all financial legislation must be introduced in the House.

The Senate however claims it has the right to amend or reject financial legislation that has passed third reading in the House.

- A bill that imposes a tax or commits the Government to spend money must be preceded by a Royal Recommendation, can only be introduced by a Minister, and cannot be introduced in the Senate.

- The allocation or expenditure of public money can only be done on the recommendation of the Governor General.

- Bills authorizing annual expenditures are based on supply motions. Bills enabling the Government to obtain revenues are based on ways and means motions.

- Over the course of the fiscal year, 20 days are set aside for debating the business of supply although the number can be changed, depending on House sittings (see next section).

In the financial realm, there are certain watchdog mechanisms, like the Public Accounts Committee, whose activities were described in the section on committees. The Auditor General also plays an important role in monitoring the use of public funds. His functions will be described in the next section.

THE HOUSE OF COMMONS AND THE EXECUTIVE

The preceding sections showed how dominant Cabinet's role is both in initiating and formulating legislation and in the area of public finance. In this section, we will look at the various means available to MPs to hold the Cabinet, and thereby the Government, accountable for its actions.

When the Government party has a majority, we can say that generally the House passes the measures proposed by Cabinet. But we live in a liberal democracy, and so no final decision is made without thorough debate. The rules of procedure in the House make it possible to sustain a dialogue between the Government, or what can also be called the Executive, and all the elected representatives of the people. These rules determine the relationships between the majority and the minorities, the Government and the opposition parties, the Executive and private Members.

Our parliamentary system guarantees freedom of expression. Any and all views may be voiced. It also provides circumstances in which the Government can be questioned, and obliged to explain and justify itself and defend its policies. In other words, parliamentary procedure offers MPs a means of monitoring the Government's actions and obliging it to account for itself. Given internal party discipline and the loyalty that

MPs owe their respective parties, the role of criticizing the Government rests mainly with the opposition parties.

As our parliamentary system now stands, we may say that this role of overseeing the Government has probably become the main function of the House of Commons. The purpose of this function is to illuminate the weaknesses in Government policies, the errors that may have been committed and the sectors that may have been forgotten, and to suggest alternative solutions. Through the media, the opposition's criticisms are conveyed directly to the general public, who are kept abreast of what the Government is said to have done wrong and what explanation it is offering. The system has the advantage not only of keeping the population informed but also of compelling the Cabinet and the administration as a whole to act prudently. Even with a comfortable majority, a Government will hesitate to propose highly unpopular measures, knowing they will provoke a public outcry.

We now turn to the specific structures through which MPs can force Government accountability.

Questions Addressed to Ministers

Question Period is not part of the legislative process and has nothing to do with it. It is a means of monitoring the Executive that the Government cannot evade.

Question Period is the subject of lively interest among the media and general public.

Question Period is undoubtedly the portion of Parliament's business that is followed with the greatest interest by the print media, radio, television and the general public who can watch it every day on the Parliamentary Channel. Interesting — and often heated — exchanges occur between Ministers and Opposition Members. Any MP can ask a question, but the time is almost exclusively set aside for the Opposition, because of the way our parliamentary conventions have developed. Members belonging to the party in power can usually obtain the information they want without having to take up time in Question Period, and the Speaker traditionally recognizes more Opposition MPs than Government MPs.

Both written and oral questions can be put to Ministers, about any area of public affairs. Naturally, the Prime Minister can also be questioned. As a general rule, we might say that written questions are put by MPs who want to obtain information, while MPs whose aim is to embarrass the Government or expose its weaknesses are more likely to ask questions orally.

Written questions must appear on the *Order Paper*. An MP may not have more than four questions there at a time. He may add a request that the Government respond to a particular question within 45 days. If it does not, he can inform the House that he intends to raise the matter during the adjournment proceedings.

An MP who wishes an oral response to his written question marks it with an asterisk. The Standing Orders set a limit of three "starred" questions per MP on the *Order Paper* at any one time. All questions must consist of a request for information expressed in simple terms and in a direct, non-tendentious style, without comments or arguments.

Often written questions are addressed to Ministers by MPs who want information on matters of local interest to their constituents. The answers are written as well, addressed to the Member who has asked the question. The tabled response is filed with the Clerk as a sessional paper and published in *Hansard*; if the answer is too voluminous for this, it is treated as an Order for Return, and the Government will table a Return which will serve as a response to the question.

It can happen as well that written questions are put to Ministers for the sole purpose of embarrassing them. Opposition MPs put such questions in an attempt to gather ammunition that they may one day be able to use against the Government. But oral Question Period undoubtedly constitutes the Opposition's favourite means of getting at the Government. It lasts 45 minutes every day, starting at 2:15 p.m. Monday through Thursday and at 11:15 a.m. on Friday. In principle, the questions must bear on a topic of sufficient urgency and importance to require an immediate response. Over the years, the guidelines governing the kinds of questions that can be put orally have evolved. On February 24, 1986, the Speaker summed up the essence when he said that guidelines should be based on certain principles aimed at making it easier to achieve the central purpose of oral questions: "the seeking of information from the Government and calling the Government to account for its actions." The Speaker may, at his discretion, allow or disallow a question. In recent years, he has generally intervened if a question was too long or of a technical nature that would be more suitable as a written question.[14]

Questions must be brief, directed to a Minister, and concern a matter within his current responsibilities and within the Government's jurisdiction. According to the guidelines, they must not express an opinion or be argumentative, request a legal or other opinion, have been answered

---

14. See the *Précis of Procedure*, 4th ed. (Ottawa: House of Commons, Table Research Branch, 1991), p. 30.

already, deal with a matter that is before the courts, or anticipate the Orders of the Day. But even these conditions are difficult to impose strictly, depending on the circumstances.

The Standing Orders also allow MPs to direct questions to a designated Member of the Board of Internal Economy as well as to a committee chairman.

Questions raised during Question Period often give rise to animated debate.

Since the aim of most oral questions is to attack the Government, they must be carefully phrased so that the Minister cannot avoid responding directly without being evasive. Asking and answering oral questions is an art in itself, with the Opposition on the one side striving to set traps for Ministers and the Ministers on the other doing their best to spot and avoid the traps. Even though a question cannot be used as a springboard for debate, the Speaker allows Members to ask supplementary questions in order to pursue the issue or obtain clarification. But Ministers have various ways of avoiding a direct reply, including evasive responses, invocations of national security, and promises that the Government will shortly be issuing a statement on the matter. Nor is there in fact any requirement that a Minister answer a question, although refusal to do so would not be a very wise move politically.

As noted earlier, Question Period places heavy demands on the Speaker of the House. He must at all times remain keenly alert and attentive, keep a perceptive eye on the whole assembly, be aware of the mood of the House and be familiar with the national and international issues likely to be raised. Insofar as possible, he must be aware of inter-party tensions over particular issues.

When an MP wishes to ask a question he rises and makes sure he has caught the Speaker's eye. The latter must, in principle, recognize in order the MPs who have in this way indicated the desire to ask a question. By tradition, many more Opposition MPs than Government MPs are recognized. The Speaker's discretion in this regard is, however, limited by certain conventions and practices. By custom, the first question of the day is asked by the Leader of the Official Opposition or his representative. This first question may be followed by two supplementaries. After that the Speaker recognizes another Member of the Official Opposition. Then the leader of the second-largest opposition party is recognized in the same way as his counterpart, i.e. he can ask an initial question followed by two supplementaries. This is the way Question Period starts every day.

Another custom is that whereby the party Whips submit to the Speaker, before each sitting, a list of the Members they wish him to recognize. The Speaker is not, of course, bound by these suggestions, and he can always recognize someone else if he thinks fit. However, since the Whips' choices are based on party strategy, and have often been the subject of negotiation either within one party or between parties, the Speaker tends to recognize the MPs who figure on these lists.

The Prime Minister can reply on behalf of the entire Government and has the right to reply to any question he wishes, about any portfolio. In the case of Ministers, it need not be the one to whom the question is directed who actually answers it.

The Adjournment Debate

The adjournment debate is also known as the "late show." Standing Order 37(3) authorizes an MP who is not satisfied with the answer he has received during Question Period, or whose question was not deemed sufficiently urgent by the Speaker to be put orally, to raise the matter during the adjournment debate. MPs who have requested, but have not received, an answer to a written question within 45 days may also raise their question during this period.

Debate on the motion to adjourn is called the "Late Show" since over the years it has taken place between 11 and 11:30 p.m.

This provision allows for a 30-minute period at the end of the day's sitting on Mondays, Tuesdays, and Thursdays, during which five mini-debates of six minutes' duration may take place. The Speaker chooses the subjects to be discussed and the order in which MPs will take the floor, basing his decision on both the order in which notices were given, and the urgency of the matters being raised. During the adjournment proceedings, a Member raising a matter has up to four minutes to speak. A Minister or Parliamentary Secretary has two minutes to reply. Thanks to this procedure, MPs can in effect have their questions debated briefly, something that is not possible during Question Period. The opposition parties use the adjournment proceedings as one more opportunity for calling the Government to account.

The Address in Reply to the Speech from the Throne

At the opening of every new Parliament, and at the start of each session within a Parliament, the Governor General reads a speech, approved by Cabinet, that sketches a general outline of the country's political and economic situation. He also voices the Government's intentions and explains the policies that it wishes to put into practice. This speech is delivered in the Senate Chamber before the assembled Members of both Houses. The Standing Orders of the House of Commons provide for a six-day debate on the Throne Speech, which at its outset gives the Leaders of the opposition parties a chance to criticize the Government, oppose its present and future policies, and deploy all the arguments

The debate on the Throne Speech gives the Government the opportunity to defend its policies and justify its expenditures.

likely to spark the interest of the media and the public. Private Members too, of every party, have the chance to speak, and they generally take advantage of it to discuss problems of concern to the voters in their ridings. MPs belonging to the party in power usually praise the Government's initiatives while working in allusions to their ridings.

The great advantage of the debate surrounding the Address in Reply to the Speech from the Throne is that it has practically no limits. Speakers can deal with any topic at all, and even with a number of topics covering a wide range of very different areas. Speaking time is limited, except in the case of the Prime Minister and the Leader of the Official Opposition, to 20 minutes. But the Standing Orders allow an extra 10 minutes after each MP has spoken, if required, during which other MPs may ask questions and make comments about his remarks.

If the opposition parties take advantage of the Throne Speech debate to attack the Government, the Prime Minister and his colleagues for their part seize the chance to defend themselves and point out all the benefits of their policies. For private Members one of the merits of the debate on the Address in Reply motion is that they are given a chance — especially if their speeches are carried in the press or by the electronic media — to show the voters at home how much local concerns are on their minds. It is an ideal opportunity for the opposition parties to make political capital, while explaining what they would do differently if they were in power.

The Budget Debate

As we saw in the section on financial matters, the presentation of the Budget by the Minister of Finance is followed by a debate of up to four days. As in the case of the debate on the Address in Reply, parliamentarians may speak for a maximum of 20 minutes each, followed by a ten-minute period for questions and comments. The Prime Minister, the Minister of Finance, the first MP who speaks for the Opposition, and the Leader of the Official Opposition, may all speak without a time limit. The debate is supposed to focus on the contents of the Budget and related areas, but in practice MPs speak on many topics which they feel should be addressed.

Supply Debates

These are related to the financial appropriations set out in the Estimates of Expenditure and offer the opposition parties more occasions to challenge the Government.

Under normal circumstances, 20 days per fiscal year are allotted for consideration of the Business of Supply: eight days for the period ending June 23, five for the period ending December 10, and seven for the period ending March 26. The last day of the period ending June 23 is devoted to consideration of the motions for concurrence in the Main Estimates and the Appropriation Bill.

Although these debates would appear to have to do with financial matters, they are in reality days allotted to the opposition parties who choose the subjects for debate, hence their place in this section. In fact, the supply debates give MPs the chance to raise almost any topic. It is easy to see how discussing the Main Estimates could open the door to discussing any and all of the Government's policies and programs.

Before the reforms of 1968, the estimates and tax proposals were debated by the Committee of Supply and the Committee of Ways and Means respectively. The abolition of these two committees did not mean that parliamentarians lost their right to debate these matters. Now that the Main Estimates are studied by standing committees, the Standing Orders provide that the Business of Supply shall be debated in the House on the "allotted" days. No MP may speak more than once or for more than 20 minutes, although an additional 10 minutes may be allowed so that others can ask questions or make comments.

Like all debates of this type, supply debates receive a great deal of publicity, and naturally the opposition parties take advantage of this for political ends. Supply debates are incontestably an excellent way of obliging the Government to defend its policies and justify its expenditures. Under the attacks and accusations of the Opposition, the Government (for obvious political reasons) makes a real point of clarifying its positions and justifying its initiatives. Usually the debates take place on non-confidence motions. Even if these motions are rejected, as they nearly always are if the Government has a majority, they still constitute official protests. Under the Standing Orders, a maximum of three motions can be designated "votable" in each supply period but no more than eight in total for the year, which means that the House will vote on them at the end of the debate. Since it is the Opposition that decides which motions will be put to a vote, it can, of course, make sure that in most cases they are no-confidence motions.

Emergency Debates

In certain cases the Standing Orders authorize debate on a motion proposing that the House adjourn. We have already seen that an MP who is not satisfied with the answer to an oral question, or who has not received an answer to a written question within 45 days of his asking it, may give notice of his intention to raise the matter during the adjournment proceedings.

A second type of adjournment debate is possible under the Standing Orders: debate on "a specific and important matter requiring urgent consideration." An MP may give notice to the Speaker of his intention to seek a debate on a matter of importance that he feels should be given the immediate attention of Parliament and the Government. The MP must ask leave to move the adjournment of the House for this purpose. The Speaker decides, without debate, whether the matter should be brought before the House immediately. In this context, "urgency" pertains to the urgency of debate rather than the subject matter. For leave to be granted, the request must meet certain criteria. The Speaker must make sure that the matter falls within the Government's administrative responsibilities. He must also consider if the matter might be brought before the House without undue delay by other means. In addition, the urgent matter must relate to an immediate crisis rather than an ongoing problem such as inflation or unemployment; and finally, the public interest must require an immediate debate. In reaching his decision, the Speaker may also take into account the general wish of the House. If the Speaker considers that the matter merits an emergency debate, it is normally scheduled for 8:00 p.m., and can go on until midnight. On Fridays, the debate occurs immediately and can go on until 4:00 p.m. No one may speak for longer than 20 minutes.

This procedure, like those described previously, gives private Members the chance to raise matters they want to publicize, and to expose failures on the part of the Government. A Cabinet Minister cannot avoid commenting on the matter at issue in the debate. Even if the MP who originally asked leave to move for an emergency debate does not succeed in convincing the Speaker that such a debate is justified, he will have succeeded in drawing the attention of the House to a problem he regards as important.

An emergency debate enables Opposition Members, and sometimes other Members too, to raise questions about Government activities that are not being discussed in the House, or about areas in which the Government is (according to the Opposition) failing to act. When a national or international event occurs unexpectedly, an emergency debate gives Parliament the opportunity to discuss it, and provides private Members with an opportunity to find out the Government's immediate reactions.

The Passage of Legislation

As we have seen, a majority Government can get the House to pass almost any legislation it wishes. However, even here the opposition parties can force the Government into a compromise, and thus exercise a certain control over its activities. The role of the opposition in committee we have already looked at in the chapter on Committees.

Despite the successive procedural reforms that have increased the Government's ability to expedite its business, the opposition parties retain a lever for putting pressure on the Government in the area of legislation. It is, in fact, over the Government's legislative program that it and the Opposition MPs clash most often.

The time element is vital to the Government's program, and an Opposition that failed to take advantage of this would be no kind of opposition at all. It knows that delaying tactics can complicate the Government's life, and so the goal of Opposition MPs is not so much to win votes in the House as to prevent the House from voting at all.[15] The legislative program can be delayed by various means, notably by protracted debate. The Opposition can use all the procedures available to it to slow the legislative process down. Nowadays "filibustering" — speaking as long as possible and using every procedural means to obstruct the legislative process — is difficult to do, thanks to closure, time allocation, and time limits on speeches (see Chapter 10). A technique used by the opposition parties in March of 1982 consisted of refusing to go to the House when the division bells rang to announce a vote. The bells rang for two weeks, and the impasse was finally resolved by inter-party negotiations. Since 1986, the Standing Orders have been amended to limit the time the division bells may ring to 15 minutes or half an hour, depending on the circumstances. Within its limits, however, filibustering may indeed interfere with the Government's plans.

The Government always has an immense quantity of legislation that it wishes to pass by the end of the session, so that delaying tactics are a very effective means of obtaining a compromise. By making use of these tactics, the Opposition can keep a careful eye on the measures that Cabinet wishes to have passed, and may also get its own amendments accepted in exchange for its co-operation.

15. John B. Stewart, *The Canadian House of Commons: Procedure and Reform* (Montréal: McGill Queen's University Press, 1977), p. 239.

Private Members' Business

In principle, one hour at each sitting is reserved for Private Members' Business.

We have looked at the role of ordinary MPs in the initiation of legislation (see "The Legislative Functions" at the beginning of this Chapter). Private Members' Business includes bills, as we have seen, and motions. Motions provide another means for Members to gain a hearing. The procedure is not, of course, reserved exclusively for Opposition MPs, but they can make use of it to their own or their party's advantage. A votable item is debated for one hour and then goes to the bottom of the order of precedence. As the House debates and disposes of the other items on the list, the votable item works its way to the top again and can be debated for a second hour, after which it goes back to the bottom. In this way, a votable item may receive up to 2 hours and 45 minutes of debate, at which point the Speaker calls for a vote. Whatever the result of the vote, the motion will have given its mover the opportunity to focus the attention of the House on a particular issue for nearly three hours.

The Public Accounts Committee

The mandate of this committee, which is chaired by an Opposition Member, has been discussed already. What we need to bear in mind here is that its function is to review the manner in which public moneys have been spent. It points out errors in financial management, either on the basis of the data in the Auditor General's report or by carrying out its own investigations. While this monitoring is indeed part of the control that Parliament exercises over the Executive, the Committee's reports, containing recommendations for improving the procedures for the use of public funds, are not often implemented (see Chapter 7). It does, nevertheless, provide a method of publicizing waste and financial mismanagement.

The Auditor General

The position of Auditor General was created in Canada in 1878, following the example of Great Britain, which appointed its first Auditor General in 1866. The incumbent is an independent civil servant appointed by Parliament, under whose authority he remains. His salary is set by Act of Parliament, and he can be removed from office for cause only by an address of both Houses of Parliament, that is to say by resolution of Parliament. His duties are defined in the *Financial Administration Act*.[16] His role is to verify that the moneys placed at the disposal of

16. R.S. (1985), c. F-11, am. 1991, c. 24.

Government departments and other Government bodies have been spent wisely and in accordance with the law, and to assess the effectiveness of the financial management of Government bodies. It is his duty to report to Parliament on any finance-related matter he considers merits its attention. He has access to departmental financial records and can bring out in his report any irregularities he may have uncovered, which gives him considerable clout. Canada's Auditors General have always guarded their independence jealously, to the point that one of them took the Government to court for refusing to produce Cabinet documents.[17]

The Auditor General's report is tabled in the House every year. This report is then referred to the Public Accounts Committee for more detailed study. The Committee works closely with the officials in the Auditor General's Office, who assist the Committee Members with their job of looking into the report's conclusions.

In general, the monitoring done by the Auditor General is useful and constructive. Even though he reports after the fact, even if the Government does not implement his recommendations, he acts as a watchdog, obliging the Government and Government bodies to be vigilant and prudent in managing the taxpayer's money. His conclusions are widely reported in the press. Furthermore, although the Government may not put all the recommended measures into law, it is hard for it to ignore them on a practical level.

The Standing Joint Committee for the Scrutiny of Regulations

The role of this Committee has already been briefly examined in the chapter on Committees. Created in 1972, its role is to review the regulations made by the Government under the authority of Acts of Parliament. Most regulations drawn up by departments or other Government bodies may be examined by this committee. To grasp why this review is so necessary, consider how many regulations are made, affecting almost every area of activity in the country. For all practical purposes these regulations are laws, often in fact referred to as "delegated legislation." The expression is very apt, since the regulations are made under an Act of Parliament that delegates to the Government the power to make suitable regulations for implementing legislation. To get an idea of the scope of delegated legislation, we need only think of the regulations

---

17. In 1989 the Supreme Court of Canada dismissed the suit brought by Auditor General Kenneth Dye, who had been trying for eight years to obtain confidential documents regarding the purchase of Petrofina by the crown corporation Petro-Canada.

that govern immigration, aviation, and food and drugs, to name but a few areas of extensive regulation. All these are decided on by the Executive. The only opportunity for Parliament to see what has been done is the review by the Standing Joint Committee for the Scrutiny of Regulations.

In practice, so great is the proliferation of subordinate legislation, that no single committee could undertake a thorough examination of all of it. The Committee therefore adopts a selective approach. Its Members must make sure that regulations are consistent with the statutes, made within the framework of the appropriate legislation and not in conflict with the *Canadian Charter of Rights and Freedoms*. It is work that requires a great deal of time, patience, and expertise. The work of this committee is useful to Parliament and enables it to keep an eye on delegated legislation.

Minority Governments

Minority governments must seek the support of Members from other parties to pass their bills into law.

The relations between Parliament and the Government as described in this chapter are considerably modified when the Government holds only a minority of seats in the House. Without a majority, a Government must constantly seek enough support among MPs from other parties to be able to get its legislative program through. The difficulties faced by a minority Government depend on a variety of factors, including the number of votes it needs to pass its legislation and the situation of other parties in the House. For example, the minority Liberal Governments from 1963 to 1968 survived without too much trouble because they were able to call upon either Social Credit or the NDP for support.

Being in this position demands greater flexibility from the Government, and obliges it to consult the opposition parties more. This was what happened in 1972-74 when the Government was obliged to consult the Leaders of the opposition parties when it wanted to bring in a bill. The various House Leaders met weekly, and the views of the Opposition carried a great deal of weight. [18]

Relations between parties depend on their political philosophy, so that a party in power with philosophical similarities to certain opposition parties will find supporters more easily. A particular issue may also bring two parties together or divide them further. It is not easy to suggest techniques that a minority Government should follow in order to implement its policies, for each minority Government is unique, and its margin of manoeuvre depends largely on the make-up of the House.

18. Richard Van Loon and Michael Whittington, *The Canadian Political System: Environment, Structure and Process*, 3rd rev. ed. (Toronto: McGraw-Hill Ryerson Ltd., 1987), p. 627.

What can be said with certainty is that when there is a minority Government, the Opposition has a greater opportunity to influence affairs of state, since it holds the balance of power and could at some point defeat the Government. It also imposes a far greater measure of responsibility on the opposition parties as it is no small thing to bring a Government down. The different opposition parties do not always agree, however, and their conflicts may be exploited by the Government.

10 The Business of the House

In this chapter the reader will find information on how the House conducts its business. Without going into technical procedural details, the chapter should give the reader an understanding of how the House of Commons operates, and this in turn may throw light on other sections of this work.

SESSIONS AND SITTINGS

Under this heading the various periods during which the House sits will be discussed. As there is some confusion about the terminology, we will begin with a few definitions.

A Parliament

The maximum term of a Parliament is five years.

By this is meant the period from the summoning of the Members, to the first meeting of a Parliament after an election, to its dissolution. This may occur when its time runs out after five years or when it is brought to an end at an earlier date. The summons, like the order to dissolve, is issued by the Governor General, at the request of the Prime Minister, who has been advised by Cabinet. The Constitution provides that a Parliament cannot go on longer than five years, but in practice, as we have seen, a Parliament usually lasts about four years (see "The Electoral System," Chapter 1). If, at the end of five years, the Prime Minister has not asked the Governor General to dissolve the House, it is deemed to have been dissolved automatically under the *Canadian Charter of Rights and Freedoms*.

Dissolution ends the life of the Parliament and is followed by a general election, the date of which is set by proclamation of the Governor General. When the Prime Minister chooses the date for the election he must take into account a provision of the *Constitution Act, 1867*, incorporated into Section 5 of the *Canadian Charter of Rights and Freedoms*, by which Parliament must sit at least once in any twelve-month period. An election cannot, therefore, be delayed indefinitely. When Parliament is dissolved the Senate does not sit.

The Opening of Parliament

After the election, the newly elected MPs, having taken the oath of allegiance administered by the Clerk of the House and signed the Test Roll, assemble in the House on the day set by proclamation of the Governor General.

Once the MPs, the Clerk of the House, and the other Clerks are in their places, and before a Speaker is elected, three knocks are heard on the door of the House. It is the Gentleman Usher of the Black Rod who announces to the Sergeant-at-Arms that he has a message. The Sergeant-at-Arms responds by advancing to the Table, bowing, and saying, "A message from the Deputy of His Excellency the Governor General." The Clerk replies, "Admit the messenger." The Gentleman Usher of the Black Rod advances to the Table in turn and announces, in English and in French, that the Deputy of the Governor General desires the immediate attendance of the Honourable Members in the Senate Chamber. This foregathering in the Senate comes from the British tradition, whereby the Sovereign never sets foot in the House of Commons.

The MPs, preceded by the Clerk of the House and the other Clerks-at-the-Table, go to the Senate Chamber. The Black Rod, the Sergeant-at-Arms (without the Mace) and several Members of the security staff walk ahead. When they arrive at the Senate Chamber, the MPs stand silently at the Bar, facing the Governor General's Deputy, who is seated at the foot of the Throne. The Speaker of the Senate transmits to the MPs a message from the Governor General, to the effect that until the Commons have chosen a Speaker, Parliament will not be opened. The MPs then return to the House to elect their Speaker (see Chapter 4). A Speaker must be chosen at the opening of each new Parliament since his term coincides with the life of the Parliament.

After the election, the Speaker thanks the MPs for the confidence they have displayed in him. Then the House adjourns until the time set for appearing before the Governor General for the official opening of the new Parliament.[1] The Gentleman Usher of the Black Rod again brings a message to the Commons, desiring them in the Governor General's name to proceed to the Senate Chamber. The newly elected Speaker goes there in procession, preceded by the Sergeant-at-Arms bearing the Mace and followed by the Clerk of the House, the other Clerks, and the MPs.

Once he has been elected to the House, the Speaker requests confirmation of the rights and privileges of the Members at the Bar of the Senate.

---

1. On two occasions the Queen has opened Parliament in person, on October 14, 1957, and October 18, 1977.

On arrival at the Senate, the Speaker takes his place on a small platform near the Bar and lifts his hat to the Governor General, who acknowledges the salutation. His Excellency is seated on the Throne, with his spouse in a chair to his left. The Prime Minister and the Government Leader in the Senate are seated to the right and left respectively of Their Excellencies. The MPs stand around their Speaker, who delivers a brief address informing the Governor General that he has been elected and requesting recognition of the Commons' rights and privileges. On behalf of the Governor General, the Speaker of the Senate confirms the Commons' constitutional privileges.

The Governor General then reads the Speech from the Throne, which, as we have seen, comprises an assessment of the country's economic and social situation and sketches the Government's plans (see "The Role of Parliament in Financial Matters," Chapter 9).

Sessions

A sitting usually lasts one day, while a session may last several months or even a year or more.

Each Parliament includes one or more sessions that may be of any length. In practice, it is the Prime Minister and the Cabinet who decide when a session should end. So far, the number of sessions has varied from one to seven. The shortest session, in 1940, lasted a matter of hours, while the longest went on without a break for 591 sitting days (1980-83).[2]

The effect of prorogation is to bring a session to an end without dissolving Parliament. The reasons will be practical or political, or both. Parliament can be prorogued by simple proclamation, but if it is sitting, a ceremony is usually observed when a session is brought to an end. At the request of the Prime Minister, the Governor General's office informs the Speaker of the House that His Excellency intends to prorogue Parliament, and the Speaker informs the Commons. At the time decided on, the Gentleman Usher of the Black Rod comes from the Senate and knocks at the door of the House of Commons to inform the Members that the Governor General (or more often his Deputy) desires their presence in the Senate Chamber. The Speaker, escorted in the usual way, and the MPs proceed to the Senate and remain at the Bar to hear the speech that will put an end to the session. At the conclusion of the speech, the Speaker of the Senate reads a message giving the date the next session will start. The Speaker of the House then leaves the Senate Chamber with his cortege. Generally speaking, prorogation takes effect the same day and the new session begins the following day. The

2. Alistair Fraser, W.F. Dawson, and John Holtby, *Beauchesne's Parliamentary Rules and Forms*, 6th ed., (Toronto: Carswell, 1989), p. 65.

Each spring, the House of Commons breaks for Easter.

immediate convening of a new session avoids a long interval during which no business could be transacted.

It is important not to confuse prorogation, which ends a session, and adjournment, which is simply the suspension of the business of the House, brought about either automatically by virtue of the Standing Orders or by passing a motion. The House, for example, adjourns at the end of every sitting day, reconvening again the next day or, in the case of a Friday adjournment, the following Monday. It can adjourn for longer periods too, as there are both regular weeks and holiday periods at Christmas, Easter, and during the summer, when it does not sit.

Dissolving Parliament puts an end to all current business. However, the Speaker remains in office to handle administrative matters until such time as a new Speaker is elected, or he himself is re-elected, both to his seat and to the Speakership. The same applies to the Deputy Speaker.

Proroguing a session does not dissolve Parliament, but it does have a similar effect on the business before the House. All current business is abandoned, committees cease their activities, and bills die. The difference between prorogation and dissolution lies in a practice that has developed in recent years, by which, when a new session starts after prorogation, some bills need not be presented again from scratch but may, with the unanimous consent of the House, be entered on the *Order Paper* for the new session at the stage in the legislative process they had reached before prorogation. The House can also authorize committees to resume their work at the point where they left off at the end of the previous session. Adjournment does not have the same effect. The House simply interrupts its deliberations temporarily and resumes where it left off.

The opening of a new session does not differ greatly from the opening of a new Parliament. The distinguishing factors are that MPs do not have to swear the oath of allegiance or sign the Test Roll at the start of a new session, a Speaker does not have to be elected nor does he have to claim the privileges of the House. Because the Speaker is elected for the life of the Parliament, he presides throughout the sessions of that Parliament. Each session opens with a Speech from the Throne. A recess is any period between two sessions of a Parliament and is also a term commonly used to denote a long period of adjournment.

Sittings

These are the hours during which the House sits continuously, ending with adjournment for the day. The Standing Orders provide that the House shall start sitting at 11:00 a.m. on Mondays, 10:00 a.m. Tuesdays, Thursdays, and Fridays, and 2:00 p.m. Wednesdays (see Table 1). This timetable can be modified by either a special order of the House or the adoption of a new Standing Order. At the end of the day (6:00 p.m. Mondays, Tuesdays, and Thursdays, 8:00 p.m. Wednesdays, and 4:00 p.m. Fridays), the Speaker adjourns the House until the next sitting day. A sitting may be extended until 6:30 p.m. Mondays, Tuesdays, and Thursdays, if there is a debate on the adjournment motion. Usually, adjournment may also be postponed by resolution or unanimous consent of the House in order to expedite business, or if an emergency debate takes place, for which the House may sit until midnight or 4.00 p.m. on a Friday. On Tuesdays and Thursdays, proceedings break off for an hour for lunch, between 1:00 p.m. and 2:00 p.m. This does not affect the sitting, which is deemed to be continuous from the morning opening to the evening adjournment.

Since 1982, the Standing Orders have provided a yearly calendar of sittings. This means that the House meets on fixed dates, allowing for variations imposed by weekends. Basically, it sits from the second Monday after Labour Day to the second Friday before Christmas Day, with one-week adjournments in October and November. It then resumes business in early February, rising for a week in March and again on the Friday preceding Good Friday. It adjourns for two weeks over Easter and then sits again until June 23, with a one-week adjournment in May. Naturally, the House can modify this calendar by extending certain periods or cutting them short, as required. In fact, since the idea of a fixed

TABLE 1

Daily Order of Business

HOURS	MONDAY	TUESDAY	WEDNESDAY	THURSDAY	FRIDAY
10:00 – 11:00		Routine Proceedings – – – – Government Orders *		Routine Proceedings – – – – Government Orders *	Government Orders
11:00 – 11:15	Private Members' Business				Members' Statements
11:15 – 12:00					Oral Questions
12:00 – 1:00	Government Orders				Routine Proceedings **** – – – – Government Orders *
1:00 – 2:00		Mid-day Interruption *	Review of Delegated Legislation ***	Mid-day Interruption *	
2:00 – 2:15	Members' Statements	Members' Statements	Members' Statements	Members' Statements	
2:15 – 3:00	Oral Questions	Oral Questions	Oral Questions	Oral Questions	
3:00 – 4:00	Routine Proceedings **** – – – –	****	Routine Proceedings **** – – – –	****	Private Members' Business **
4:00 – 5:00	Government Orders *	Government Orders *	Notices of Motions for Production of Papers – – – – Government Orders *	Government Orders *	
5:00 – 6:00		Private Members' Business **		Private Members' Business **	
6:00 – 6:30	Adjournment Proceedings *	Adjournment Proceedings *		Adjournment Proceedings *	
6:30 – 7:00			Private Members' Business **		
17:00 – 8:00					

* – Possible extension or delay pursuant to Standing Order 33(2) respecting Ministerial Statements.
** – Could be delayed pursuant to Standing Order 30(7) respecting a day appointed for the consideration of the Business of Supply and pursuant to Standing Order 33(2) respecting Ministerial Statements.
*** – If required, House to sit at 1:00 p.m. for the review of Delegated Legislation pursuant to Standing Order 128(1).
**** – Possible extension of Routine Proceedings to complete Introduction of Government Bills pursuant to Standing Order 30(4).

Source: House of Commons.

schedule was adopted, the House has frequently sat longer than expected. The House of Commons calendar for 1994 appears in Appendix C.

Sometimes it proves necessary to recall the House while it is adjourned. Standing Order 28(3) provides that the Speaker can recall the House if, after consultation with the Government, he is convinced that the public interest requires the House to reconvene earlier than scheduled in the Standing Orders or under the terms of the adjournment motion. In fact the Speaker must rely on the Government's advice, because the Standing Order makes no mention of an emergency. The only criterion mentioned in the Standing Order is "the public interest." He then gives notice that he is satisfied of the need for the House to meet early, indicating a date. The House reassembles on that day and resumes work as though it had originally adjourned to that date.

ROUTINE PROCEEDINGS

When the House is in session, it sits five days per week. There is nothing to prevent it from sitting late into the evening and in practice this often happens. It can even happen that circumstances require the House to sit on a holiday or during a weekend. That is why sessions of the House are not divided into "days" but into "sittings."

A portion of each sitting is devoted to Routine Proceedings.

Each sitting of the House begins with prayers, after which the Speaker says, "Let the doors be opened." Only then may strangers[3] enter the galleries and television broadcasting of the debates begin. Every day the House deals with Routine Proceedings, which fall under various headings set out in the Standing Orders.

During Routine Proceedings, the Speaker calls each heading one after another and gives the floor to MPs who have an item to present or a bill to introduce. Usually MPs give prior notice to the Speaker or one of the Table Officers of their intention to intervene under one or more headings during Routine Proceedings.

The Tabling of Documents

This is the first activity under Routine Proceedings. Ministers may table reports, papers, or documents provided they deal with matters within the Government's administrative competence. We saw earlier that a committee may ask the Government to table a response within 150 days of the presentation of a report. This response may be tabled by

---

3. In parliamentary language, the term "stranger" means anyone who is not a Member of Parliament or an official participating in the sitting. See Norman Wilding and Philip Laundy, op. cit., p. 728.

a Minister or a Parliamentary Secretary when Tabling of Documents is called. This is also the time for the Government to table responses to petitions and announcements of Order-in-Council appointments.

The Government has two ways in which to table documents in the House "by the front door" or "by the back door." The first, "by the front door," is done by tabling the document in the House during Routine Proceedings while the second, "by the back door," consists of submitting the document to the Clerk at any time. All documents tabled are recorded in the *Votes and Proceedings*.

Statements by Ministers

The time period allotted for statements by Ministers allows Ministers to speak, if they wish, on issues having to do with Government policy. Most important news on action taken by the Government is conveyed in this way. For example, the Secretary of State for External Affairs may announce that diplomatic relations have been established with another country, or express the Government's reaction to an important international event that has just occurred.

The Speaker then gives the floor to representatives of the opposition parties for brief comments. The Speaker limits the duration of these statements at his discretion; certainly they should not take more time than the Minister making the statement. The purpose of Statements by Ministers is to communicate information, not to give rise to debate.

Although it is not part of Routine Proceedings, there is a practice that has been current since 1968 and deserves to be mentioned: the Thursday Statement. Normally on Thursdays at the end of Question Period, the Speaker gives the floor to the Opposition House Leader, who inquires about future business. The Government House Leader responds by announcing the business expected or planned for consideration the following week.

During the "Thursday Statement," the Opposition House Leader can question the Government House Leader about the following week's business.

Presenting Reports from Inter-parliamentary Delegations

Leaders of inter-parliamentary delegations who have travelled outside the country are required to present a report to the House within 20 sitting days of their return to Canada. An inter-parliamentary delegation may be composed of several parliamentarians or of only one. When the Speaker leads a delegation, he may ask another Member of the delegation to table the report. The report may be accompanied by oral explanations. The requirement to present a report applies only to official parliamentary delegations.

Presenting Reports from Committees

Each committee has a mandate from the House to consider or investigate a matter and report to the House. The report usually contains recommendations, or in the case of the consideration of a bill, possibly amendments. When this heading is called, the chairman of the committee, or in his absence another member of the committee, rises and is given the floor by the Speaker. The committee chairman says a few words, briefly explaining the contents of the report. In the section on the committees, we saw earlier that since April 1991, it has been possible to append to the report a statement of supplementary or dissenting opinions or recommendations. When this happens, a committee member from the opposition may rise in order to provide a brief explanation.

The Introduction of Government Bills

Government Bills appear on the *Order Paper* in chronological order, following a minimum of 48 hours' notice. The Speaker calls on Ministers by their title. A Minister wishing to introduce a bill nods, and the Speaker proposes the motion to the House, asking whether leave is granted to introduce the bill. The motion is deemed to be carried without debate, amendment, or a vote. Leave to introduce the bill having been given automatically, the Speaker proposes that the bill be read a first time and printed. This motion for first reading and printing is also deemed to be carried without debate, amendment, or a vote.

Parliament devotes a good deal of time to the examination of bills.

Once a bill has been passed on first reading, the Speaker asks the House when the bill will receive second reading. In all cases, the second reading is set for the next sitting of the House, that is, the next sitting at which the bill will be considered. The Government has the right to determine the sequence in which its orders are called. In order to ensure that the Government will be able to introduce its legislation, the Standing Orders provide that the House shall complete its proceedings under Introduction of Government Bills every day, suspending Private Members' Business or sitting beyond the normal hour of adjournment if necessary.

The Introduction of Private Members' Bills

The Standing Orders expressly provide that MPs may introduce public bills. In fact, hundreds of such bills are introduced during each session. The procedure parallels that explained earlier for bills introduced by Ministers for the Government. The Speaker calls Introduction of Private Members' Bills. An MP wishing to introduce a bill notifies the Speaker in advance. Leave to introduce the bill having been given automatically, the MP may then provide a brief explanation of the bill. In practice, MPs almost always speak at this time, since it is an opportunity for them to draw the attention of the House to their proposals. The Speaker then proposes to the House that the bill be read a first time and printed. This motion is carried without debate, amendment or a vote, and the bill then appears on the *Order Paper* under the appropriate heading. As we saw earlier, however, this does not mean that the House will consider it on second reading. Only bills that appear on the order of precedence, after having been subject to the draw, may be considered by the House on second reading (see "The Legislative Functions," Chapter 9).

Although the procedures for the introduction of Government Bills and Private Members' Bills are nearly identical, three differences must be noted. Firstly, private Members may never introduce money bills providing for the imposition of a new tax or the introduction of a program that would require public expenditure. Introducing such bills is the prerogative of the Government. Secondly, unlike Ministers, MPs may not have another MP replace them when their bills are introduced. Individual MPs must sponsor their bills at the various stages of the legislative process. Lastly, the Standing Orders do not provide, as they do in the case of Government bills, that the House shall complete the routine proceedings on items under this heading every day.

First Reading of Senate Public Bills

When the Senate has passed a bill, a message is sent to the House informing it of this fact. The Speaker informs the House, which is equivalent to granting leave to introduce the bill, and the bill then appears on the *Order Paper* under First Reading of Senate Public Bills. The MP or Minister sponsoring the bill gives agreement by nodding when the Speaker calls this item. The motion that the bill be read a first time is not subject to amendment or debate. However, the question must be submitted to the House, where a vote may be required.

As soon as the motion is carried, the Speaker asks whether the bill will be read a second time at the next sitting of the House. If the House agrees, the order for second reading appears in the Orders of the Day under Government Orders if the bill is sponsored by a Minister or under Private Members' Business if sponsored by a private Member.

It was stated earlier that the Senate does not have jurisdiction to initiate money bills, whose purpose is the expenditure of public money or the collection of a tax. In addition, as was explained earlier, a money bill introduced in the House must be recommended by the Governor General. As well, the notice of first reading of a Senate public bill may be struck from the *Order Paper* if the bill infringes on the Government's prerogative of introducing money bills.

Motions

Motions that may be presented to the House at this time most commonly concern the business of the House, and are usually moved by the Government. They may alternatively open discussion on committee reports, in which case they are usually moved by a private Member. The Standing Orders also enumerate other motions that may be presented at this time during Routine Proceedings. Essentially, these are technical or administrative motions. These motions and those having to do with concurrence in committee reports are debatable.

Presenting Petitions

Petitions may take up a maximum of fifteen minutes at each sitting.

A period not to exceed 15 minutes is provided for MPs to present petitions. A petition is a request by means of which individuals address Parliament, requesting that action be taken in response to a specific problem. The right to petition Parliament is fundamental. However, ordinary citizens must first approach an MP, who becomes the sponsor of the petition. There are conditions for presenting petitions. Petitions must be submitted to the Clerk of Petitions, who examines them for form and content and certifies them. The MP who presents a petition does not sign it as a petitioner but must endorse it. The fact that a Member agrees to present it does not necessarily mean that he shares the opinions expressed in it.

When given the floor by the Speaker, the MP presenting the petition may make a brief statement informing the House of its contents, but must not read the petition. It should be noted that a petition may also be deposited with the Clerk of the House at any time during a sitting, and in this case the MP does not make an oral statement. A copy of the petition is sent to the Privy Council Office, which then sends it to the responsible department or Government body for a response to be prepared. The response must be tabled in the House within 45 days of the presentation of the petition. The MP receives a copy of the response the same day.

Questions on the Order Paper

It was noted in the section on relations between the House and the executive that MPs may ask oral or written questions. An MP who asks a written question must give 48 hours' notice and may request an answer to the question within 45 days of this notice. The MP may also specify whether the answer is to be given orally in the House or in writing. When the notice period has expired the question or questions are transferred from the *Notice Paper* to the *Order Paper*. When Questions on the *Order Paper* are called during Routine Proceedings, a Parliamentary Secretary rises to indicate which questions, if any, the Government intends to answer during that sitting. The Government has two options. It may indicate the numbers of the questions which the Government will answer. The text of the answer then appears in that day's *Debates* as if the Minister to whom the question had been directed had informed the House of the answer. The Government may also ask the House to make the question an order for return. The House then "orders" the Government to table the documents that will serve as the answer to the question.

Since the questions tend to accumulate faster than they can be answered, outstanding questions are removed from the *Order Paper* at the end of the month and appear in the *Monthly Supplement to the Order Paper — Questions*, where they remain until they are answered, withdrawn, or made orders for return.

We have seen that MPs who ask for a Government response within 45 days and do not receive satisfaction may raise the subject during the adjournment proceedings of the House. When Questions on the *Order Paper* are called, MPs may rise and give notice of their intention to do so. Their questions are then removed from the *Order Paper*.

Statements by Members

These statements are provided for in the Standing Orders. Although they do not form part of Routine Proceedings, it is appropriate to explain what they are. For a period of 15 minutes just before Question Period, each MP may speak for not more than one minute on a subject of his choice. The Speaker gives the floor to approximately 15 MPs in succession, taking into consideration the representation of the parties in the House. Those who exceed the time allowed are interrupted. This procedure gives MPs an opportunity to speak briefly on a subject or problem of particular concern to them. If the proceedings of the House do not begin right on time, the time allowed for Statements by Members is shortened accordingly and may even be completely eliminated from the sitting.

During the period devoted to Statements by Members, MPs who have obtained authorization from the Speaker may treat a subject of their choice for one minute.

THE RULES OF DEBATE

Most parliamentary business takes the form of debate. It is therefore necessary that there be certain rules to ensure that the House can get on with its business as smoothly as possible. Some of the applicable rules are to be found in the Standing Orders, some arise from usage and convention, and others are part of the body of precedents formed by the rulings of the Speaker and his predecessors.

An MP who wishes to speak must rise in his place to catch the Speaker's eye. He may not start to speak until he has been recognized by the Speaker. He may speak in either official language, since simultaneous interpretation will ensure that the debate can proceed without difficulty (should an aboriginal language be used, simultaneous interpretation can be provided if the Member concerned gives advance notice.)

As a general rule, an MP may not speak twice on the same subject, except to provide clarification. When he speaks, he must address himself to the Speaker. He may not respond directly to one of his fellow MPs, even if he is giving an explanation requested by that MP.

There are norms governing who may speak and in what order. The Whips provide the Speaker with a list of their party Members who would like to take part in a debate. Normally the Speaker will call on an MP from each party in turn, in the same proportion as the parties are represented in the House. Despite conventions and agreements designed to ensure participation by all parties, it is ultimately up to the Speaker to decide on the order in which he will recognize Members. He must make sure that independent or dissident MPs are not left out, and that all sides of an argument are heard.

Motions as the Basis of Debate

A motion is a proposition presented by a Member or a Minister, about which the House is called upon to make a decision.

One of the characteristics of parliamentary business is that it starts with a motion. Any debate, any discussion in the House, must be initiated by a motion. A motion is a proposition enunciated in the House by a Minister or a private Member, about which the House is called upon to make a decision. An ordinary MP moving a motion must do so in person, rising when the Speaker recognizes him, and this motion must then be seconded by another MP. A Minister wishing to move a motion may be represented by another Minister.

Once a motion has been moved and seconded, the Speaker reads the motion to the House. The motion is then formally before the House and debate can begin. The motion can be discussed, amended, rejected or withdrawn, depending on the decision of the House. Once the debate has concluded, the Speaker puts the motion to a vote. If, for some reason, the mover wants to withdraw his motion, he needs the unanimous consent of the House.

There are various types of motions and a range of procedural details which will not be explored here. The essential thing is that, apart from

Question Period, nothing can be discussed in the House without some kind of motion having first been moved.

Voting

All decisions made by the House result from the Speaker's putting a motion to the MPs for a vote. The vote is affirmative when 50 percent plus one of the MPs taking part in the vote answer yes ("yea") to the question being put. There are two types of vote, the voice vote and the "recorded division."

The Speaker holds a voice vote by saying, "Those who are in favour of the motion will please say 'yea.' Those who are opposed to the motion will please say 'nay.' " After listening to the voices of the MPs, who respond in chorus to each of the questions, the Speaker says, "In my opinion the yeas (or nays) have it." Members who want to make sure the vote is not considered to be unanimous can at this point call out, "On division," and the Speaker then confirms the vote "on division," to indicate that there were dissenting voices.

If five or more MPs rise to demand a recorded vote, the Speaker orders, "Call in the Members." The Sergeant-at-Arms then has the division bells rung for either 15 or 30 minutes, depending on the case, and the Whips gather their respective MPs. Committee meetings are interrupted for recorded divisions. When the bells fall silent the MPs take their places, and the Chief Government Whip and the Official Opposition Whip walk together down the centre aisle of the Chamber towards the Chair, bow to the Speaker and to each other and take their seats. The Speaker reads out the motion (he may with the permission of the House dispense with this if the text is very long), and puts the question. The MPs are called by name as they rise, one at a time, by a Clerk-at-the-Table, the "yeas" rising first, followed by the "nays." Once everyone has voted, the "yea" and "nay" votes are tallied by two other Clerks and the results given to the Clerk of the House of Commons, who announces them out loud to the Speaker, who then states: "I declare the motion (or the amendment) carried (or lost)."

When a recorded division is necessary, the bells ring to call the Members to the House.

Pairing

In the past, MPs established a practice that enabled them to be absent from the House without prejudicing their party's chances should a division be called. When an MP knew, for example, that he could not be in Ottawa on a given day, he would look for an MP on the opposite side of the House who also had to be absent, or who was willing, even if present, to refrain from voting. Their agreement had the practical consequence of cancelling out their votes without affecting the result of a vote by the House. Arrangements were made through the Whips. This informal system worked more or less successfully for years. As an interesting aside we note that in 1926 the Meighen Government was defeated because of a misunderstanding about pairing.[4]

In 1991, the House decided to institutionalize this informal arrangement, and added a Standing Order that provided for a Register of "paired" Members. Under the responsibility of the Clerk of the House, the Clerks-at-the-Table keep a register containing the names of MPs who have mutually agreed that they will not participate in any recorded division on a given date. The two MPs who have reached this agreement have their names entered by their respective Whips. Independent MPs sign the register themselves. The names of "pairs" are published together in the *Debates* and the *Votes and Proceedings* at the end of the text dealing with any recorded division held that day.

Time Limitation

For reasons of efficiency the House has adopted a number of measures aimed at limiting the length of debates. In previous chapters we saw that in a variety of circumstances the length of an MP's remarks may be limited by provisions of the Standing Orders. Another time limitation is that imposed by "closure." This procedure enables the Government to put an end to a debate, in particular when the subject is controversial and the discussion shows signs of going on forever. Although it can be used for any matter under debate, it is usually invoked only when the House has before it a controversial issue on which the parties cannot reach a compromise.

A Minister of the Crown, having announced his intention to do so at a previous sitting, invokes closure by moving that the debate not be further adjourned. The House votes on the motion and in so doing decides whether or not closure shall apply. The Canadian rule is less rigid than that in Great Britain, where closure applies immediately. In Canada, the Standing Orders allow debate to continue until 11:00 p.m., after a motion for closure is carried.

The Standing Orders also make provision for time allocation, which is a device for planning the use of time during the various stages of consid-

---

4. *Debates of the House of Commons*, July 1, 1926, p. 5311. Apology of Mr. Bird: "I wish to explain to the House, and with extreme regret, that I was paired with the hon. member for Peace River who had to retire from the House in account of indisposition, and I cast my vote inadvertently." See also Eugene Forsey, *The Royal Power of Dissolution of Parliament in the British Commonwealth*, (Toronto: Oxford University Press, 1968), p. 159, and MacGregor Dawson, *The Government of Canada*, op. cit., p. 355.

eration of a bill, rather than for bringing the debate to an immediate conclusion. Setting limits on the time allocated at various stages is similar to closure, but in this case the limitations may be the subject of negotiations with the opposition parties. The provision enables the Government, with the consent of the other parties, to draw up a schedule for passage of a piece of legislation. Here again, the implied threat tends to have a persuasive effect on the opposition parties. If their consent is not forthcoming, the Government, by noting that agreement could not be reached, can always proceed unilaterally by moving a motion without the agreement of the opposition parties.

Point of Order

The raising of points of order enables Members to draw attention to any deviation, real or alleged, from the Standing Orders, the customs governing debate, or any matter of parliamentary procedure. Every MP has the right and the duty to point out to the Speaker anything that in his view is out of order or to seek the Speaker's guidance. He may interrupt the debate to explain his objection succinctly to the Speaker, but he must do so the moment he becomes aware of an irregularity. He may intervene in any circumstances except during Members' Statements or Question Period, as long as he is not interrupting the Speaker. An MP rising on a point of order may name the Standing Order that in his view has been breached or ignored. He may also quote from published parliamentary authorities to substantiate his case. The Speaker's role is to interpret the practice and the Standing Orders. He may hand down his ruling immediately or defer it. It is also his duty to draw the attention of the House to any irregularity he may observe in debates or other proceedings, without waiting for an MP to rise.

> The Speaker's task is to apply the Standing Orders in a fair and impartial manner.

The Rules of Relevance and Repetition

It can occur during debate that MPs repeat themselves and occasionally stray from the subject. Sometimes this is done for emphasis or to make a special point. Usually it is unintentional. This can make the process of debate, already a weighty one, even more so. Furthermore, such techniques could be used deliberately by speakers who want to exploit every delaying tactic possible to paralyze the business of the House.

To rectify this situation, rules have been formulated to protect the House against irrelevancy and repetition. The rules are designed to prevent waste of the House's time and to enable the Speaker to intervene if he sees that MPs are deliberately slowing down the business of the House. He can call an MP to order when the latter repeats arguments that have already been made, whether by the same MP or by someone else. (Naturally this applies only to arguments put forward at the same stage of a debate.) Nor may an MP allude to a decision made by the House during the current session. Reading letters aloud, even in support of an argument, is also regarded as an inefficient use of the time reserved for the business of the House. These rules are difficult to apply since the different stages of the legislative process supply many opportunities for echoing previous remarks, and in fact multiply such opportunities.

The rule of relevance can be invoked when Members stray too far from the issue. In general, remarks are ruled out of order when their connection with the topic is not sufficiently obvious. The rule applies in particular to the various stages of the legislative process. For example, at second reading, when debate is limited to the principle of the bill, discussing the details of individual clauses would be out of order. As we have already seen, the rule is applied less rigorously during the debate on the Address in Reply to the Speech from the Throne and the Budget Debate.

It can be difficult to judge the relevance of a remark. In practice, the Speaker relies mainly on his discretionary power and the rule does not tend to be applied very strictly. Its purpose is to empower the Speaker to deal with deliberate obstruction.

Unparliamentary Language

Members are usually called by their riding names in the House. One MP addresses another as "the Honourable Member" or "my Honourable Friend."

Debates must take place in an atmosphere of courtesy. All MPs are, in their capacity as MPs, equal, and enjoy the same rights; they must thus all be treated the same way. By custom, no MP refers to another MP in the House by his name, saying instead "The Member for [the name of the riding]." He never addresses another MP directly, but always uses the third person. The usual expressions are "the Honourable Member" or "my Honourable Friend."

When he speaks in the House, an MP must use acceptable language and not refer to his colleagues with abusive epithets. Many words and phrases have been deemed to be "unparliamentary," but it is impossible to draw up an exhaustive list because so much depends on context, tone of voice, and the manner in which the remarks were made. A word that in one context might be acceptable could well be deemed unparliamentary in another. Words like "liar" and "dishonest," and those conveying threats and insults do not leave much room for doubt. In all cases, it is up to the Chair to decide. The use of unparliamentary language can be drawn to the attention of the House by any MP, or by the Speaker. It should be done as soon as the language is used and if done by an MP must take the form of a point of order.

The rule concerning unparliamentary language enables the Speaker to ensure that MPs express themselves temperately and in a manner consistent with the dignity of the House.

The Sub Judice *Convention*

In the interest of justice, parliamentary custom expects MPs in the House to refrain from talking about matters that are before the courts. This limitation on MPs' freedom of expression is accepted willingly by them because to raise such matters could be to violate the rights of an accused person or of any other person who might be affected by the outcome of a case. Since this convention is not covered by a Standing Order, its application can be unclear in some circumstances.[5]

Certain rules have, however, been established by precedent. The situation is clear when the case in question is a criminal one, where the *sub judice* convention applies until the verdict has been handed down. Once the verdict has been made public, the convention no longer applies, but will apply again if an appeal is launched. The *sub judice* convention does not apply to bills, because nothing must interfere with Parliament's fundamental right to legislate. The situation is less clear when a civil case is involved. Even though the convention may not really apply, the Chair has always recommended prudence, noting that though there may be no precedent distinguishing between civil and criminal proceedings, an unresolved dispute is in either case still before the courts.

The convention applies only to cases before courts of record, and so does not apply to matters before a royal commission. However, MPs do tend to refrain from commenting on the proceedings of a commission of enquiry.

The core of the problem lies in the need to protect the rights and interests of private citizens, to the extent that this protection can be reconciled with the national interest. In the last analysis, it is up to the Speaker to decide, because he is the protector of MPs' rights and, in this context, of the rights of citizens outside the House of Commons.

PARLIAMENTARY PRIVILEGE

Parliamentary privilege consists of all the privileges and immunities Parliament and parliamentarians enjoy, without which they could not carry out their functions. The classic definition of parliamentary privilege was formulated by Erskine May:

---

5. Philip Laundy, "The *Sub Judice* Convention in the Canadian House of Commons," *The Parliamentarian*, July 1976, Vol. LVII, No. 3, p. 211.

Parliamentary privilege is the sum of the peculiar rights enjoyed by each House collectively as a constituent part of the High Court of Parliament, and by Members of each House individually, without which they could not discharge their functions, and which exceed those possessed by other bodies or individuals. Thus privilege, though part of the law of the land, is to a certain extent an exemption from the ordinary law.[6]

Parliamentary privilege protects MPs from legal action as a result of what they say in the House or in committee.

These privileges were won over the centuries by the Parliament of England in order to enable it to carry out its functions without let or hindrance. Section 18 of the *Constitution Act, 1867*, repeated in Section 4 of the *Parliament of Canada Act*, provides that the privileges, immunities, and rights of the Parliament of Canada may be determined by an act of Parliament but may not exceed those of the House of Commons of the Parliament of the United Kingdom. The concept of privilege and its applications have evolved to allow Parliament to carry out its functions in the context of today's society. By tradition, the first act of a newly elected Speaker of the House of Commons is to ask that parliamentary privilege be confirmed (see "Sessions and Sittings" at the beginning of this Chapter).

The purpose of privilege is not to place Parliament and parliamentarians above the law, but rather to allow them to carry out their duties independently and effectively, in the national interest. It is important to note that parliamentary privilege has been conferred on MPs not for their personal advantage, but solely in order to make it easier for them to carry out their functions. Members may not invoke any privilege or immunity unless it is related to their functions in the House of Commons.

There are two major categories of privilege: privileges associated with the House collectively, and those MPs enjoy individually.

Rights and Powers of the House Collectively

The House has certain powers acquired through custom or conferred by law. Under these powers, the House and its committees may institute inquiries, require the attendance of witnesses, and order the production of papers. The *Parliament of Canada Act* gives the House the right to administer oaths to witnesses. The House has very wide latitude in maintaining its authority and ensuring that its deliberations are made in an atmosphere in keeping with that authority.

6. Erskine May, *Treatise on the Law, Privileges, Proceedings and Usage of Parliament*, 21st ed., edited by Clifford Boulton, (London: Butterworths, 1989), p. 69.

Among the rights and powers of the House in this field, the two that are essential are its exclusive right to regulate its own affairs, and its disciplinary power.

The House is solely responsible for its internal affairs. In other words, it has absolute control of its agenda, and adopts and amends procedures at its convenience and as it requires. For this reason, the courts may not intervene in the work of Parliament. We saw that the House, for its part, accepts by convention that MPs do not discuss matters which are *sub judice* (cases under adjudication by a court or tribunal) in debate in the House or its committees (see "The *Sub Judice* Convention" earlier in this chapter). They are under no legal obligation to refrain from such discussion.

The exclusive right of the House of Commons to regulate its internal affairs has been interpreted to mean that local and provincial legislation does not usually apply in the parliamentary precincts. Similarly, the internal regulation of House of Commons activities is not governed by federal legislation unless specific provision to the contrary is contained in an act of Parliament.

The other exclusive right of the House of Commons is its right to take the disciplinary measures required to penalize any act that would jeopardize its authority. The House has the power to penalize anyone — a Member or a stranger — who is guilty of misconduct that the House considers a breach of privilege or contempt of the House. The distinction between the two types of breach of the authority of the House is not very clear. As is stated in the document on parliamentary privilege prepared by the Table Research Branch:

> *...all breaches of privilege are contempts of the House, but not all contempts are necessarily breaches of privilege. A contempt is any conduct which offends the authority or the dignity of the House, even though no breach of any specific privilege has been committed.*[7]

The Standing Orders contain provisions on the disciplinary power of the House. For example, the House may refuse entry to the public galleries or corridors to strangers who have previously misconducted themselves.[8]

However, the power of the House is not limited to cases provided for in the Standing Orders, as everyone who comes within the jurisdiction of the House is subject to its discipline for any form of misconduct.

---

7. *Privilege in the Modern Context* (Ottawa: House of Commons, Table Research Branch, June 1992), p. 6.
8. Standing Order 158.

The House of Commons has the right to reprimand individuals and take them into custody until the end of the session, although, since the *Canadian Charter of Rights and Freedoms* was passed, one might question the constitutional nature of Parliament's right to sentence someone to incarceration. The House may suspend a Member who is disorderly or uses unparliamentary language and persistently refuses to apologize. The House is also empowered to expel Members but would only do so in the most extreme circumstances. An expelled Member is not precluded from running again as a candidate in a constituency. In general, the House of Commons is hesitant to use its disciplinary power, and Canadian parliamentary history records only a few instances of its having done so.[9]

Rights and Immunities of Parliamentarians Individually

The most important privilege is certainly the freedom of expression.

The privilege of freedom of speech is certainly the most important and least disputed among parliamentarians' rights and immunities. It was guaranteed by the *Bill of Rights* in Great Britain in 1689. By virtue of this privilege, MPs may speak freely during sittings of the House or in committees with complete immunity from criminal or civil prosecution for what they may have said. They are thus protected from any legal action for libel or slander.

This privilege allows parliamentarians to express themselves frankly and to make the statements and comments they consider necessary in complete freedom, without having to be concerned with the legal consequences their words might have. This freedom allows the House to carry out its functions properly and consider the matters before it fully.[10]

The parliamentary privilege attached to freedom of speech applies only to MPs' statements in the House or in committees. Reports of proceedings or debates published in newspapers or by other persons outside Parliament are protected by qualified privilege. This means that reports are protected if they are fair and accurate but not if they are selective or malicious. Parliamentary privilege would not protect MPs publishing their own speeches in local newspapers. The *Debates* are protected if circulated in the form they are published as the complete record of a sitting.

It must not be deduced from these explanations that MPs are entirely free to say anything at all about anyone at all. The Speaker warns MPs

9. *Parliamentary Privilege*, (Ottawa: Office of the Law Clerk and Parliamentary Counsel, 1988), p. 5.
10. J.A.G. Griffith, M.A.J. Wheeler-Booth and Michael Ryle, *Parliament: Functions, Practice and Procedures*. (London: Sweet and Maxwell, 1989), pp. 85-86.

Parliamentary immunity associated with freedom of speech applies in the House or in committee, but not outside the Parliament Buildings.

who abuse this privilege. Although MPs need to be able to express their opinions freely, citizens' reputations also need to be protected and they should not be attacked unjustly. There are other restrictions on freedom of speech that have already been mentioned. Under the *sub judice* convention, MPs refrain from discussing certain cases before the courts. Another restriction may be imposed when the Speaker asks an MP to withdraw an unparliamentary remark. This is an example of the right of the House to regulate its own affairs.

Another privilege MPs enjoy individually is protection from arrest in civil matters. Originally, this privilege was conferred on parliamentarians so that the House would not be deprived of the presence of its Members. Today, this right is primarily historical in nature, since arrests are no longer normally made in civil matters. Members of Parliament are not, however, above the law. If they commit criminal offences, they are subject to criminal law and may not claim immunity from arrest or imprisonment on criminal charges.

Since the Speaker is the authority responsible for administering the House and the buildings that are part of it, he has the right to control security and the activities of the police within the precincts of the House of Commons. It may happen that members of outside police forces may wish to enter the precincts of the House of Commons in order to arrest or question someone or conduct a search. On one such occasion the question arose as to whether the police could freely enter the Parliament Buildings and execute their warrant or whether they had to respect certain rules. A committee considered this question and concluded that outside police forces on official business may not enter the precincts of Parliament without first obtaining the permission of the Speaker, who is the guardian of the privileges of the House.[11]

This permission is not just a formality. In 1979, Speaker Jerome refused to authorize the RCMP to search a certain MP's office on the ground that no charge had been laid, and that it appeared the investigation which had been initiated was unrelated to any alleged offence on the part of the Member.[12]

In these matters, the Speaker is placed in a sensitive position. He must ensure that the rights and privileges of the House and those of the MPs are respected, so that the business of Parliament is not hindered. At the same time, he must not interfere with the administration of criminal justice.

Parliamentarians are excused from jury duty.

Another privilege granted to parliamentarians in order to enable them to carry out their functions is exemption from jury duty and the requirement to testify in court. However, MPs who consider that their testimony is indispensable to the course of justice may waive this privilege. Some officials of the House are also exempt from jury duty. In fact, these exemptions make it possible for MPs and officials who fulfil essential functions to carry on their work without interruption. There is no shortage of persons eligible for jury duty, and this privilege is therefore justified for practical reasons.

There is another privilege that protects MPs from obstruction and intimidation. If an MP complains of interference in the carrying out of parliamentary duties, the Speaker determines whether at first glance there appears to be a breach of privilege and therefore whether there is a case to investigate.

Any actual or presumed breach of privilege or contempt of Parliament must be brought to the attention of the House immediately. When MPs raise a question of privilege, they must be brief and concise. The task of the Speaker is to determine whether the question of privilege appears to be well-founded and should be given priority. This decision is the responsibility of the Speaker, who may rule on the spot or postpone his decision in order to consider the question at greater length.

11. Canada, House of Commons, *Journals*, September 21, 1973, p. 567.
12. Canada, House of Commons, *Debates*, November 30, 1979, p. 1891.

If the Speaker concludes that, at first glance, the question of privilege is indeed well founded, an MP makes a motion whose general purpose is usually to submit the question to the Standing Committee on House Management. If the motion is agreed to, the matter is referred to the Committee. After considering the matter, the Committee presents its report in accordance with the same conditions applicable to the other work of the committees. It is also open to the House to take the matter into consideration immediately without referring it to the Committee.

Members often invoke parliamentary privilege concerning matters that have nothing to do with privilege. In fact, privilege is a frequently misunderstood concept.

11 Management of the House

Different organizations assist the Speaker in his administrative duties.

The Speaker's position in the House is like that of the Minister in a department, that is, he is the senior authority where management of the House is concerned. However, given the special nature of the House of Commons, the organizations that assist the Speaker in the task of managing reflect the composition of the House. It must also be noted that in recent years the management systems have been developed and structured in order to meet the needs of MPs and the House as a whole.

ADMINISTRATIVE ORGANS OF THE HOUSE

The Board of Internal Economy

The Board of Internal Economy acts as a sort of board of directors of the House, and is provided for in Section 50 of the *Parliament of Canada Act*. This Act was amended in April 1991 in order to set out and enhance the powers of the Board of Internal Economy.[1] The Board of Internal Economy derives its powers from the *Canada Parliament Act*, the *Standing Orders of the House of Commons* and the *Parliamentary Employment and Staff Relations Act*. The Board is composed of the Speaker of the House of Commons, who chairs the Board, the Deputy Speaker, two Ministers (at the present time the President of the Treasury Board and the Government House Leader), the Leader of the Opposition or his representative, and four other MPs. Two of the latter are Members of the party in power; the two others, from the opposition parties. One member from the opposition parties is from the Official Opposition; the other, from the second-ranking opposition party, provided it has at least twelve MPs. The Act specifies that if the second opposition party does not have at least twelve MPs, the Official Opposition party has two members on the Board in addition to the Leader of the Opposition or his nominee.

1. *Canada Parliament Act*, R.S. (1985), c. P-1, am., (1985), c. 31 (1st supp.), c. 38 (2nd supp.) 1991, c. 20.

The members of the Board are required to take a solemn oath or affirmation of fidelity and secrecy concerning various aspects of the Board's activities that must not be disclosed. Five Members, including the Speaker, form a quorum. If the Speaker is unable to be present, the Deputy Speaker replaces the Speaker. When Parliament is dissolved, members of the Board retain their functions until they are replaced. The Clerk of the House of Commons is the secretary of the Board and is assisted in these duties by a secretariat managed by a procedural clerk.

The Board is responsible for administrative and financial matters concerning the House of Commons and MPs, and therefore determines all policies of the House in these matters. It is a legal entity and, in exercising its powers, may enter into contracts, memoranda of agreement or other arrangements on behalf of the House of Commons or on its own behalf.[2] In administrative matters, it is responsible for managing the premises, services, and personnel of the House as well as the goods, services, and premises made available to MPs for the carrying out of their functions. The Board makes all administrative decisions concerning use of the premises. It is also the Board that has recommended to the House policies on broadcasting the deliberations of Parliament and approved action taken in Parliament to enforce the *Non-smokers' Health Act.*

In accordance with the requirements of the *Parliamentary Employment and Staff Relations Act,*[3] the Board was designated as the official employer of all House of Commons employees. The Board is responsible for the conditions of employment of House of Commons employees, but MPs hire their own employees, and they are not members of the House of Commons staff. As the employer, the Board authorizes officials of the Human Resources Directorate to negotiate the renewal of the collective agreements of unionized employees, and approves salary scales for non-unionized employees.

The Board of Internal Economy has very important financial responsibilities. The fact that the President of the Treasury Board sits on the Board of Internal Economy allows the Board to receive information on Government policies directly from the source. Knowledge of these policies, particularly where conditions of employment are concerned, is important. For example, the Government's intentions concerning salary raises (or freezes) should be known so that similar measures are adopted for House of Commons employees.

2. *Canada Parliament Act,* 52.2.
3. *Parliamentary Employment and Staff Relations Act,* R.S. (1985), c. 33 (2nd supp.) am., 1985 (4th supp.), c. 1.

The House of Commons Estimates are prepared at the Board's request. After the Board has studied and approved them, it sends them, through the Speaker, to the President of the Treasury Board, who tables them in the House with the Government's departmental estimates for the fiscal year. Amounts thus allocated to the House of Commons — operating and administrative expenses of the House, including the salaries of its employees — are managed by the Board, as are amounts payable to MPs such as sessional indemnities, expense allowances, and travel and telecommunications costs.

The Board of Internal Economy is charged, among other things, with deciding on the funds that should be allocated to the committees.

Under Standing Order 121, the Board is responsible for approving and monitoring the committees' expenditures. The Board decides the amount to be budgeted for all committees. A global amount is allocated to the standing committees. It is then the responsibility of the Liaison Committee of the House of Commons, composed of the chairmen of the standing committees, to distribute the amount allocated among the standing committees and then to present the entire calculation to the Board for its approval. The Board allocates to the legislative and special committees the amounts necessary for their operation following their submission of detailed budgets. Legislative committees are not obliged to furnish budgets if their expenses do not exceed $50 000. Each year, the Clerk of the House supplies a comprehensive financial report to the Board of Internal Economy, outlining the expenditures incurred by each standing, special, or legislative committee during the year ended. The report is appended to the *Votes and Proceedings* of the day on which it is presented.

One amendment made to the *Canada Parliament Act* in 1991 authorized the Board to make by-laws governing MPs' use of the funds, goods, services and premises made available to them. We saw earlier that individual MPs receive an overall authorization for their staff, travel, and constituency office costs. The Board now has exclusive jurisdiction to assess the propriety of the use of these funds and goods. In the course of a judicial investigation, a peace officer may ask the Board of Internal Economy to provide such an assessment, but the Board may also give one on its own initiative.

Other regulations that apply to the Board include a provision of the *Canada Parliament Act* stipulating that when the Board makes by-laws, the chairman must table them in the House of Commons within 30 days. In another area, the Standing Orders provide that MPs may question a member of the Board, specially designated for this role, during Question Period.

The Board of Internal Economy meets regularly while the House is sitting, usually every second Wednesday evening. The Clerk of the House regularly attends these meetings, since he is secretary of the Board. The two other sector heads, the Sergeant-at-Arms and the Administrator, attend as well, in order to respond to requests for information and provide any necessary documentation. The Speaker as Chairman also attends, accompanied by his Chief of Staff.

The Board of Internal Economy Secretariat schedules meetings and prepares agendas in consultation with members of the Executive Committee. It is responsible for preparing minutes of proceedings and records of decisions.

The Standing Orders provide that, within 10 days of the opening of each session, the Speaker shall table in the House of Commons a report of the proceedings of the Board of Internal Economy during the preceding session.

The Standing Committee on House Management

This committee was set up during the major procedural reform that took place in 1991. It replaced the Striking Committee, whose functions it retained. In addition, it took over the functions of the Standing Committee on Elections, Privileges, Procedure, and Private Members' Business and those of the Standing Committee on Management and Members' Services. It is thus an extremely busy committee with a very broad mandate.

Like the other standing committees, it is appointed for the duration of a Parliament. It is composed of 14 members, in the same proportion as membership on the other committees, so as to reflect the proportion of seats occupied by the official political parties in the House. The three Whips and Deputy Whips sit on this committee, although this practice is not formally provided for in the Standing Orders. Their presence on this committee is logical in view of their role and that of the committee.

Acting as a striking committee, at the beginning of each session, the Committee on House Management must draw up the list of MPs who may sit on each standing committee and those who will act for the House on joint committees.[4] As well, when debate on second reading of a bill that must be sent to a legislative committee has begun, it selects the MPs who will compose this legislative committee if the House passes the bill on second reading. Obviously, the Standing Committee on House Management must replace members of committees as required. It has made one of its subcommittees, composed of the three Whips, responsible for selecting and replacing MPs who sit on committees.

The Standing Committee on House Management looks after activities related to the Parliamentary Library, among other duties.

4. Standing Order 104(1).

Standing Order 108(3)(a) describes the mandate of the Standing Committee on House Management. In general, it is responsible for reviewing and reporting to the House and the Board of Internal Economy on issues concerning the management of the House and the provision of services and facilities to MPs. Under the Standing Orders, it is directly responsible to the House for reviewing and reporting on the effectiveness, management, and operational plans of the House and the provision of services and facilities to MPs. It may receive requests from MPs, conduct studies and make recommendations, which it includes in its report to the House, and make suggestions to the Board of Internal Economy.

This committee reviews the effectiveness of all joint operations by the two Houses, such as the Library of Parliament and the Parliamentary Restaurant. The Committee may deal with any matter related to these operations and in all cases may present a report to the House.

Having taken over the mandate of the former Standing Committee on Elections, Privileges and Procedure and Private Members' Business, this Committee is responsible for reviewing the Standing Orders, procedure and practice in the House and its committees, as well as questions of privilege which are referred to it by the House and matters having to do with the *Canada Elections Act*. It therefore examines the operation of the House and its committees on a regular basis, deals with any matter it considers appropriate and then makes recommendations to the House.

In 1992, this committee tabled many reports that the House approved. These reports concerned, among other matters, the television broadcasting of committee meetings,[5] Private Members' Business,[6] and the membership of legislative committees.[7]

The Standing Committee on House Management decides which items of Private Members' Business will be considered votable and also looks after matters relating to private bills. It has given this mandate to a subcommittee composed of one member of each party and chaired by a member of the party in power.

The budget estimates of the House of Commons are considered by this committee in the same way as other committees consider departmental estimates. The committee hears the Speaker and senior officials who provide explanations and justifications.

5. Twenty-third report, presented February 14, 1992 and concurred in by the House on March 27, 1992.
6. Twenty-seventh report, presented March 11, 1992 and concurred in by the House on April 29, 1992.
7. Twenty-eighth report, presented March 18, 1992 and concurred in by the House on April 29, 1992.

The committee is an excellent complement to the Board of Internal Economy where all House management matters are concerned. It is in a good position to investigate these matters and then make recommendations to the Board of Internal Economy. Although the Committee was created only recently, it has inherited the mandate of the former Committees and its relations with the Board of Internal Economy can be expected to be similar to those of its predecessors.

The Standing Committee on House Management constitutes an excellent complement to the Board of Internal Economy.

The Executive Committee

This committee is chaired by the Speaker of the House of Commons and also includes the Deputy Speaker and the three sector heads: the Clerk of the House, the Sergeant-at-Arms, and the Administrator. The Procedural Clerk of the Board of Internal Economy's Secretariat acts as Recording Secretary of the Committee.

Essentially, this committee's role is to approve certain measures taken by the Administrative Committee, to make decisions in matters referred to it by the Administrative Committee, and to prepare for the meetings of the Board of Internal Economy. The Committee approves all appointments of senior officials except persons appointed by Order-in-Council. It meets regularly, late in the morning of the day the Board meets. In this way, the three sector heads can inform the Speaker about any developments in matters that must be discussed by the Board. Together, they review the documentation to be distributed to members of the Board.

The Administrative Committee

The Administrative Committee is composed of the three sector heads and is chaired by the Clerk of the House. The General Legal Counsel, the Comptroller, and the Director General of Human Resources regularly attend these meetings as advisors. Other officials of the House are sometimes invited to take part in this Committee's discussions on subjects in their respective fields of responsibility. The Executive Assistant to the Clerk of the House acts as Recording Secretary of this Committee.

The Committee is responsible for administrative matters such as the hiring of contract employees, review of budgetary proposals, and security matters. It also considers other matters, on which it makes recommendations to the Executive Committee.

These two committees, the Executive Committee and the Administrative Committee, have no statutory basis. They have been set up for reasons of practicality and efficiency, and they are well served by their hierarchical structures, ordered according to the importance of the matters with which they deal. In addition, having the three sector heads participate in the work of these two committees and that of the Board of Internal Economy facilitates committee discussions and ensures effective communication between the various administrative units and the members of the Board. The sector heads do not play the same role on these committees as they do with the Board, where they do not take part in decision-making. Their liaison role is nonetheless essential to the smooth operation of the organization.

THE ADMINISTRATOR'S SECTOR

The Administrator is one of the three senior officials of the House and the head of one of the three sectors. While the Clerk of the House of Commons and the Sergeant-at-Arms are appointed by Order-in-Council, the Administrator is appointed by the Board of Internal Economy. Like the other sector heads, the Administrator reports directly to the Speaker of the House of Commons. The Administrator is responsible for four important services: Program Evaluation and Internal Audit; the Office of the Comptroller (management and financial control); Support and Information Systems; and Human Resources.

As we saw earlier, the Administrator is a member of the Administrative Committee and the Executive Committee, and also attends meetings of the Board of Internal Economy. Of the four services for which the Administrator is responsible, the first is managed by a Director, the second by the Comptroller, and the remaining two by Directors General.

The Program Evaluation and Internal Audit Directorate

The main purpose of the Directorate is to ensure the integrity of administrative and financial decisions by providing independent reviews, evaluations, examinations and financial audits. The Directorate provides advice on the appropriateness of means used by administrative units in reaching goals of the House of Commons.

The Office of the Comptroller

The Office of the Comptroller oversees the financial administration of the House.

The Office of the Comptroller is responsible for the financial administration of the House. The Comptroller is available to MPs and heads of administrative units in the House in order to provide them with advice and opinions on financial management. He is responsible for three branches.

THE FINANCIAL MANAGEMENT BRANCH

This Branch is responsible, in general, for budget planning and financial control for the House. It prepares the annual departmental estimates, by co-ordinating the various elements of which they are composed, and then prepares comprehensive estimates for the House of Commons as a whole. It regularly prepares the documentation and financial analyses required by the Administrative Committee, the Executive Committee and the Board of Internal Economy, and also provides these services for the Liaison Committee, made up of the chairmen of standing committees.

THE FINANCIAL POLICY AND SYSTEMS BRANCH

This Branch is responsible for developing and applying financial policies and systems that will meet the needs of MPs and managers in the House. These policies apply to manual and computerized accounting operations, the pay system and financial control, as well as to all administrative units in the House.

The Branch prepares documents and manuals on financial policies and their application. For example, it writes and updates the *Members' Manual of Allocations and Services*, an informative publication that is very helpful to parliamentarians, and the *Committee Financial Policy Manual*. It also looks after the delegation of financial signing authority, ensuring that the applicable procedures are respected, and monitors their implementation. This Branch, like the preceding one, provides advice and assistance to MPs and managers in the House.

THE ACCOUNTING OPERATIONS BRANCH

In light of the nature of the services provided, this Branch is divided into two units. The unit responsible for Accounting Operations provides accounting services for the administrative units in the House, the Parliamentary Restaurant, and MPs. It processes accounts payable, does banking transactions, and invoices accounts receivable. Employees from this unit are available to MPs who want explanations of benefits to which they are entitled and financial policies and procedures in effect in the House of Commons.

The other unit in this Branch is responsible for pay and benefits for all MPs, their employees, and House of Commons employees. It therefore maintains attendance and leave records, performs all pay calculations, and administers benefit programs. It provides advice and opinions to MPs and managers on all compensation matters.

The Support and Information Systems Directorate

The Directorate is run by a Director General, who is responsible for five services.

THE INFORMATION SYSTEMS DIRECTORATE

In the era of electronic communications, extensive services ensure the automatic transfer of information for the House.

The three branches that make up this Directorate are: Computer Systems, Electronic Services, and OASIS User Support. They are responsible for acquiring and maintaining all equipment for automated information systems and the OASIS system: computers, automated publishing systems for producing parliamentary publications (*Hansard, Votes and Proceedings, Issues and Committee Reports*), and all other management information systems used in MPs' offices or by managers in the House. These units also design the software required by various administrative units and provide training for MPs' employees and House employees who use the OASIS system.

The Electronic Services Branch provides the electronic equipment required for the recording and simultaneous interpretation of the deliberations of the House, the Senate, and their committees. Along with food services, and the postal and distribution services, this is one of the rare services provided to both Houses. In all other cases, the Senate has its own administration, separate from that of the House. It should be noted that the Houses of Parliament have a vast array of electronic equipment for the simultaneous interpretation, recording, transcription, and audiovisual reproduction of their deliberations. All the technical aspects of installing and maintaining this equipment are the responsibility of the Electronic Services Branch.

Another unit, Telecommunications, is responsible for all services required to install, move, and maintain telephone and related services. This unit allocates and monitors the use of Bell Canada credit cards and authorization codes for calls made on the Government network. These cards, identified by number codes, allow MPs and officials to make official telephone calls within Canada using the Government telecommunications system.

THE SUPPORT SERVICES DIRECTORATE

The Directorate is responsible for the following units: Purchasing, Materiel Management, Printing, Press Gallery services, Transportation and Parking, and Furniture Repair and Auxiliary Services.

The Purchasing unit purchases supplies, equipment, and furniture for MPs' offices and all administrative units in the House. It is also responsible for obtaining contracts for equipment rental, repair and maintenance, laundry and other services.

The Materiel Management unit is responsible for materiel storage, paper supplies, inventory control and, when necessary, the disposal of assets on behalf of the House of Commons. It also manages the souvenir shop located in the main hall of the Centre Block.

The Printing unit provides printing, photocopying, and photomechanical reproduction services for MPs and House administrative staff.

Another unit is responsible for providing administrative services, equipment and staff for members of the Press Gallery, in order to enable them to carry out their duties as parliamentary journalists. This unit must also organize the recording and interpretation services required during press conferences held on Parliament Hill.

The Transportation and Parking unit provides minibus service among the buildings on Parliament Hill for authorized users, as well as a truck delivery service as required. This unit issues parking permits and monitors their use.

The Furniture Repair and Auxiliary Services unit looks after the repair, construction, restoration and installation of movable assets belonging to the House of Commons and certain repairs in buildings occupied by administrative units of the House.

THE FOOD SERVICES BRANCH

The Parliamentary Dining Room, three cafeterias, and three snack bars are managed and operated by this Branch. It is also responsible for special events such as receptions and official dinners for which catering services are used.

THE ACCOMMODATION, MANAGEMENT AND PLANNING DIRECTORATE

This Directorate plans needs for space in buildings and manages all construction within the parliamentary precincts. It is also responsible for the use of space and conservation services. It provides liaison with Public Works Canada.

The Room Allocation unit makes reservations for conference rooms, committee meeting rooms, and other space required for special occasions.

The Curator's office is responsible for maintenance and inventory control of works of art and antiques in the House of Commons.

The Tenant Services unit is responsible for maintaining, repairing, and renovating all space in commercial premises rented by the House of Commons.

THE POSTAL AND DISTRIBUTION SERVICES BRANCH

Postal services in all buildings in which MPs' offices are located are the responsibility of this branch. It also looks after the distribution of official documents in all the buildings of Parliament for MPs, Senators, employees of both Houses and members of the Press Gallery.

The Messenger unit ensures that messages and documents are delivered to MPs and officials of the House. Messengers also provide security inspection and delivery of material delivered by commercial messenger services. On foot or using public transit, they make deliveries in the parliamentary precincts and within a certain radius of Parliament Hill.

The Human Resources Directorate

This Directorate is run by a Director General and includes three services.

When this photograph was taken (1902), messengers were kept busier delivering mail than they are in our days of electronic communications.

THE STAFF RELATIONS DIRECTORATE

This Directorate makes sure that harmonious employer-employee relations are maintained. It ensures that labour legislation is enforced and the provisions of collective agreements respected, and interprets the terms and conditions of that legislation and those agreements. Its officers deal with the unions on behalf of the employer when collective agreements governing the working conditions of various categories of unionized employees are negotiated. This division handles grievances and ensures that they are dealt with according to the applicable procedures. It is also responsible for occupational safety and health programs.

Employees hired by MPs are not House employees, nor are they part of the federal public service, although their conditions of work are similar. Unions were introduced in the House of Commons in 1986. As is the case in the public service, most employees, except for senior managers, are unionized.

The Directorate acts in an advisory capacity to officials on all matters concerning staff relations or the application and interpretation of collective agreements.

THE PERSONNEL OPERATIONS DIRECTORATE

The services offered by this Directorate are available to all MPs, their employees, managers in the House and all officials of the Board of Internal Economy. These services include staffing and hiring. Although MPs hire their employees directly, they may, if they wish, request assistance from the Directorate in hiring staff.

Position evaluation plans, salary scales, and benefit policies are developed by the Personnel Operations Directorate. The classification and compensation system for positions in the House of Commons is drawn up taking into consideration uniformity, internal comparisons, and pay equity, as well as established standards. Positions are paid at rates comparable with those in the public service.

Hiring is done using the merit principle and the process illustrated in the Figure 5. The Personnel Operations Directorate is also responsible for implementing an employment equity program for persons with disabilities or impairments and members of minorities.

THE POLICY, PLANNING AND TRAINING DIRECTORATE

This Directorate is responsible for developing and implementing human resources policies. As we saw earlier, these policies must be approved by the Board of Internal Economy. The Directorate also monitors and evaluates these policies.

FIGURE 5

Staffing Process

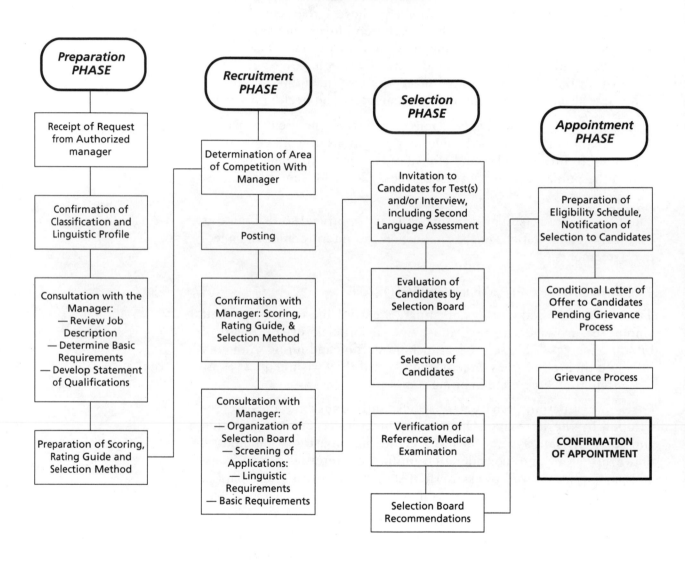

Source: Human Resources Directorate, House of Commons.

A division of the Directorate has a mandate to provide information to employees on all matters related to their employment and career development. Orientation courses are provided for new House employees.

The Directorate is also responsible for training programs, including courses and seminars organized by the Human Resources Directorate and, for employees who so wish, the possibility of taking professional development courses at educational institutions or elsewhere. These costs are paid from the budgets of the appropriate sponsoring administrative units. Language training programs are also part of the Directorate's responsibilities. Members of Parliament, their employees, and House employees may take language training courses in either official language given by teachers employed by the Directorate.

The Directorate is also responsible for the health units available to parliamentarians and employees in case of urgent need or routine medical attention in the case of minor ailments. The nurses who work in these units are employed by the Directorate.

AFTERWORD

Against the backdrop of the 125th anniversary of Confederation, there is much that we as Canadians have to be profoundly grateful for, much that we can take great pride in. Not only are our institutions of governance a source of pride but, beyond this, they stand at the very centre of our prosperity, our freedom, and the way of life which binds us together. The institutions which our ancestors established to sustain and defend democracy in this country are still with us today, more than two hundred years later. If we examine the history of Canada, one fact among all others stands out: the creation, growth, and development of parliamentary institutions have been very much an effort shared by all Canadians.

Initially, the challenge to create a democratic society was undertaken by our French- and English-speaking ancestors. Subsequently others, not a few of them attracted by our free and democratic institutions, have made Canada their home and joined their efforts with ours to preserve our foundations of governance and build upon them. And they have added their strength and wisdom to ours as we strive to give democracy its fullest meaning.

It is worth recalling that this common project of ours has had a long history. I have always maintained that those who claim that Canada began in 1867 are mistaken. The events which laid the foundation of this country occurred much earlier. Canada's native peoples had developed effective and sophisticated systems for governing their social and political affairs. Well before 1867, our ancestors worked together to establish the basis for our institutions of parliamentary democracy. I think it quite important to stress that this process, although at times turbulent, has been a peaceful one with relatively peaceful beginnings. As others have noted, this stands in marked contrast to the French and the American experience, where citizens paid the heavy price of revolution to gain their democratic rights.

Yet we cannot in all conscience claim that the process of building parliamentary democracy in Canada has been an untroubled one, or even that it represents a goal which has been fully attained. For all our protracted constitutional debates, however, what seems to me truly extraordinary is that we are of a remarkable accord, namely, that full democratic rights for all citizens is what we want to achieve and that parliamentary institutions represent the best means by which this can be attained.

Within this framework, debate and diversity have flourished exactly as was intended. Some say that it is remarkable that we have survived this long as a country. They view the intense debates taking place, shake their heads and forecast Canada's impending demise. They have lost sight of the fact that the turbulence they perceive is a sign of health, a sign of vitality, a sign of life. And a sign that our democratic institutions, by legitimizing debate and disagreement, by offering a forum for the expression of ideas, have succeeded remarkably well.

While some of us in this country have overlooked this simple fact, it has not gone unnoticed elsewhere. You do not have to take my word that our parliamentary system is an effective means of realizing the democratic aspirations of this country's citizens. Representatives from nations around the world come here to observe our institutions in action and to consult with our parliamentarians.

Most recently, Canada has been serving as a model for the new democracies of Eastern Europe who, still reeling from what has been called "the shock of freedom," see in this country an example of how peoples of diverse backgrounds can govern themselves peacefully while preserving their distinctiveness.

For two years now, my office has had the honour and privilege of sponsoring seminars on the functioning of government in this country for Eastern Europeans. These seminars and exchanges have brought together representatives from such nations as Bulgaria, Hungary, the Czech and Slovak Republic, Roumania, Poland, Russia, Lithuania, Latvia, Estonia and the Ukraine, all of them anxious to learn what makes a society as diverse as Canada work and how our institutions make it governable. Needless to say, our parliamentary institutions are the principle mechanisms which facilitate our desire to live together while enabling us to preserve our precious diversity. And the attention given these institutions by these distinguished visitors should give pause to any of us who have doubted the worth of our parliamentary heritage.

Not only do representatives of the nations of the world come to this country to learn from us — we actively reach out to share our knowledge of parliamentary institutions with others. Canada has been, and is, a leading participant in organizations designed to promote inter-parliamentary co-operation and understanding. Needless to say, the resulting exchange of ideas is one which I personally find deeply rewarding. These organizations provide an invaluable means of enhancing the understanding and growth of parliamentary democracy.

However, despite all I have just said, there is a dark cloud on the horizon. The good that others have recognized in our parliamentary system has not been so readily acknowledged here at home. We cannot ignore the fact that the institutions that we have worked so hard together to build have fallen into disrepute. Although there are many possible causes for this sorry state of affairs, I would argue that in large part this is due to a lack of understanding of how those institutions function to further the best interests of all Canadians. Clearly, one of the solutions involves a concentrated effort to make sure that the public develops a better understanding of how these institutions work. This means that parliamentarians in particular have a special responsibility to explain how parliamentary institutions function and why they provide certain advantages which are not offered by other systems. That is why I have endeavoured to share my knowledge of our parliamentary institutions in this book.

Yet this is not an easy assignment. News media have more than ever assumed the task of interpreting government to citizens and increasingly, the tone of that interpretation is negative. Rather than being told of the positive accomplishments of their governing institutions, Canadians are mainly exposed to their shortcomings. Is it any wonder that an ever larger number of our citizens lack confidence in government and politicians?

If the institutions of parliamentary democracy are worth preserving, the duty to explain them to the people they are meant to serve becomes vitally important. It is in the interest of our entire community, and in particular of the young men and women who are our children, that the institutions which guarantee democratic freedoms in our country be kept whole and intact.

Our efforts to explain the institutions of parliamentary democracy to those they serve are one of the best investments of time I can think of. When people develop a better understanding of the way their system of government works for them, the benefits will be numerous and immediate. To name only a few, criticism of the system should become more constructive; rather than destroying existing institutions completely, people instead will think of ways in which they might be improved. Communication between government and citizens will be enhanced. The needs of citizens will be more effectively addressed by their elected representatives. Respect for the institutions and those who labour in them will be restored. And once these institutions are seen to be effective, citizens will be encouraged to participate more actively in the public life of their community.

Our institutions of parliamentary democracy have been built on the basis of hard work and co-operative efforts of all citizens. The structures established by our ancestors and subsequent generations of new arrivals from other nations have served us well. They are the living testimony to the desire of all of the communities in Canada to work together in peace and harmony, in mutual respect, and mutual caring. They are the embodiment of our collective democratic will.

With proper care and nurturing, with an effort to improve understanding, the institutions of Parliament will continue to serve us and serve our children well into the future. An awareness of our past can give us confidence to meet the challenges of the future. We can be inspired by the vision and the integrity of those who came before us. We can take solace in their struggles and successes, and we can learn from their mistakes.

The institution of Parliament is our surest means of achieving both individual and collective freedom. In the words of George-Étienne Cartier ". . . the most vital and the most incontestable of a people's rights is to have a parliament that protects the people's freedoms . . ."[1] [*Translation*]

---

1.   Cited by Jean-Charles Bonenfant in *Les idées politiques des premiers ministres du Canada*, Marcel Hamelin éditeur, Les éditions de l'Université d'Ottawa, 1969, p. 40.

APPENDIX A

Canadian Prime Ministers
since 1867

Prime Ministers	Party	Years in Office
1. Rt. Hon. Sir John A. Macdonald	Liberal Conservative	1867-1873
2. Hon. Alexander Mackenzie	Liberal	1873-1878
3. Rt. Hon. Sir John A. Macdonald	Liberal Conservative	1878-1891
4. Hon. Sir John J.C. Abbott	Liberal Conservative	1891-1892
5. Rt. Hon. Sir John S.D. Thompson	Liberal Conservative	1892-1894
6. Hon. Sir Mackenzie Bowell	Conservative	1894-1896
7. Rt. Hon. Sir Charles Tupper (Baronet)	Conservative	1896
8. Rt. Hon. Sir Wilfrid Laurier	Liberal	1896-1911
9. Rt. Hon. Sir Robert L. Borden	Conservative	1911-1917
10. Rt. Hon. Sir Robert L. Borden	Conservative	1917-1920
11. Rt. Hon. Arthur Meighen	Conservative	1920-1921
12. Rt. Hon. William Lyon Mackenzie King	Liberal	1921-1926
13. Rt. Hon. Arthur Meighen	Conservative	1926
14. Rt. Hon. William Lyon Mackenzie King	Liberal	1926-1930
15. Rt. Hon. Richard Bedford Bennett (became Viscount Bennett, 1941)	Conservative	1930-1935
16. Rt. Hon. William Lyon Mackenzie King	Liberal	1935-1948
17. Rt. Hon. Louis Stephen Saint-Laurent	Liberal	1948-1957
18. Rt. Hon. John G. Diefenbaker	Progressive Conservative	1957-1963
19. Rt. Hon. Lester B. Pearson	Liberal	1963-1968
20. Rt. Hon. Pierre Elliott Trudeau	Liberal	1968-1979
21. Rt. Hon. Charles Joseph Clark	Progressive Conservative	1979-1980
22. Rt. Hon. Pierre Elliott Trudeau	Liberal	1980-1984
23. Rt. Hon. John Napier Turner	Liberal	1984
24. Rt. Hon. Martin Brian Mulroney	Progressive Conservative	1984-1993

Speakers of the House of Commons since 1867

Speakers	Years in Office
1. James Cockburn	1867-1874
2. Timothy Warren Anglin	1874-1878
3. Joseph-Godéric Blanchet	1879-1882
4. George Airey Kirkpatrick	1883-1887
5. Joseph-Aldéric Ouimet	1887-1891
6. Peter White	1891-1895
7. James David Edgar	1896-1899
8. Thomas Bain	1899-1900
9. Louis-Philippe Brodeur	1901-1904
10. Napoléon-Antoine Belcourt	1904-1905
11. Robert Franklin Sutherland	1905-1908
12. Charles Marcil	1909-1911
13. Thomas Simpson Sproule	1911-1915
14. Albert Sévigny	1916-1917
15. Edgar Nelson Rhodes	1917-1922
16. Rodolphe Lemieux	1922-1930
17. George Black	1930-1935
18. James Langstaff Bowman	1935-1936
19. Pierre-François Casgrain	1936-1940
20. James Glen	1940-1945
21. Gaspard Fauteux	1945-1949
22. Ross Macdonald	1949-1953
23. René Beaudoin	1953-1957
24. Roland Michener	1957-1962
25. Marcel Lambert	1962-1963
26. Alan Macnaughton	1963-1966
27. Lucien Lamoureux	1966-1974
28. James Jerome	1974-1980
29. Jeanne Sauvé	1980-1984
30. Lloyd Francis	1984
31. John Bosley	1984-1986
32. John Fraser	1986-

APPENDIX C

House of Commons Calendar 1994

Standing Orders 24(1) and 28

JANUARY						
D	L	M	M	J	V	S
						1
2	3	4	5	6	7	8
9	10	11	12	13	14	15
16	17	18	19	20	21	22
23	24	25	26	27	28	29
30	31					

FEBRUARY						
D	L	M	M	J	V	S
		1	2	3	4	5
6	7	8	9	10	11	12
13	14	15	16	17	18	19
20	21	22	23	24	25	26
27	28					

MARCH						
D	L	M	M	J	V	S
		1	2	3	4	5
6	7	8	9	10	11	12
13	14	15	16	17	18	19
20	21	22	23	24	25	26
27	28	29	30	31		

APRIL						
D	L	M	M	J	V	S
					1	2
3	4	5	6	7	8	9
10	11	12	13	14	15	16
17	18	19	20	21	22	23
24	25	26	27	28	29	30

MAY						
D	L	M	M	J	V	S
1	2	3	4	5	6	7
8	9	10	11	12	13	14
15	16	17	18	19	20	21
22	23	24	25	26	27	28
29	30	31				

JUNE						
D	L	M	M	J	V	S
			1	2	3	4
5	6	7	8	9	10*	11
12	13*	14*	15*	16*	17*	18
19	20*	21*	22*	23*	24	25
26	27	28	29	30		

JULY						
D	L	M	M	J	V	S
					1	2
3	4	5	6	7	8	9
10	11	12	13	14	15	16
17	18	19	20	21	22	23
24	25	26	27	28	29	30
31						

AUGUST						
D	L	M	M	J	V	S
	1	2	3	4	5	6
7	8	9	10	11	12	13
14	15	16	17	18	19	20
21	22	23	24	25	26	27
28	29	30	31			

SEPTEMBER						
D	L	M	M	J	V	S
				1	2	3
4	5	6	7	8	9	10
11	12	13	14	15	16	17
18	19	20	21	22	23	24
25	26	27	28	29	30	

OCTOBER						
D	L	M	M	J	V	S
						1
2	3	4	5	6	7	8
9	10	11	12	13	14	15
16	17	18	19	20	21	22
23	24	25	26	27	28	29
30	31					

NOVEMBER						
D	L	M	M	J	V	S
		1	2	3	4	5
6	7	8	9	10	11	12
13	14	15	16	17	18	19
20	21	22	23	24	25	26
27	28	29	30			

DECEMBER						
D	L	M	M	J	V	S
				1	2	3
4	5	6	7	8	9	10
11	12	13	14	15	16	17
18	19	20	21	22	23	24
25	26	27	28	29	30	31

* Possible extension of sittings (Standing Order 27(1))
Note: Coloured areas indicate sitting days.
Projected number of sitting days: 133

Source: House of Commons.

GLOSSARY OF PARLIAMENTARY TERMS

This glossary is presented to the reader as an introduction to parliamentary vocabulary. Its basic explanations of often complex concepts should not be considered definitive.

Act of Parliament A bill which has been passed by both the House of Commons and the Senate and received Royal Assent.

Address in Reply to the Speech from the Throne An Address expressing the Commons' thanks to the Sovereign for the Throne Speech, adopted after a debate of up to six days dealing with various aspects of the Government's program.

adjournment The termination by the House of its own sitting (either by motion or pursuant to Standing or Special Order) for any period of time within a session.

adjournment proceedings A thirty-minute period, held three times a week prior to the daily adjournment, during which Members raise matters they feel were not satisfactorily dealt with during Question Period, and receive a reply by a Government spokesperson.

allotted day A day reserved for the discussion of the business of supply, the actual topic of debate being chosen by a Member in opposition. Also called *supply day* or *opposition day.*

amendment An alteration proposed to a motion, a bill, or a report.

appropriation bill A bill to authorize government expenditures, introduced in the House following concurrence in the Estimates. Also called *supply bill.*

bar (of the House or Senate) A brass barrier inside the south entrance to each Chamber demarking the area where non-members may be admitted. It is here that witnesses must appear when formally summoned.

bell An electronic bell used to summon Members at the beginning of a sitting, for the taking of a vote or because the House lacks a quorum. When used with respect to a vote, it is called a *division bell.*

bill A proposed law submitted to Parliament for its approval. It may originate either with the Government or with a private Member and may relate either to public or private interests.

Board of Internal Economy A nine-member body, presided over by the Speaker, responsible for all matters of financial and administrative policy affecting the House of Commons.

breach of privilege Any act or omission which infringes on the privileges of the House or its Members in such a way as to obstruct them in the carrying out of their functions.

Budget speech A presentation made in the House by the Minister of Finance introducing the Government's plans concerning revenues, expenditures, and general economic policy. It is followed by a debate of up to four sitting days.

business of supply The process by which the Government submits its projected annual expenditures for parliamentary approval. It includes consideration of Main and Supplementary Estimates, interim supply and motions debated on allotted days.

business of the House Any question, motion, or bill with which the House is seized.

casting vote A vote by the Speaker in the House or by the chairman in a committee meeting, to break a tie.

chairman The Member elected as the presiding officer of a committee. Joint committees have co-chairmen, one from each Chamber.

clause-by-clause study Detailed study of a bill by a committee during which each clause of the bill is considered individually.

Clerk of the House The chief procedural advisor to the Speaker and to Members of the House of Commons, responsible for a wide range of duties relating to the proceedings and official records of the House.

closure A procedure precluding further adjournment of debate on any motion or on any stage of a bill by requiring that the matter come to a vote at the end of the sitting in which it is invoked.

committee A body of Members, or Members and Senators, selected to consider such matters, including bills, as the House may refer to it. There are several types of committees: standing, legislative, special and joint committees as well as Committee of the Whole.

Committee of the Whole All of the Members of the House meeting as a committee. Presided over by a chairman rather than by the Speaker, it studies appropriation bills and any other matters referred to it by the House.

contempt of Parliament Any offence against the authority or dignity of Parliament, including disobedience to its commands or libel against it or its Members.

Daily Proceedings of the House A generic designation for prayers, statements by Members, and oral questions, which occur daily in the House but are not part of routine proceedings.

deferred division A recorded division which, in accordance with the provisions of the Standing Orders, is not held at the close of a debate but at a later time.

delegated legislation Regulations made by departments, boards, or agencies by virtue of the power conferred on them by an Act of Parliament.

dilatory motion A motion intended to delay consideration of the question before the House (e.g. a motion to adjourn the debate or to adjourn the House).

dissolution The bringing to an end of a Parliament, either at the conclusion of its five-year term or by proclamation of the Governor General. It is followed by a general election.

division A recorded vote. The dividing of Members into two groups (the yeas and nays) in order to reach a decision.

division bell see **bell.**

Estimates The departmental expenditure plans. They consist of Main Estimates, tabled annually and Supplementary Estimates, tabled as required.

emergency debate A debate held on a motion to adjourn, devoted to the discussion of a specific and important matter requiring immediate and urgent consideration.

first reading A purely formal stage in the passage of a bill, immediately following the granting of leave to introduce the bill in the House. It includes the printing of the bill and is decided without debate, amendment, or question put.

free vote A division on a question during which party discipline is not imposed on individual Members.

galleries Areas in the House set aside for the public, the press, and distinguished visitors who wish to attend a sitting.

Gentleman Usher of the Black Rod An officer of the Senate who delivers messages to the Commons when their attendance is required in the Senate Chamber by the Governor General or the Governor General's deputy.

government bill A bill introduced by a Minister addressing a matter of public policy. Numbered in the House from C-1 to C-200, they are the only bills which may contain financial provisions.

government business Any bill or motion introduced in the House by a Minister or Parliamentary Secretary.

Government House Leader The Government Minister responsible for managing the Government's business in the House, including negotiations with the House leaders of the opposition parties.

Government Order An order of the House placed on the agenda (the *Order Paper*) dealing with business, usually presented by a Minister or a Parliamentary Secretary.

House of Commons The elected lower House which with the Senate and the Crown comprise the Parliament of Canada. Made up of 295 Members in 1993, the House alone is constitutionally authorized to introduce legislation concerned with the raising or spending of funds.

interim supply Funds approved by the House pending approval of the Main Estimates to cover government expenditures for the period from April 1 to June 23 each year.

introduction of a bill The first presentation of a bill to the House for its consideration. Leave to introduce a bill is granted automatically without debate, amendment, or question put.

joint committee A committee made up of a proportionate number of Members of both the House of Commons and the Senate. It may be either a standing or a special committee.

"late show" see **adjournment debate.**

legislative committee A committee created under the Standing Orders on an ad hoc basis to study a bill in detail after second reading. The committee may only report the bill, with or without recommendations.

Mace The symbol of authority of the House of Commons. When the Speaker takes the Chair, the Mace is placed on the Table by the Sergeant-at-Arms.

Main Estimates A series of Government documents providing a breakdown of its expenditure plans for the coming fiscal year.

Member of Parliament A person elected to a seat in the House of Commons as a representative of one of the 295 constituencies into which Canada is divided at the time of writing (1993).

Minister A member of the Cabinet named by the Governor General on the advice of the Prime Minister, usually chosen from among Members and Senators.

motion A proposal made for the purpose of eliciting a decision of the House.

naming a member A disciplinary procedure used by the Speaker to maintain order in the House. A member named is usually suspended for the rest of the sitting.

non-confidence motion A motion which, if adopted, indicates that the Government has lost the confidence of the House. The Government then either resigns or requests the Governor General to dissolve Parliament and issue election writs.

notice of motion An announcement, either oral or written, of an intention to present a motion at a subsequent sitting. Depending on the type of motion and its mover, the notice period varies from 24 hours to 2 weeks.

opening of Parliament The ceremony opening the first session of a new Parliament at which the Speaker claims the rights and privileges of the Commons. It is followed by the Governor General's Throne Speech in the Senate Chamber giving the reasons for summoning Parliament.

Opposition critic A member of a party in opposition, responsible for presenting that party's policies in a given area and commenting on those of the Government.

opposition day see **allotted day.**

order A decision of the House giving a direction to its committees, members or officers, or ordering its proceedings.

order for return An order of the House to the Government to table a document.

order of reference An order of the House to a committee instructing it to consider some matter or defining the scope of its deliberations. It may be incorporated in the Standing Orders or be adopted to deal with a specific issue.

Panel of Chairmen One of four groups composed of the Deputy Speaker and Chairman of Committees of the Whole, the Deputy Chairman of Committees of the Whole, the Assistant Deputy Chairman of Committees of the Whole and six other Members appointed by the Speaker, from whom the chairmen of legislative committees are chosen. Each Panel is attached to a specific envelope (that is, an administrative grouping of standing and legislative committees).

pairs Two Members, who would otherwise vote on opposite sides of a question, who have agreed to abstain from voting and been so recorded in the Register of Paired Members.

parliamentary procedure The rules by which the House conducts its business, based on statutes, the *Standing Orders*, authoritative procedural works and tradition.

Parliamentary Secretary A Member of the Government party named for a period of one year to assist a Minister as the Minister directs.

petition A request to Parliament for some action made by Canadian residents. Such a request can only be presented to the House by a Member.

point of order A question raised with respect to any departure from the Standing Orders or customary procedures, either in debate or in the conduct of House or committee business. Points of order are decided by the Speaker, whose decision is final, or, in committee, by the chairman, whose decision may be appealed to the committee.

precedent A Speaker's ruling or practice of the House taken as a rule for subsequent cases of a similar nature. Not all decisions and practices constitute precedents.

previous question A debatable motion preventing any amendments to the question before the House. If the previous question is passed, the main motion is immediately put to a vote; if negatived, the main motion is superseded.

private bill A bill designed to exempt an individual or group from the application of the law, such as a bill to incorporate a private company. It can only be introduced in the House by a Member who is not a Cabinet Minister.

private Member Strictly, a Member who is not a Minister. Sometimes, Parliamentary Secretaries and Opposition critics are excluded from this designation.

Private Member's Bill A bill sponsored by a Member who is not a Cabinet Minister. The term usually refers to public bills only.

Private Members' Business Bills and motions sponsored by private Members. A one-hour period is devoted to this business each day.

privilege of Parliament Those rights and immunities enjoyed by the House as a collectivity and by each Member individually, without which Members could not carry out their duties and the House could not fulfill its functions.

prorogation The ceremonial ending of a parliamentary session, which abolishes all pending legislation and halts all committee work.

public bill A bill concerned with matters of public policy; it may be sponsored either by a Minister or by a private Member.

put the question To put the motion before the House to a vote. At this stage no further debate or amendment is possible.

Question Period A daily period in the House when oral questions may be addressed to Ministers and committee chairmen.

quorum The number of Members, including the Speaker, necessary to constitute a meeting of the House for the exercise of its powers. In the House, it is set by the Constitution at 20; in a committee, it is a majority of the committee members.

reasoned amendment An amendment expressing specific reasons for opposing the second or third reading of a bill.

recess The period between prorogation and the beginning of a new session. Often loosely used to refer to a long adjournment.

recorded division A division where the names of those voting for and against a motion are registered in the official record of the House or one of its committees.

report stage The stage at which the House considers a bill as reported by a committee, with amendments, if any. It is at this stage that Members may propose amendments to individual provisions of the bill.

report to the House A statement by a committee to the House, oral or written, giving the results of an inquiry or requesting additional powers. For a committee studying a bill, the bill itself, and any amendments, constitutes its report.

resolution A declaration of opinion or purpose made by adopting a motion.

Routine Proceedings Business of a routine nature for which a daily period is set aside in the House. It includes such items as tabling documents, presenting committee reports, presenting petitions and introduction and first reading of bills and statements by Ministers.

Royal Assent Ceremony during which a representative of the Crown gives approval to a bill passed by the House and the Senate, making it into an Act of Parliament.

Royal Recommendation A message from the Governor General, required for any vote, resolution, address or bill for the appropriation of public revenue. Only the Government can obtain such a recommendation.

second reading The stage at which the principle and object of a bill are debated and either accepted or rejected. Detailed consideration is not given to the clauses of the bill at this stage.

Sergeant-at-Arms An officer of the House, responsible for security and the maintenance of the Parliament buildings. This officer attends the Speaker with the Mace on ceremonial occasions.

session One of the basic periods into which parliamentary time is divided, it begins with a Throne Speech and is ended by prorogation.

sessional paper Any document tabled in the House during a given session and filed with the Clerk. All such documents are open to public scrutiny.

sitting A meeting of the House of Commons.

six months' hoist An amendment at second or third reading which has for effect the rejection of a bill. It proposes that the bill not now receive second (or third) reading, ". . . but that it be read a second (or third) time this day six months hence."

Speaker The Member elected to serve as spokesman for the House and to preside over its proceedings. In particular, he or she is responsible for maintaining order and decorum and interpreting the rules and practice of the House.

special committee A group of Members, or of Members and Senators, appointed to study a particular matter. Once it has made its final report, the committee ceases to exist.

Speech from the Throne A speech by the Governor General at the opening of a session of Parliament, which outlines the Government's legislative plans for the session.

standing committee A permanent committee established in the rules of the House. It may study matters referred to it by Standing or Special Order or undertake studies on its own initiative.

Standing Orders The written rules of the House which it has adopted to govern its proceedings.

steering committee A subcommittee established at the organization meeting of a standing, special, or legislative committee to plan the committee's work. It is also called the Subcommittee on Agenda and Procedure.

subamendment An amendment to an amendment. As such, it must be directly relevant to the amendment it seeks to modify, not to the original question.

subcommittee A committee of a committee, to which the latter may delegate its responsibilities. Not all committees are granted the power to establish subcommittees.

subcommittee on agenda and procedure see **steering committee**

sub judice **convention** A convention whereby Members refrain from making reference to certain matters, particularly criminal cases, which are before the courts. It does not apply to bills.

substantive motion An independent motion complete in itself. Normally such motions require notice before they can be moved in the House.

superseding motion A motion intended to replace the question under discussion. It may be either a dilatory motion or a motion for the previous question.

Supplementary Estimates An expenditure plan introduced to provide funds to meet new or increased costs to the Government.

supply see **business of supply**

supply bill see **appropriation bill**

supply day see **allotted day**

Table Officers The clerks who provide procedural advice during sittings of the House, take the votes, and keep the minutes of proceedings.

third reading The last stage of consideration of a bill, at the conclusion of which the bill as a whole is either finally approved or rejected.

Thursday statement A statement at the end of Question Period on Thursday, outlining the government business to be considered the following week. It is made by the Government House Leader, usually in response to a question from the Opposition House Leader.

time allocation The allocation of a specific period of time for consideration of one or more stages of a public bill. A procedure which can only be invoked by the Government.

voice vote An oral vote without recording individual Members' votes or the number of yeas and nays.

vote 1. The formal expression of opinion for the purpose of reaching a decision. 2. An individual item in the Estimates indicating the amount of money required by the Government for a particular program or service.

ways and means motion A motion proposing to introduce a new tax, to increase an existing tax, to continue an expiring tax or to extend the application of a tax. If adopted, it becomes an order that a bill based on its provisions be introduced.

Whip A Member charged with keeping other Members of the same party informed concerning House business and ensuring their attendance in the House, especially when a vote is anticipated.

Source: Prepared by the Table Research Branch and published in the 4th ed. of the *Précis of Procedure*, House of Commons, Ottawa, 1991.

CITED WORKS

BOOKS

BAKVIS, H. *Regional Ministers: Power and Influence in the Canadian Cabinet*. Toronto: University of Toronto Press, 1991, 378 p.

BRODIE, J. and VICKERS, J. *Canadian Women in Politics: An Overview*. Ottawa: Canadian Research Institute for the Advancement of Women, 1982, 60 p. (CRIAW Papers, 2)

The Legislative Process. 2nd ed. Ottawa: Parliament of Canada, Table Research Branch, 1992, 27 p.

The Legislative Process in Canada. Ottawa: Department of Justice, 1987, 28 p.

Parliamentary Privilege. Ottawa: House of Commons, Office of the Law Clerk and Parliamentary Counsel, 1988, 19 p.

Précis of Procedure. 4th ed. Ottawa: Parliament of Canada, Table Research Branch, 1991, 425 p.

Privilege in the Modern Context. Ottawa: House of Commons, Table Research Branch, June 1992, 30 p.

CLEVERDON, C.L. *The Women Suffrage Movement in Canada*. with an introduction by Ramsay Cook. Toronto: University of Toronto Press, 1974, 324 p.

CHRISTIAN, W. and CAMPBELL, C. *Political Parties and Ideologies in Canada: Liberals, Conservatives, Socialists, Nationalists*. 2nd ed. Toronto: McGraw-Hill Ryerson, 1983, 247 p.

DAWSON, R.M. *The Government of Canada*. 7th ed., edited by Norman Ward. Toronto: University of Toronto Press, 1987, 373 p.

FORSEY, E.A. *The Royal Power of Dissolution of Parliament in the British Commonwealth*. Toronto: Oxford University Press, 1968, 316 p.

FRANKS, C.E.S. *The Parliament of Canada*. Toronto: University of Toronto Press, 1987, 305 p.

FRASER, A., DAWSON, W.F. and HOLTBY, J.A. *Beauchesne's Parliamentary Rules and Forms*. 6th ed. Toronto: Carswell, 1989, 472 p.

GRIFFITH, J.A.G., WHEELER-BOOTH, M.A.J. and RYLE, M. *Parliament: Functions, Practice and Procedures*. London: Sweet & Maxwell, 1989, 538 p.

LAUNDY, P. *The Office of Speaker in the Parliaments of the Commonwealth*. London: Quiller, 1984, 274 p.

MACKAY, R.A. *The Unreformed Senate of Canada*. Rev. ed. Toronto: McClelland and Stewart, 1963, 216 p. (The Carleton Library, 6).

MALLORY, J.R. *The Structure of Canadian Government.* Rev. ed. Toronto: Gage Publishing, 1984, 472 p.

MAY, Sir T.E. *Erskine May's Treatise on The Law, Privileges, Proceedings and Usage of Parliament.* 21st ed., edited by C.J. Boulton London: Butterworths, 1989, 1079 p.

MAY, Sir T.E. *Erskine May's Treatise on The Law, Privileges, Proceedings and Usage of Parliament.* 16th ed., edited by Sir E. Fellowes and T.G.B. Cocks London: Butterworths, 1957, 1139 p.

MEISEL, J. "The Decline of Party in Canada," In *Party Politics in Canada*, 6th ed., H.G. Thorburn, 1991, pp. 178-201.

STEWART, J.B. *The Canadian House of Commons: Procedure and Reform.* Montreal: McGill Queen's University Press, 1977, 337 p.

VAN LOON, R.J. and WHITTINGTON, M.S. *The Canadian Political System: Environment, Structure and Process.* 3rd rev. ed. Toronto: McGraw-Hill Ryerson, 1987, 879 p.

WHEARE, K.C. Sir *Federal Government.* 4th ed. New York: Oxford University Press, 1964, 266 p.

WILDING, N.W. and LAUNDY, P. *An Encyclopaedia of Parliament.* 4th rev. ed. London: Cassell, 1972, 931 p.

ARTICLES

BARLAS, R.D. "The Role and Qualifications of a Clerk in the 1970s," *The Parliamentarian*, 49 no. 4 (October 1968): 222-6.

CAIRNS, A.C. "The Electoral System and the Party System in Canada, 1921-1965," *Canadian Journal of Political Science.* 1 no. 1 (March 1968): 55-80.

DAVIES, J.M. "Red and Green," *The Table* 37 (1968):33-40.

DRIEDGER, E.A. "Money Bills and the Senate," *Ottawa Law Review* 3 no. 1 (Fall 1968):25-46.

FORSEY, E.A. "Alexander Mackenzie's Memoranda on the Appointment of Extra Senators, 1873-4," *Canadian Historical Review* 27 no. 2 (June 1946):189-190.

"Appointment of Extra Senators under Section 26 of the British North America Act," *Canadian Journal of Economics and Political Science* 12, no. 2 (May 1946): 159-167.

LAUNDY, P. "The *Sub Judice* Convention in the Canadian House of Commons," *The Parliamentarian* 57, n° 3 (July 1976):211-214.

LOVINK, J.A.A. "On Analysing the Impact of the Electoral System on the Party System in Canada," *Canadian Journal of Political Science* 3, no. 4 (December 1970):497-516.

MALLORY, J.R. and SMITH, B.A. "The Legislative Role of Parliamentary Committees in Canada: the Case of the Joint Committee on the Public Service Bills," *Canadian Public Administration* 15, no. 1 (Spring 1972):1-23.

NORTON, P. "Government Defeats in the House of Commons: Three Restraints Overcome," *The Parliamentarian* 59, no. 4 (October 1978): 231-8.

MAIN CANADIAN LAWS CITED

Abbreviation used:

am.	amended	R.S.	revised statute
c.	chapter	supp.	supplement
Geo. V	George V		

Canada Elections Act, R.S. (1985), c. E-2 am., R.S. (1985), c. 27 (2nd supp.), 1989, c. 28.

Canada Parliament Act, R.S. (1985), c. P-1 am. (1985), c. 31 (1st supp.), c. 38 (2nd supp.) 1991, c. 20.

Lobbyists Registration Act, R.S. (1985), c. L-12.

The Military Voters Act, 1917, 7-8 Geo. V, c. 34.

War Time Elections Act, 1917, 7-8 Geo. V, c. 39.

Act to Confer the Electoral Franchise upon Women, 1918, 8-9 Geo. V, c. 20.

Dominion Elections Act, 1920, 10-11 Geo. V, c. 46.

Interpretation Act, R.S. (1985), c. I-21.

Financial Administration Act, R.S. (1985), c. F-11, am. 1991, c. 24.

Parliamentary Employment and Staff Relations Act, R.S. (1985), c. 33 (2nd supp.) am., 1985 (4th supp.), c. 1.

SOURCES

Public Information Office, House of Commons, Ottawa, p. 10; Canada Elections Act, Ottawa, p. 20; National Capital Commission, p. 28; National Archives of Canada, C 3987, p. 29 (left); National Archives of Canada, C 38765, p. 29 (right); National Capital Commission, p. 29 (bottom); National Archives of Canada, PA 45626, p. 30 (top); Public Information Office, House of Commons, Ottawa, p. 30 (centre); National Capital Commission, p. 30 (bottom); National Capital Commission, p. 33; National Archives of Canada, PA 8338, p. 35; Public Information Office, House of Commons, Ottawa, p. 36 (top); Public Information Office, House of Commons, Ottawa, p. 36 (bottom); Public Information Office, House of Commons, Ottawa, p. 38; Public Information Office, House of Commons, Ottawa, p. 40; National Archives of Canada, PA 126745, p. 46; Public Information Office, House of Commons, Ottawa, p. 48; Public Information Office, House of Commons, Ottawa, p. 49; National Archives of Canada, PA 8375, p. 65; Public Information Office, House of Commons, Ottawa, p. 71; Martine Bresson, p. 88; National Capital Commission, p. 96; Public Information Office, House of Commons, Ottawa, p. 97; Senate Archives, Ottawa, p. 111; National Capital Commission, p. 137; National Capital Commission, p. 155; National Capital Commission, p. 161; National Archives of Canada, C 37983, p. 168.

INDEX

Prepared by the Index and Reference Service, Parliamentary Publications Directorate.